THE
POLITICAL
TEACHINGS
OF JESUS

EDITED BY TOD LINDBERG

*Beyond Paradise and Power: Europe, America,
and the Future of a Troubled Partnership*

THE
POLITICAL
TEACHINGS
OF JESUS

Tod Lindberg

HarperOne
An Imprint of HarperCollinsPublishers

HarperOne

A hardcover edition of this book was published in 2007 by HC, an imprint of HarperCollins Publishers.

HarperCollins books may be purchased for educational, business, or sales promotional use. For information please write: Special Markets Department, HarperCollins Publishers, 10 East 53rd Street, New York, NY 10022.

HarperCollins Web site: http://www.harpercollins.com
HarperCollins®, 📖®, and HarperOne™ are
trademarks of HarperCollins Publishers.

FIRST PAPERBACK EDITION PUBLISHED IN 2008

Designed by Kris Tobiassen

The Library of Congress Cataloging-in-Publication Data is available upon request.

ISBN 978–0–06–137394–7

08   09   10   11   12   RRD(H)   10   9   8   7   6   5   4   3   2   1

FOR TINA

CONTENTS

PREFACE

This book is about the political (rather than the religious) teachings of Jesus—his guidance for people about how to live in *this* world and how to build a just society among and for themselves. I'll often refer to this political teaching as the "Jesusian" teaching (which I pronounce *jay-SOO-sian*) in order to distinguish that aspect of what Jesus had to say from the Christian religious teaching pertaining to such matters as the immortality of the soul, divine judgment, salvation and damnation, and so on. In the Introduction that follows, I'll say a little more about the relationship of the political teaching and the religious teaching and why I think it is both possible and valuable to examine the political teaching on its own terms. Here, I would like to clarify the sense in which "politics" is at issue.

The detailed exploration of the political teachings of Jesus readers will find here is very different from the deployment of the Christian Gospels in support of a contemporary political agenda. People sometimes find it convenient to dip into the Bible to search for material that seems to support their views or undermine their opponents' views on matters of current partisan controversy. We will not be doing that here.

I want to be perfectly explicit on this point: Jesus was neither a progressive Democrat bent on income redistribution nor a neoconservative Republican promoting a radical democracy agenda. It is impossible to determine from the Gospels whether Jesus would favor or oppose private accounts for Social Security. Jesus did not address the question of what the optimal rate of taxation of capital gains is. In my view, mining the New Testament for insight into such questions is anachronistic—and worse than useless. In how many cases has someone with a political agenda consulted scripture only to have scripture reveal that his or her agenda is all wrong?

Such exercises have the perverse effect of introducing even more distance between ourselves and a fuller understanding of what Jesus had to say. The Jesusian teaching is extraordinarily rich in content, and it does indeed have profound implications down to our time. But to fully appreciate it, we need to broaden our understanding of what "politics" is from the set of political questions that confront twenty-first-century Americans.

While it is unreasonable to call Jesus a "progressive" in the context of modern American politics, it is entirely reasonable to call Jesus *the progressive* in the context of his day—and in that sense, ever since. Into a world of imperial occupation, deprivation, cruelty, slavery, injustice, hereditary privilege, persecution, tribal conflict, collective punishment, piracy, the arrogance of the strong, the hopelessness of the weak, and the banishment of the sick, Jesus introduced the idea of universal freedom and the equality produced when people recognize the freedom of others by treating others the way they themselves would like to be treated. Dead set against politics based on the rule of the strong, or of an elite, or of the mob, Jesus proposed instead a political order organized on the principle of shared recognition of freedom and equality—a community of goodwill. This basic question of how people should organize worldly affairs to settle their disagreements is the "political question" at issue in the Jesusian teaching—and our subject.

It's my hope that readers will see that the political teaching of Jesus is now widely accepted, though rarely understood as such. On their good days, people in the modern world believe they should live in accordance with universal principles of freedom and equality. They also expect others in their societies to share this view of how to live, and they act accordingly, although they recognize that people have their bad days and do bad things and that some people think they can get away with rejecting their obligations while demanding that others adhere to theirs. The pangs of conscience people sometimes feel when they misbehave come from knowledge that they have failed to live up to this Jesusian guidance. These taken-for-granted elements of modern life frame our current political disputes and mostly prevent them from rising to anything like the level of contention—routine violent struggle—that politics entailed at the time of Jesus.

No one today can read the Sermon on the Mount and take it the way it fell on the ears of those who first heard it in Galilee—who first heard Jesus pronounce that the meek are blessed and shall inherit the earth. For modern readers, there is a paradox: Because the politics of the modern world is substantially Jesusian in character, the influence the political teachings of Jesus have had on us is easy to miss. His teaching comes down to us not only directly, through his own words, but also through various religious and secular filters, from the doctrinal teaching of particular churches to the thought of philosophers indebted to him even if they rebelled against him. Our access to the Jesusian teaching does not begin with hearing a preacher spell out his ideas in a sermon delivered from a hillside or with the formal study of the Gospels, but with the daily activity of our own lives lived in large measure according to principles Jesus espoused. Some of us may be unaware of this influence, or only dimly aware, but it is there. And having enjoyed the benefits of living this way and not another—as slaves of a cruel tyrant, for instance—we can and should go back and see where this way of living comes from. Because today there are many more people in the world who are free than there were during Jesus's time and because people today mostly believe that all people should be free (at least ideally), they have a leg up on understanding what Jesus meant by saying "you will know the truth, and the truth will make you free" (Jn. 8:32).

In what follows, readers will find much to take away on the question of how to live their lives and what obligations they have toward other people. The Jesusian teaching remains rich in the insight it provides into the question of how we should approach our relations with others. We will see that when we seek an unfair advantage for ourselves at the expense of others, we are unnecessarily jeopardizing not only their well-being but also our own. We will see guidance on how to structure our relations with others so that a gain for me is a gain for you, too. We will see why it follows from the Jesusian teaching that those who are well-off have a special obligation toward those who are not, why this is true with regard not only to those whose *material* circumstances are lesser but also to those who find themselves down in the dumps or dispirited, and why the fulfillment of this special obligation is good not only for others but also for those lucky enough to be in a position to incur such obligations.

All this is true even within the modern world, where society operates at a pinnacle of peace and prosperity unfathomable to those of Jesus's time. Yet the politics of daily life-and-death struggle and oppression is still the politics that confronts much of the world today. The modern, Jesusian world is real, and it is robust, but it is hardly the whole world. Indeed, some have sought and some still seek to overturn the foundations of the modern world in the name of one violent and coercive ideology or another, and we need to know how to go about preserving the political achievement the creation of this world represents against its opponents.

The key political challenge of our time is extending the benefits of the political and social world we inhabit to others. In some cases, we will find that this effort of outreach will be met with ready reciprocation, as those to whom we extend a hand quickly understand the benefit of such relations. But, of course, the task is complicated, as it has always been, by the fact that some political actors today are just as resourceful in their ruthlessness and cruelty as some of those in Jesus's time. Jesus, as we shall see, anticipated this problem as well. The most difficult political challenges of our day, though much diminished in scope by the spread of the Jesusian teaching, remain the same as those that Jesus set out to relieve two thousand years ago. A return to the source will both illuminate the success we have had and guide us on the question of what to do next.

INTRODUCTION

When the crowds heard this, they were astonished
at his teaching.

(MATTHEW 22:33)

The purpose of this book is to take Jesus seriously as a political thinker:
to examine carefully the words attributed to him about how people
should live in *this* world. In order to do that, we will have to put aside
(at least for the length of this book) the possibility that God *commands*
us to live in a certain way on the promise of eternal rewards and punishments. Instead, we will take what Jesus had to say as an *invitation* to
live a life on earth in accordance with his teachings based on whether
we are persuaded by them. If we want to, we can accept what Jesus has
to say as the path to salvation, but we are equally free to accept or reject this counsel solely on its merit as political advice or guidance for
how to live in the here and now. The question, then, is whether Jesus's
political teachings offer guidance about how to live a life that we can
find satisfying *in this world*, quite apart from any promises with regard
to the next.

It may be argued that to strip the theological implications from the
message of Jesus is to try to take God down from the cross and put up
a mere man in his place. And it is true that the past has seen efforts to
reduce Christianity to a secular social or ethical teaching—"updating"

Jesus in secular terms, so to speak, and recasting him as a modern-day classical liberal, or in some cases as a revolutionary. These efforts, some more intellectually interesting and rewarding than others, have consistently failed. As a general matter, they seek to cope with the explicitly religious element of Jesus's teaching, which they find inconvenient, by subsuming it under the "social Gospel." This won't do, not if we are to retain any sense of fidelity to what Jesus thought he was up to. He had a program for the salvation of souls and life everlasting.

It is not my intention to consider theological questions of salvation, of whether one can be saved by right conduct or simply by faith in God. Futhermore, it is not my purpose here to address or pass judgment one way or another on the questions surrounding the immortality of the soul, the possibility of salvation, and the like. I ask readers for whom these are truly the most important questions to grant that there are also subsidiary questions of great relevance—those pertaining to how to live on earth in relation to other people. Jesus counseled exactly this. For those readers who reject the notion of an afterlife and a God who judges one's earthly conduct, I invite them to consider the possibility that the most serious question they will then face is how to live the life on earth they have. And I mean to show that the words of Jesus, whatever else they offer, provide a coherent account of how to live in the world, one based on a profound understanding of what makes people tick, including their potential for acting on his words and the obstacles that stand in the way of their ability or willingness to do so.

This "Jesusian" society—let us not call it "Christian," since we are confining our investigation to this world—is one in which the freedom of each person is recognized by the other in all aspects of life, from the mundane world of the customer and the shopkeeper, to the relation of citizen to state, to the obligation of the individual to charity toward others. In this model, the freedom of each is secure only when the freedom of all is secure, each to each. The minute I attempt to secure my freedom—free rein for my preferences—at your expense, I disrupt not only the security of your freedom but also the security of my own, for I invite a world in which the next person to come along may seek to fulfill his or her wishes at *my* expense. My desire to secure my own freedom, Jesus explains, can be satisfied only by an accompanying desire to respect the freedom of others. In so respecting one another, we are equals. Note that no law, divine or natural, dictates this real-world outcome of equal respect; it is something people have to work out among themselves.

Jesus offers guidance on how. He describes an ideal of proper conduct that in turn regulates and extends freedom and equality. His most economical formulation of this principle is so familiar as an adage that many now fail to grasp its profundity: "Do unto others as you would have them do unto you." Not *as they have done unto you*, but *as you would have them do*. Jesus here proposes a revolution in the idea of freedom. Freedom is no longer merely the ability to do what you want as a master lords it over a slave. Now, in deciding how to treat a slave, the master must put himself in the place of the slave— and in deciding how to respond, the slave must put himself in the place of the master. But this, of course, yields an end to masters and slaves. It ushers in a new type of freedom, freedom grounded in equality. To get there, one must set aside past slights along with all supposed obligations that conflict with the primary obligation of treating the other as one would wish to be treated. One must see oneself as a person through the eyes of another and look on others as if one were looking on oneself.

Jesus does not counsel passivity, as we shall see through a careful analysis of his admonition to turn the other cheek. Rather, he counsels active measures to recruit people to this freedom in equality, with a view toward its universal extension.

Our procedure will be to carefully examine what Jesus has to say in the Gospels of Matthew, Mark, Luke, and John. Jesus apparently wrote nothing himself,[1] instead preaching in and around Galilee and Jerusalem. In general, we shall try to approach him as directly as possible through the words attributed to him. Sometimes he offers his guidance directly. Often, however, he teaches by indirect means, speaking to people in parables or other figurative language. Much of the preaching and many of the parables go to the question of afterlife, as noted, but the Sermon on the Mount is not *exclusively* concerned with salvation to the point of its irrelevance to the question of how to live in this world. The parables are distinctive for their potential to offer *several* layers of meaning, one of which goes to the question of the eternal, but one of which also addresses the question of life properly lived in the here and now.

We will begin with a close analysis of the most famous of the teachings of Jesus, the Sermon on the Mount. We will then take up thematically the parables Jesus told and some of his statements from other scenes depicted in the Gospels.

For our purposes, it's most useful to start with the question of *to whom* Jesus said what he said: Was he preaching to a crowd, or was he talking to a small number of his disciples in private? The difference is that we can be sure, when he was talking to a crowd, that he was *teaching*: What he said in public, along with the example he set in his public life, *is* his teaching, including his political teaching. When Jesus was preaching, he was explicitly addressing *all* of his listeners. There was nothing he said that was intended for half the crowd but that the other half could not be allowed to hear. These were public events, often massive. In one case, the crowd is put at 5,000 men plus women and children (Mt. 14:21). Even allowing for imprecise counting or exaggeration, the number is huge for a time before electronic amplification.

Jesus could also be reasonably sure that what he said would be repeated elsewhere. Of course, there might be some distortions in

---

[1] The only instance in the Gospels in which Jesus is depicted writing is in the story of the woman accused of adultery. He stoops to write something on the ground after her accusers present her to him and again after he tells them that whoever is without sin should cast the first stone (Jn. 8:6,8). What these words might have been, the Gospel does not record.

individual accounts. People forget or misremember. However, especially in the case of his public statements, we should recall that he was, after all, a major public figure (to slip into the idiom of today), and there were, quite simply, a lot of witnesses. He spoke, moreover, in a cultural milieu in which illiteracy was widespread and the oral tradition of paying attention to, remembering, and repeating the spoken word was accordingly very much alive.

Throughout this exploration, we will ask ourselves what the political and social meaning of his words is: how he wants people to live, the changes in political and social arrangements he proposes through the reform of conduct. We will ask, for example, how he might intend us to respond to his claim that it is easier for a camel to pass through the eye of a needle than for a rich man to enter the kingdom of heaven. In the first place, where is this kingdom? Purely in the next world? Actually, no; there is ample reason to conclude that Jesus is referring not exclusively to a world beyond but also to this world as reorganized according to the principles he espouses. What, then, should the rich man do? Give up his riches? As it happens, it is no small task for a poor man or anyone to act in such a fashion on earth as to participate in the kingdom of heaven—which is to say, among other things, to act rightly on earth. The eye of the needle is still small. The twofold point is that the demands of right conduct on one with wealth are vastly greater on account of that wealth, and above all, wealth at any level, or concern over material possessions, must never interfere with the performance of these difficult obligations. But they are not impossibly difficult, as Jesus also says.

As we work through this interpretive exercise, we will be able to analyze the political teaching of Jesus more thematically. We will be able to ask what society organized in accordance with his political teaching would look like and whether such a society is plausible on its own terms. We will see the social and political forces—competing claims about how human affairs should be organized—against which the political teachings of Jesus contend. The question is how we should think about getting from *here* (whether we mean the Jerusalem of two millennia ago or our own time) to *there*—i.e., the realized teaching of Jesus. Should we see this as essentially utopian? More to the point, did Jesus view this as an impossible task?

The answer is that Jesus saw his political teaching as attainable in this world, and so should we. The ideal he describes is within people's grasp, not beyond, and therefore, it is worth pursuing, even if there is also reason to wonder whether it will ever be *fully* realized. Against the backdrop of the freedom to accept or reject the counsel he offers, Jesus provides a detailed description of how people can organize their relations with one another so as to secure their freedom. If heaven is an all-encompassing circle where sits an all-powerful and all-seeing God who both loves people and pronounces eternal judgment upon them, life on earth is an inner circle for which Jesus's words provide full and sufficient knowledge of right conduct toward others—an idea of justice. In the inner circle, our equal being "before God" becomes our being with others toward a common idea of justice that is put into place by the action of people in relation to one another as equals.

Perhaps paradoxically, near-universal acceptance of the *political* teaching of Jesus is plausible in a way that a comparably universal acceptance of the divinity of Jesus and his teachings on salvation is not. As far as his guidance for *life on earth* is concerned, one can find adequate reason to accept and live by his principles whether or not one crosses over into the encompassing circle of the divine. Likewise, one can accept those principles even if one embraces a different religious faith altogether. One may also accept those principles, while explicitly rejecting the notion of an encompassing circle (and thus religion) entirely.

Here we will see the extent to which people have actually accepted Jesus's guidance for life on earth. This question is distinct from the admittedly related and better-studied question of how the Christian religion spread. One may be Jesusian in conduct without being Christian in religion, and of course, one may profess Christianity without being especially

Jesusian in conduct. These considerations were not lost on Jesus. Yet despite the pounding that the political teaching of Jesus has taken from certain philosophers, the human imperfection of the Christian religion as practiced, and the supposed advance of secularism in the world, the political teaching of Jesus is in fact alive and well, taking deeper root in modern life and continuing to spread throughout the world.

Please note that, unless otherwise specified, scripture quotations come from the New American Standard Bible.

PART I

THE SERMON
ON THE MOUNT

Your kingdom come. Your will be done, on earth as
it is in heaven.

(MATTHEW 6:10)

1.

THE BEATITUDES

The Sermon on the Mount is the most influential piece of preaching ever, a summary of the most important elements of the teaching of Jesus. The Gospel of Matthew places it front and center in its account of Jesus's life and ministry. It comes as the climax of the first section of Matthew's Gospel, a sort of answer to the question of what all the fuss over Jesus is about. In the opening pages of the Gospel, we hear about Jesus's genealogy and birth; John the Baptist dramatically preparing the way for "he who is coming" (Mt. 3:11); Jesus's baptism and temptation; and the beginning of his preaching career, in which he recruits his first disciples. The Gospel of Matthew notes: "Jesus was going throughout all Galilee, teaching in their synagogues and proclaiming the gospel of the kingdom. . . . The news about him spread throughout all Syria. . . . Large crowds followed him from Galilee and the Decapolis and Jerusalem and Judea and from beyond the Jordan" (Mt. 4:23–25). People were willing to travel scores of miles to hear this preacher and teacher—vast distances when the way from here to there was by foot.

One finds in these passages of Matthew a sense of mounting excitement: *Jesus began preaching and drawing crowds—and* this *is what he had to say*. The Sermon on the Mount has long been rightly understood as both a starting point and a summation of Jesus's teaching. No less than with regard to his religious teaching, the Sermon on the Mount is also the foundation and the first concise summary of the political teaching of Jesus.

The Sermon on the Mount begins with a dizzying commentary designed to turn upside down the political and social world of the Roman Empire of Caesar Augustus and of the Jewish religious elite of Judea and Jerusalem. As if this were not enough, it is also the opening move of a more drastic and fundamental reassessment of political and social affairs, applying not only to its own time but also to all future times, down to our day. More still: it points to the increasing fulfillment *in this world* of the promise of the human condition as such—and of the struggle against vast and daunting but not insurmountable obstacles that such fulfillment will require.

Jesus begins by describing those who are truly fortunate, the lucky ones of their day. But it is not emperors, conquerors, priests, and the wealthy who enjoy this favor. Rather, it is the common people, those whom earthly success has largely passed by: the poor, the meek, the persecuted, the peacemakers. How can this be? Because though they may have been denied worldly success, what cannot be taken away from them is their potential to live rightly by one another. It is all too easy for those who enjoy the pleasures of this world to try to float above such obligations. Jesus goes on to say that so long as ordinary people stand for the right things and do not retreat in their rightness before those who seem to have more power, what's right will prevail. It's *their* kingdom—a kingdom organized not from the top down, but from the bottom up.

Superficialities, such as worldly success, are accordingly no indication of true worth. Jesus is appalled by the way mankind, supposedly in possession of the law, has used the technicality of the law's commands to subvert its spirit. He says his mission is to fulfill the law. He directs people to look within themselves to discover their true obligations, and he remonstrates against those who think they have complied with the law merely by following its letter.

Some of the laws that have come down from ancient times are themselves incomplete, and Jesus means to flesh them out. The principle of "an eye for an eye," which comes from Exodus (21:24), was an improvement on the practice of taking *both* eyes for an eye: A principle of proportion replaced an older principle of justice according to which any infraction against the social code or political order warranted a sentence of death. But it is an inadequate improvement, Jesus contends. Likewise, "You shall love your neighbor and hate your enemy" (Mt. 5:43). The first part of the passage, which comes from Leviticus (19:18), is important guidance for those inclined to hate not only their enemies *but also* their neighbors, but this ancient rule still leaves a world organized around the permanent existence of friends and enemies. Jesus seeks to undermine that juxtaposition and move toward a world beyond enemies.

The effect of Jesus's correction of the law in these cases is to drive people's thoughts inward: Outward compliance with the law is not enough; the question of where the heart is also matters—indeed, is most important. Jesus invites people to confront what drives them in the direction of wrongdoing *before* they do wrong. Following a law against doing wrong, under penalty of death, is a start, but not until people begin to overcome their interior urges to do wrong will a true community come into being.

Jesus further explores the importance of the interior life by asking why people give to the poor, pray, or fast. Do they give alms to the poor for *the sake of* the poor or simply for their own sake, in order to be praised for their generosity? Do they pray and fast because they are pious or simply to be hailed for their piety? If all they care about is their reputation—the outward appearance they present—then they will have lost the true benefit that giving to the poor conveys. They should see in the poor an *obligation* they owe, not an opportunity for their own reward. Jesus reinforces this point metaphorically, admonishing his listeners that the true treasures are not those one can accumulate materially, but the treasures of the heart. When the heart's treasures are secure, material matters assume their proper, secondary place.

Having focused his listeners' attention on what goes on within their own hearts, Jesus turns to the question of their relations with others. First, he warns of the dangers of passing hasty judgment: Can we ourselves hold up under the scrutiny we seem to have an almost irresistible impulse to apply to others? A candid look within ourselves will reveal how difficult such scrutiny would be to withstand. We have a responsibility to clean up our own conduct. Only then can we approach the misconduct of others in the spirit of helping them, not condemning them. Approaching our own flaws in this fashion yields the single most important ethical and political precept Jesus offers to his followers, the "Golden Rule": "In everything, therefore, treat people the same way you want them to treat you" (Mt. 7:12; Lk. 6:31).

Jesus warns that the course he proposes is not an easy one; the distractions are many. Success is not merely a matter of repeating what Jesus says or *outwardly* doing as he prescribes, as one might follow a set of instructions or rules. Rather, successful adherence to his teaching is a matter of what goes on within. To hear the Sermon on the Mount is only the beginning. It is a foundation for what comes next. What people build for themselves on earth will either rest on a secure foundation—Jesus's political and ethical teaching—and so will last because it is true on its own terms, or, built on sand, the human project will be at the mercy of the rain, the floods, and the winds—erratic fortune—and may fall.

At the center of the Sermon on the Mount—at the very heart of this reflection on the importance of the heart—Jesus gives instruction to people on what to say when they pray. It includes the lines: "Your kingdom come. Your will be done, On earth as it is in heaven" (Mt. 6:10). From the Sermon on the Mount itself, we can see that this is not mere beseeching for the arrival of divine justice on earth. The teaching of Jesus amounts to a program for the creation of a just order in this world.

THE BEATITUDES BEGIN

The Sermon on the Mount begins with the Beatitudes (Mt. 5:3–12), Jesus's delineation of categories of people who enjoy special favor. There is a corresponding section, with differences in detail, in Jesus's Sermon on the Plain in Luke (6:20–23). They are all familiar to us as sayings, the best known being *Blessed are the meek, for they shall inherit the earth*. But what, really, are the Beatitudes? Is Jesus *merely* pronouncing a blessing, offering good wishes to those whom he chooses to single out? In fact, there's more to the story than that because each of the Beatitudes includes not only a statement about who is blessed but also a short description of what is in store for each category of those who are blessed: The meek shall inherit the earth. Are those *predictions* Jesus is making? Or *promises* about what the future holds? If so, where? Only in the next world or in this world as well?

In order to see the answers to these questions, we have to look at the Beatitudes not just individually, but in relation to one another. With these nine categories, Jesus offers a portrait of the ways in which it is possible to be a good person with respect to others—a description of the various forms human goodness, in this social sense, can take. This description is as true today as when he spoke these words, and if we are looking for the ways in which it is possible to be a good person today, we really need look no farther.

As for the predictions or promises, what Jesus has done with them is to imagine the consequences of a world comprised of more and more people attuned to the social good as he has described it. He offers in these few lines a description of what the world looks like when good people prevail over bad people—and he makes the bold claim that such a world will come to pass.

Jesus calls those who belong to the nine categories he specifies in Matthew "blessed." The sense of the term here is "fortunate" or "prosperous." Who are the lucky ones? The "poor in spirit" are prosperous; "those who mourn" are fortunate; so are "the gentle"; and "those who hunger and thirst for righteousness"; and "the merciful"; and "the pure in heart"; and "the peacemakers"; and "those who have been persecuted for the sake of righteousness"; finally, says Jesus, fortunate are "you when people insult you and persecute you, and falsely say all kinds of evil against you because of me."

By now, we are used to the idea of wishing well for those who are downtrodden, who are oppressed, who can't get a break, who have fallen on hard times. This is, in no small measure, a product of the teaching of Jesus itself, in this passage and elsewhere. Those in his time who heard him speak words such as these, however, had a different general outlook and set of expectations. Theirs was a world in which robbers could leave a man for dead on the side of a road, and it was unclear whether anyone would stop to help.[1] The exalted were truly exalted—the rich, the royal, the Sadducees and Pharisees, the imperial Roman officers, the tax collectors—and they often treated have-nots with undisguised contempt.

Here, Jesus proposes a different hierarchy. To see whom he elevates in the Beatitudes, it may be helpful to conjure a list of qualities opposite to the ones he lists. Cumulatively, what emerges from this collection of "anti-Beatitudes" is a portrait of a privileged class, one that sees those below as essentially inferior. For "the poor in spirit," the opposite number might be someone arrogant in his righteousness and sense of superiority. For "those who mourn," we can substitute those whom the world has given cause for rejoicing. For "the gentle," the overbearing. For "those who hunger and thirst for righteousness," we may find a contrast in those who are complacent on account of their privileges and defend them vigorously. For "the merciful," the unforgiving, perhaps the cruel: those who, when they have an advantage over another, even a temporary one, don't hesitate to exploit it.

Opposite "the pure in heart" are those who are cunning in pursuit of their private gain. Opposite "the peacemakers" are those who act to

---

[1] See Luke 10:29–37, the "Good Samaritan."

create or aggravate conflict. Opposite "those who are persecuted for the sake of righteousness" are those doing the persecuting, as opposite "you when people insult you . . . because of me" are those seeking to put down Jesus's teaching and those who follow it.

Far from feeling any sense of obligation toward those below, this elite dismisses them as irrelevant—or worse, sees them as objects to be used to its own advantage. In addition, the elite seek to perpetuate their advantages, if necessary by silencing those (such as Jesus) who speak up for the downtrodden. There was much for the elite to lose if the teachings of Jesus caught on. Indeed, from the beginning of his career, Jesus understood quite clearly the high stakes involved in his political teaching.

Perhaps privileged *classes,* in the plural, captures the essence a little more precisely. It is an oversimplification to see the problem as simply one of haves versus have-nots. The have-nots have in common that they are oppressed, but their oppressors come in different guises, from the elite of the temple to the occupying Romans. And we must bear in mind *how little* it takes to oppress. Some who are oppressed by the powerful above them may in turn oppress those below them with yet less power. Oppression can manifest itself in as little as a declined opportunity to show mercy out of the enjoyment of one's position of relative power—one's sense of superiority.

As it turns out, though, the have-nots have more going in their favor than they realize, and this is Jesus's message. For the poor in spirit, "theirs is the kingdom of heaven." Those who mourn "shall be comforted." The gentle "shall inherit the earth." Those who hunger and thirst for righteousness "shall be satisfied." The merciful "shall receive mercy." The pure in heart "shall see God." The peacemakers "shall be called sons of God." As for those who have been persecuted for the sake of righteousness, again, "theirs is the kingdom of heaven." And for those who are insulted, persecuted, and falsely accused because they adhere to and seek to exemplify Jesus's teaching, he tells them "rejoice and be glad, for your reward in heaven is great."

At first, it seems that Jesus sees the rectification of the worldly troubles of those whom he has described as "blessed" coming only in the next world, referring to heaven in three of the Beatitudes and in a fourth promising the sight of God. However, it is not *only* the next world to which Jesus refers. Most conspicuously, "the gentle," he says, "shall inherit the earth." This statement could not be more emphatically rooted in *this* world. It promises no less than *this world itself* to the gentle (or meek or humble). Note that Jesus does not say the gentle will take over the world or conquer the world: The way in which the gentle come to possess the world is not by becoming something other than what they are. Rather, the world comes to them—as an inheritance, a bequest. The language is striking. One obtains an inheritance upon the death of one's benefactor. This raises the question: a bequest from whom? We will soon see the answer.

Four of the nine promises or predictions of the Beatitudes are at least as grounded in this world as they are in the next: *Where* will those who mourn "be comforted"? Where will those who hunger and thirst for righteousness "be satisfied"? Where will the merciful "receive mercy"? Come the time that the gentle do indeed "inherit the earth"— should such a world come to pass—it seems plausible that those who mourn will find the comfort Jesus has promised in such a world, that those who desire righteousness will find it and the merciful be shown mercy there.

Furthermore, we must also ask why the "pure in heart . . . will see God" only in heaven, since perhaps the uncorrupted heart could have access to a vision of the divine on earth as well. Jesus does not speak of a "reward [explicitly] in heaven" here, as he does elsewhere. As for the peacemakers, who will be called "sons of God," will they be called this in heaven only? Or perhaps on earth, where they may be said to be doing the Lord's work—earthly emulators of Jesus with regard to the pursuit of peace.

Jesus speaks of this world prospectively: The gentle have *not yet* inherited it, those who desire righteousness are not yet satisfied. But whatever consolation they may draw in the present moment, listening to Jesus speak on the mountainside, that their hunger for righteousness will be satisfied in the next world, the future that Jesus describes points to a form of satisfaction in this world also.

THE STRUCTURE OF THE BEATITUDES

The Beatitudes are organized according to a scale running from passivity and paralysis in this world, through increasing levels of engagement with it in accordance with the Jesusian teaching, up to a pinnacle of earthly conduct Jesus describes. The categories he delineates describe people we can recognize in our own day, from homeless shelters and nursing homes to the halls of power, at least on those occasions when people rise above their private ambitions and work for the public good.

We begin with the "poor in spirit." It is an ambiguous phrase, but one that evokes a sense of those incapable of taking care of themselves at all: the dejected, the demoralized, those in whom the spark has gone out. They have given up, resigning themselves to their lonely place at the bottom, beyond reach of all others.

Next come the mourners, whom we may think of as the temporarily incapacitated. For now, they are overwhelmed by a sense of grief and loss. They are perhaps unable to take care of themselves or to fulfill their responsibilities toward others. They once felt a connection to another or others—strongly enough to be reduced to incapacity by the loss. The loss of that connection in turn imperils all their other connections. Because they were once more robust, however, now there is at least the possibility that one day they will again be so, having recovered from their mourning.

Then there are the gentle, or meek or humble. They walk softly on the earth, seeking to impose themselves on others as little as possible. They see to their obligations as best they can, but they take nothing from others and ask for nothing from them for themselves. They are satisfied with what they have, however meager it may be. They do not strive, but accept their circumstances.

The gentle are followed by those who desire righteousness. They, unlike the gentle and still less the poor in spirit, have surveyed the world around them and are dissatisfied with it, wishing instead for a world in which their desire for righteousness is fulfilled. Here, Jesus uses metaphorical language: He speaks of those who "hunger and thirst" for righteousness. All people get hungry, all people get thirsty. Hunger and thirst are primordial and universal bodily desires.

Here, however, the desire Jesus speaks of—the desire for righteousness—is something whose satisfaction, unlike hunger and thirst, is not *of* the body. Having passed from the permanently dispirited (the poor in spirit), to the incapacitated (those who mourn), to the unstirred spirit of acquiescence (the gentle or meek), we arrive now at the moment when the human spirit becomes an active entity for the first time. People are no longer merely operated on—passive objects played with by natural forces or the will of other, stronger human beings. Instead, they stir of their own will, seeking for themselves something outside themselves.

In the desire for food and drink, people are no different from other members of the animal kingdom. Jesus goes on to specify an object of desire that is distinctly human: the desire for righteousness. He invites us to take the desire for righteousness as the first stirring in all those who are not content *simply* to be, in the passive or debilitated senses he has already evoked.

So far, Jesus has not specifically said what this "righteousness" people desire is, but his language offers some clues. First of all, the Beatitudes categorize *groups* of people. He does not say, "blessed is *the one* who is poor in spirit," but rather "blessed are the poor in spirit"; not "the mourner" but "those who mourn." From the start, Jesus's teaching is directed not merely to each solitary person who will one day stand before God for eternal judgment; instead, it includes an element that is social or political. It invites listeners—including the most downtrodden and oppressed—to recognize that they are not alone and to think beyond themselves. Wherever one of his listeners may fall, whether in one of his categories of the "blessed" or somewhere outside, the listener is not alone: Jesus calls people to think of themselves in relation to others like them, even if the others are people with whom they previously have felt nothing in common.

The second point concerns the specific group of "those who hunger and thirst for righteousness." This Jesusian category describes a *common* desire. Although this desire is felt by individuals—I can feel or intuit or experience *my* desire in a way that I cannot feel *yours*, even if I know you are feeling it, too—it is not unique to each person who feels it. Rather, it is a desire common to all. Jesus reinforces this sense of universality by saying that those who feel the desire for righteousness will be "satisfied"—that is, this universal desire will be fulfilled universally.

One person's desire for righteousness, in Jesus's teaching, doesn't necessarily bring that person into conflict with another's desire for righteousness. In fact, if two or more—indeed, many more—people are "blessed" in their desire for righteousness and "shall be satisfied," then the satisfaction of their respective desires for righteousness would result in their mutual satisfaction. They would be satisfied as individuals, but all individuals desiring righteousness would likewise be satisfied. No individual's satisfaction could come at the price of another individual's failure to obtain satisfaction or the denial of satisfaction to the other. If someone's desire for righteousness necessarily conflicted with another person's desire for righteousness, then the generalization Jesus proffers, namely, that "those who hunger and thirst for righteousness . . . shall be satisfied," would not work out. Jesus holds out the prospect of reconciliation of each individual's desire for righteousness and universal fulfillment.

But what if I, as an individual hungering and thirsting for righteousness, conclude that I can obtain satisfaction for myself only at the expense of others? Well, it is clearly no solution if others who hunger and thirst for righteousness find out that I have obtained my fulfillment at the expense of their ability to find satisfaction. Another way to put this is that I have confused an *advantage* I have obtained over them with the satisfaction of my desire for righteousness. The conclusion, therefore, is that what I think of as the desire for righteousness within myself is actually something else—or, more simply, that I am wrong to think that what I have desired and obtained can properly be called "righteousness." Nevertheless, there *is* the desire, which *seems* like the desire for righteousness. What it needs is proper channeling.

Similarly, what if I satisfy myself at the expense of others and the others either don't see it or don't object? What if they are, for example, so poor in spirit, so ground down by oppression, that they cannot imagine anything different? Does this acquiescence somehow vindicate my claim to righteousness in satisfying myself at their expense? Can I say that I am in the right because of my natural or otherwise-given superiority over them, as demonstrated by their acceptance of my position of privilege? Jesus's answer is clearly "no." And the reason is simply this: *They* may not be able to speak up for themselves, but others can speak up for them—starting, of course, with Jesus. No overlord's sense of his own vindicated righteousness stands unchallenged. Such supposed righteousness is wrong-headed. A true desire for righteousness is of the kind that can be satisfied along with everyone else's true desire for righteousness.

An important distinction that Jesus makes is that to desire righteousness is not necessarily to act on that desire. How, then, should one obtain satisfaction for one's desire? The beginning of the answer becomes clear in Jesus's next category of the blessed, the first category that specifies righteous action: In one's relations with other people—when one reaches beyond oneself toward another—one should be merciful.

Mercy is a quality within reach of everyone at one time or another. All mercy requires is a position of the barest advantage over another, even for the most fleeting of moments. When someone is down—whether physically, psychologically, or emotionally—do you kick him or not? To show mercy is an action that doesn't necessarily require activity: In certain cases, no more than the refusal to press an advantage one has is an act of mercy.

The next deemed blessed are the "pure in heart." Such people will act out of no bad motive, but always in accordance with the purity of rightness within them. Uncorrupted inwardly, the pure in heart will act toward others without corruption, since it would not occur to such a person to cheat a friend or steal from a stranger or tell a lie. As we shall soon see, what transpires in the heart or inner desire is, in Jesus's view, the *most* reliable predictor of how someone will behave toward others.

After the "pure in heart" come "the peacemakers." Jesus's intention here is clearly broad, encompassing not only relations between nations and peoples but also all subsets of conflict, down to those between two people. Here, we take another step outward. If purity of heart relates to how I govern my own conduct toward others, peacemaking has the potential to take me outside myself.

It may be that the peace I am trying to make is between me and someone else. In that case, I am seeking to remove from my own conduct the sources of conflict between me and you. But I have to go further, to recruit another to the cause of peace—to persuade another that the benefits of peace are sufficiently great to justify the other's removal of internal impediments to it, and then to provide the other with the benefits of peace once it has been made.

Clearly, the Jesusian instruction here will not be fulfilled through the imposition of the peace of the victor upon the vanquished. Nor will it be fulfilled by the purchase of peace at the cost of surrendering what is right. Neither "I win" nor "I surrender" will do. Peace must be *made*: At a minimum, there is a condition of mutuality involved between the parties. Along those same lines, peace*making* also becomes a matter of peace*keeping*: ensuring that the conditions for peace remain. Here, peace is more than the (temporary) absence of conflict, and by saying that "the peacemakers" are blessed, Jesus points to the importance of aspiring toward permanent peace and universal peace.

In some instances, peacemaking of the sort Jesus endorses here will be an exercise in reaching even further beyond oneself, interposing between others in conflict to help them remove the sources of discord between them. With such peacemaking attempts, the presupposition is that such a peacemaker is already at peace with each of the two parties in conflict (otherwise, the type of peacemaking described in the preceding paragraph would have to come first). But this suggests that my peace with each of them must not come at the expense of the continuation of their conflict with each other. If I perceive the conflict between them as a benefit to me, then I am failing to uphold peacemaking in its broadest, Jesusian sense. Making one's personal peace, whatever it entails, does not fulfill the Jesusian prescription. Such a peace is insufficient if others remain in conflict, and it is incumbent upon one who is at peace with others to make peace *among* the others as well. As we will see later, Jesus regards the obligations of those who enjoy the benefits of living in a world shaped by his political teaching to be especially high with respect to those who are not so fortunate.

Jesus does not say specifically whether he refers to peace between and among individuals, families, tribes, societies, nations, or some other grouping. His lack of specificity invites the conclusion that he is referring to all of these levels of peacemaking, which in turn raises a troubling question: What if there is a conflict between the requirements of peace among individuals or families, for example, and the requirements of peace between nations? As an illustration, think of the American Civil War, in which, famously, brother sometimes fought against brother. Or think of Sophocles's story of Antigone, who was caught between her obligation to obey the command of her king and her obligation to provide a proper burial for her brother. If a broad peace is truly possible, there will have to be a way of eliminating or reconciling such conflicts. This is a subject to which Jesus will speak later.

Jesus next mentions "those who have been persecuted for the sake of righteousness." In this group, we find those whose desire for right has been translated into action—the *pursuit* in the world of what is right, in some fashion that is perceptible to others in the way mere "hunger and thirst," or desire, is not. Perhaps it is by demanding right treatment for themselves or for others. In any case, persecution may follow—from those whose wishes stand to be thwarted by the ones demanding what is right. The demand for righteousness comes as a threat to the advantage some enjoy over others. Those who have the advantage may take action to protect what they have—what they think of, erroneously according to the Jesusian teaching, as rightly theirs. Of course, it is quite possible that those trying to be peacemakers will find themselves in this position, their efforts having failed not for want of trying but because they have given offense to those with the power to persecute.

Last mentioned are "you when people insult you and persecute you, and falsely say all kinds of evil against you because of me." Jesus reserves pride of place for the followers of his teaching. That's because he believes his teaching is true. Considered as such, his teaching is the highest possible expression of righteousness. Jesus is perfectly aware that those who take his message to heart, act on it, and espouse it to others may run great risks in doing so. After all, his teaching is based on the proposition that people's hunger and thirst for righteousness can be universally satisfied, which in turn threatens those for whom vindication of their own, erroneous sense of right comes only at the expense of others. Such overlords are apt to resist.

Jesus promises possession of "the kingdom of heaven" to those in two of his categories: the poor in spirit and those who have been persecuted for the sake of righteousness. As for those who run afoul of the overlords because they are following his teaching, he says "Rejoice and be glad, for your reward in heaven is great; for in the same way they persecuted the prophets who were before you."

Jesus seems to be suggesting that the prophets' reward is great because they anticipated the message he brings. He will make this point more explicitly later on. As for "rejoice and be glad," we must ask what the alternative is? To be ground down by the persecution one must suffer; to give up; to let go of the message of Jesus and to wallow, paralyzed, in one's despair; to become *poor in spirit*. In the Beatitudes, we have before us a full circle of good conduct, a complete typology of the "good person" or "good soul" (taking soul in the this-worldly sense of the part of a person that is not merely body)—from the lowest of the low (who harm no one but themselves) to the most exalted (those persecuted for their actions on behalf of what's right).

It is no accident that the first category of the blessed, the poor in spirit, and the eighth and ninth, the persecuted, have in common the promised reward of heaven. Jesus is under no illusion about the difficulty of the advance of his message in this world. For some—those who have given up and those who are persecuted—he can promise no earthly reward at all (though he does promise a heavenly one). This is a harsh pronouncement, and we must not shrink from it.

Jesus's categories in the Beatitudes have in common his description of those who belong to them as "blessed." Clearly, it is good to be "blessed," and one can find favor in any of the groups. However, the amount of activity required to qualify for membership in each of them—the activity of taking care of oneself and others—progressively increases from one category to the next. The "poor in spirit" are indeed "blessed," but that does not mean one should *emulate* the poor in spirit or seek spiritual impoverishment for oneself if one is capable of doing more, first for oneself, then with others. While "theirs is the kingdom of heaven" in the case of both "the poor in spirit" *and* "those who have been persecuted for the sake of righteousness," that doesn't mean we have no basis for preferring to join one category over the other if we are fortunate enough to have a choice. The latter category clearly entails a higher level of activity in working for the good of others than the former, whose members simply can't do more.

What makes working for righteousness higher, however, is not the superiority on the part of someone who has the possibility of making such a choice over someone who is debilitated by circumstance. It is that if one *can* reach out and help others by the pursuit of righteousness, one *should* do so and not avoid it for selfish reasons. Likewise, it is good to be gentle—and certainly better than to mourn inconsolably, but to be gentle alone is not quite as good as to desire righteousness or to act on behalf of righteousness if one can. One should not aspire to be "pure in heart" *instead of* acting as a peacemaker if one has the capability of working to end conflict.

The categories Jesus describes sometimes come into conflict with one another. It is a strain to suppose that one can always be gentle or meek while also being an activist on behalf of righteousness. Similarly, it is easy to envision someone who is less than pure in heart acting as a peacemaker. The progressively higher level of activity described as one moves from one of the categories to the next doesn't necessarily entail incorporation of all previously specified attributes in their original form.

Moreover, there is no suggestion that motion can be in one direction only. One could revert to a lower level of activity. One could become less active in the pursuit of the Jesusian vision of righteousness. Indeed, at the highest level—"you when people insult you and persecute you and falsely say all kinds of evil against you because of me"—there is an implied warning of the danger of falling back not just a little, but to the very bottom. "Rejoice and be glad" even through persecution, Jesus instructs, because as long as you are doing so, you are reaching out to and for others in the name of righteousness. But realize this: From even the highest point in the Jesusian hierarchy of the "good person," it is but a single step to the lowest, the poor in spirit. It's the difference between bearing one's persecution gladly and breaking under its weight. And it's not necessarily within your control.

We have seen that the character of the Beatitudes becomes clearer if we view the categories Jesus calls "blessed" in light of their opposites: the spiritually self-confident in contrast to the poor in spirit, the persecutors of those who follow the Jesus teaching in contrast to those persecuted.

These opposites, too, form a hierarchy—of potential activity in opposition to the Jesusian categories of good. Here, then, is the typology of the "bad person," each stage reflecting a greater degree of activity on behalf of the old political order, which Jesus seeks to overturn: those who offer the lowest of the low only their own sense of superiority; those unmoved by or contemptuous of people suffering from great loss or adversity; those whose response when they encounter the meek and gentle is to lord it over them; those who embrace a doctrine defending their position of privilege at the expense of others; those in a position of power who show no mercy to the powerless; those corruptly seeking advantage over others; those obstructing a just peace or fomenting conflict; those who persecute people who seek what's right; those who persecute the followers of Jesus's teaching. Jesus's first message to those in any of these categories is, quite simply, stop. Stop expressing contempt for others, stop promulgating strife, stop your persecution.

Accordingly, there are also worldly repercussions for individuals who exemplify these qualities of bad conduct. Those who define themselves by their sense of superiority will live in a world governed not by justice but by persecution, one in which the tables may turn on them without a moment's notice. Those who have contempt for the fellow-feeling that underlies mourning will be unmourned. Those who abuse the meek will lose their claim on a world they think is theirs. Those who defend their position of privilege at the expense of others will remain unsatisfied. Those who show no mercy will live their lives in fear of a world in which no mercy will be shown them. Those whose inner corruption drives them to seek ill-gotten advantage will find themselves mired in it, deprived of the ability to appreciate or apprehend anything that is good or pure. Those who obstruct peace will find their names reviled. Those who persecute the just will live in a world in which justice means nothing next to the arbitrary power of persecution, a power from which they will have no protection should it turn on them.

Except, of course, that the world of the "bad person" is the one to which Jesus is opposed and which he seeks to overturn. According to his prescription, the world will indeed come to be governed by justice—what's right—and not by persecution. And he offers those currently prone to the temptations of the "bad person" a chance to overcome them by embracing his teaching and stopping their own unjust conduct. These are real-world admonitions. Anyone in a position of privilege who heard Jesus speak and thought seriously about what he had to say would find his guidance on the reform of personal conduct difficult to mistake. But whether such a person would act on these words is another question altogether.

At first glance, the main purpose of the Beatitudes seems to be to offer various consolations to the downtrodden. But while Jesus does this, he also propounds a stern standard of judgment and offers strict guidance for good behavior for those who find themselves in a position of privilege. This injunction takes the form of a warning: The days of abusive privilege are numbered. Jesus's is not merely an ethereal threat, bound up in the afterlife and a world to come, which the nonbeliever can spurn with contempt in favor of worldly enjoyment. It is a threat based on changes coming to *this world*. It is a threat dangerous to ignore in the here and now.

Nevertheless, the question remains: Is this all to be taken literally? Come the revolution, of course, heads may roll, but surely Jesus cannot be saying that all those who enjoy privilege without righteousness are going to suffer for it in this world. Surely he is aware that some will hear all of what he has to say, spurn it, and get away with it scot-free for the rest of their earthly lives. Moreover, there is a potential for large-scale contradiction based on misreading here: If the point is to show mercy, even those who have themselves been unmerciful should be shown mercy, should they not?

True. Jesus says that what is right, according to the Beatitudes, "shall" come to pass; he does not say when. However, the cumulative effect of the positive, stated promises of the Beatitudes and the negative, unstated repercussions for those who oppose righteousness point to a question that *will* be asked in this world about those who have come before: What side were you on? Did you defend your privileges at the expense of others or work to uplift those who found themselves downtrodden? Did you act only for yourself, or did you think of others as best you could, whenever you could? Did you run risks for what's right, or was the risk you ran that the righteous would prevail? The merciless, the persecutors, the purveyors of conflict, the defenders of privilege—Jesus's point is that they live in a world governed by fear, and he invites them to reflect on what might happen if the world turned on them and they suddenly became the ones with cause to fear.

But that world is not the world Jesus is promoting. In a world ordered according to Jesusian principles, there will be no persecution, even for those who have made a transition from a world in which they were persecutors. Even those who have been unmerciful will be shown mercy. Their fear of a world in which the tables are turned on them is in fact displaced fear of a more primordial—one might say existential—kind: a world that has no place for them. A world in which the attributes of privilege that they believe are essential to their being have been obliterated. A world in which they, in their conception of themselves, cannot continue to *be*. A world in which *they* must change, if they are to remain. Jesus confronts the "bad person" not with something so simple—and easy to reject—as a competing model of how to live a better life. Rather, he forces a radical confrontation within the "bad person" over the very possibility of his or her continued existence.

More than that. What would the world look like if those in a position of privilege decided to comport themselves in accordance with the implicit guidance of the Beatitudes? And how, in turn, would that affect membership in the categories Jesus has described as "blessed"? The result here is most interesting.

If no one persecutes people for following the teaching of Jesus, then the category of the "persecuted" disappears. If no one persecutes those who seek righteousness, then this category, too, disappears. And if the response to the poor in spirit is not to show contempt for them but to uplift them, to encourage them to find the value in their lives that they have somehow lost sight of, then that category, too, disappears. Thus, these three categories of the blessed for which Jesus makes promises only with regard to heaven *disappear entirely wherever the Jesusian teaching takes root on earth.* This explains why Jesus assigns no earthly reward for people in these three categories. His silence anticipates that once people follow his guidance, there will be no one left in these conditions. His ambitious political agenda is to rid the world of both persecuted and persecutors—opposites sides of the coin of persecution.

In the world, we will always have among us those in mourning and the gentle; we will always have a need of those who desire righteousness, of those who are merciful, of those who act out of pure intentions, and of those who seek peace. But if or when the world is organized in accordance with the principles embedded in the lives of those Jesus here deems "blessed," we will no longer have the persecuted and the unvalued, nor their persecutors and tormentors. The Jesusian political agenda is thus organized around the pursuit of righteousness by those who are able—at potential risk to their own lives—for the sake of a world in which the unvalued (including they themselves when they are persecuted) are at last fully valued as human beings.

How, then, does Jesus envision that the gentle will come to inherit the earth? Because the once-mighty, under pressure of precisely this kind, will die out as a type. They will change their minds about defending their privileges at the expense of others. And the world will be their dying bequest to the gentle.

SALT AND LIGHT

Immediately following the Beatitudes are four verses that complement and complete the preceding thoughts (Mt. 5:13–16). We have seen how Jesus draws a portrait of the ways in which people may be good in relation to one another. The result, between and among them, is a community of goodwill in which repression no longer exists—a world where people enjoy a sense of equality among themselves, born of the recognition that the only true way for anyone's desire for righteousness to be satisfied is for everyone's desire for righteousness to be satisfied. In today's world, wherever people have come to the conclusion that repression is no longer an option for their relations with one another, they have succeeded in implementing this aspect of the Jesusian teaching as far as their relations with one another are concerned. But as we look around us, we see parts of the world where repression still reigns. Clearly, the desire for righteousness that people feel in these areas is not being satisfied in the truest sense. Jesus will soon elaborate on why and how we can reach out to others in an effort to include them in the world beyond repression. But first, he means to reassure us about what that effort entails.

Jesus shows another property of the community of goodwill. When we seek to extend it, we can do so in the confidence that its extension won't necessarily result in the diminishment or dilution of its essential unifying quality, that common feeling of goodwill. (Of course, as Jesus will explain later, there are practical considerations related to the extension of the community of goodwill, especially to those who remain determined to pursue their satisfaction at the expense of others.)

Here, Jesus speaks as if those listening have already embraced his teaching. He tells them that they are "the salt of the earth" and "the light of the world," following each remark with what seems to be an admonition: In the first example, "but if the salt has become tasteless, how can it be made salty again?" Rather, it is useless, fit only for throwing away. Second, with regard to the light, he notes that no one lights a lamp in order to cover it up. Doing so is self-contradiction. Therefore, "let your light shine before men that they may see your good works" and accordingly glorify "your Father who is in heaven."

As a matter of first impression, these metaphors seem to warn those whom Jesus's teaching has made, at it were, "salty" and "shiny" not to lose their saltiness or shininess by ceasing to follow the teaching. This

risk would seem to be the reversion of the world to a pre-Jesusian business as usual: the extinguishing of the Jesusian teaching.

But let's look more closely. How, exactly, can salt lose its saltiness?
Its taste and its properties with regard to bodily needs as well as its
utility as a means of preserving food are inextricably bound up with
what it is. If you are salt, then you must be salty. It's not, in Jesus's
metaphor, that the salt is in people, commingling with who they are—
an influence on them that might recede or be eliminated—but that
they *are* salt. You can't separate those who are salty from the properties
of salt within them.

Those who do not follow the Jesusian teaching would seem to be
something other than salt. What distinguishes people who *are* salt,
metaphorically speaking, is that they can break off a small piece of
themselves and salt others—a process that may have the effect of beginning the transformation of the others into "salty" beings themselves.

As for the metaphorical sense in which followers of the Jesusian
teaching are the light of the world, again, his followers are the light as
such. Where did the light come from? Who lit the lamp? The answer is
Jesus, in propounding his teaching. And he did not do so in order for it
to be extinguished. He intended the light to "shine before men in such
a way that they may see your good works" (Mt. 5:16). The light illuminates as the salt seasons. Once again, it is the initiation of a process in
which the light shows people what they need to see—in order to begin
their own transformation into a source of light. There is only the one
light source in this metaphor, and that is the collective body of the followers of the Jesus teaching. It is a torch from which people can light
other torches ad infinitum.

In these passages, Jesus is indeed exhorting his followers to continue, but what at first seems an exhortation based on the possibility
that the Jesusian teaching is at risk of being extinguished (in the case of
the light metaphor) or losing its essence (in the case of the salt) turns
out on closer examination to pose the matter both more optimistically
and more radically: One is "salty" in order to salt others and "shiny" in

order to light the way for others, that the others may in turn become "salty" and "shiny." There is something about the essence of the Jesusian teaching as embodied in his followers that is permanently transformative, at least in a collective sense. His teaching has transformative power: Your saltiness makes you salty enough to salt others.

His clear implication is that this process has no limit. So we need have no fear that when we reach out to others, we are necessarily weakening our grip on what unites us.

2.

THE ANCIENT LAW

It is already quite clear, from only the first few verses of the Sermon on the Mount, that Jesus has something radically new to say. The Beatitudes turned the world of his day upside down to show us the various qualities present in a "good person." Now it is time for him to offer his guidance on how people should act in order to begin to bring the world he envisions into being. In short, he is about to lay down the law.

This is a new kind of lawgiving, however. Whereas the rulers of his day set down the law and expected it to be obeyed, Jesus instead issues an invitation, something for his listeners to consider. They are free to accept or reject what he has to say; his law is not binding in this world except to the extent that people bind themselves to it.

Of course, the world in which he preaches the Sermon on the Mount is not anarchical or lawless. There are the laws of the Roman occupation, and more important to most of his listeners at the time, the ancient law of the five books of Moses, the Torah, especially as spelled out in Exodus, Deuteronomy, and Leviticus. So the question arises: What is the status of the ancient law in his teaching? Is what's new in what he has to say the equivalent of a revolution against the old law? If not, what is the relationship between his law and the ancient law?

These questions, however, are not just matters for the time of

Jesus. The problem he describes and addresses here—namely, how his teaching fits into the ancient law of the Israelites—has implications down to our time for the spread of the community of goodwill. To begin with, in keeping with the way Jesus invites others to follow his teaching (rather than commanding them to do so), the extension of our community of goodwill must be based on an invitation to join it, not a command to do so. Jesus is not a builder of empire, but an enabler of voluntary association and affiliation. The clear implication for our own day is that as we reach out to others, we need not and must not demand that they make a clean break with every aspect of their past. Rather, our invitation consists of an offer to accept them as they are, providing only that they share the goodwill that characterizes the community.

Addressing the Ancient Law

Jesus begins this section of the Sermon on the Mount with a sweeping statement with regard to the ancient law: "Do not think that I came to abolish the Law or the Prophets; I did not come to abolish but to fulfill" (Mt. 5:17). He then admonishes his listeners in no uncertain terms to follow the ancient law (Mt. 5:18–20). He continues with an analysis of specific ancient laws that elaborates what he means by "fulfill" in six passages that take the general form "You have heard [X]. . . . But I say to you [X does not go far enough]. . . ." (Mt. 5:21–48).

The first thing to remark is that the Sermon here takes on a somewhat defensive tone. There seems to be an underlying subtext, a contemporaneous dialogue about the meaning of the teaching of Jesus that has taken place or is taking place out of earshot. As becomes explicit in subsequent Gospel accounts depicting confrontations between Jesus and the established religious order, what Jesus has been saying in and around Galilee has caused some to call into question his allegiance to the ancient law. Jesus here moves to set the record straight. Not so much as the serif of a single letter, he says, "shall pass from the Law until all is accomplished" (Mt. 5:18). He promises heavenly condemnation for anyone who "annuls" the law or teaches others to do so and great heavenly reward for those who keep to the law and teach it (Mt. 5:19). He adds that "unless your righteousness surpasses that of the scribes and Pharisees" (Mt. 5:20)—the religious leaders of the day—there will be no place in heaven for you.

While in a sense this is a resounding affirmation of the ancient law, it also has two important twists. Consider Jesus's remark about the scribes and Pharisees. Clearly, he knew whom he was setting himself up against: key elements of the contemporary religious establishment. Now, perhaps one should understand his statement as the ultimate call to virtuous conduct: Given the known and conspicuous and even officially acknowledged righteousness of scribes and Pharisees, any follower of Jesus's teaching for this world, he says, will have to meet and surpass that very high standard.

The other side of this two-edged remark suggests that, as Jesus sees it, the righteousness of the scribes and Pharisees themselves isn't quite up to the standards that heaven demands. To put it in this-worldly terms, Jesus expects better behavior from his followers than the conduct exhibited by the official religious establishment.

He thereby puts the members of that establishment into an awkward position. They can claim that (a) no higher standards than the ones they exhibit are necessary, since conduct in accordance with the standards they uphold is good enough. Or they can claim that (b) they are already meeting the highest standards, the ones Jesus is going about setting for his followers. But in doing so, they would implicitly be endorsing his teaching. Or they can claim that (c) they (and only they, not everyone else) possess true knowledge of what the standards are and can follow them properly—in this case, the ancient law and the tradition of interpretation that surrounds it. What they cannot acknowledge is the truth of Jesus's claim to be articulating a universal, higher standard. Their defense is necessarily partial; it's particular to them. Jesus's statement therefore has the effect of undermining their authority—their status as the acknowledged arbiters of compliance with the only true law.

By implication, the other twist is that when "all is accomplished," whatever that may mean, the law *can* change. At a minimum, what Jesus is saying is that the law is not permanent. Those who say otherwise—that it is eternal, forever binding, because God has given it as part of a covenant with his chosen people—are mistaken, in his judgment. It is binding now because "all is [not yet] accomplished."

We may take this a step farther. What does it mean to say that the law is binding until "all is accomplished"? First, that the law as it is now is incomplete: More needs to happen. This point is consistent with Jesus's claim that he came "to fulfill" the law. Second, Jesus takes the position here that the law (as it is currently understood, that is, in its unfulfilled form) is not an end in itself, and therefore, someone who abides by the law, even fully, has not thereby achieved the full human potential for good or proper conduct. The law as it is points to a higher end and is really only a way-station to that end: the fulfilled law, which Jesus is offering. At which point, when "all is accomplished," Jesus pregnantly suggests, some element or elements of the current law will indeed "pass." He doesn't say what.

We cannot miss the radicalism of the Jesusian teaching here, cloaked though it may be in language of respect for the law and for the scribes and Pharisees, the official upholders of the law. The ancient law is not just a matter of a series of free-standing edicts, any one or more of which might "pass" without effect on any of the others. Collectively, the specific ancient injunctions form a whole, *the* law, whose authority rests on its supposedly divine status as a complete statement of the obligations incumbent on the people governed by it. Jesus acknowledges as much when he warns of the peril facing anyone who "annuls *one of the least* of these commandments" or who "teaches others" to annul even the least (Mt. 5:19, emphasis added). To question so much as a single element of this law is to question the entire edifice. Nevertheless, this is what Jesus does: He points to a time, however far in the future, when "all is accomplished" and therefore aspects of the law "pass." To say this is to say that the law as a whole, traditionally construed as an inviolable body, will pass. There is no escaping the implication. And no wonder Jesus raised the issue in the manner of someone who knows that what he is saying may get him into trouble.

How do we square this startling conclusion with Jesus's admonition to his listeners to keep the law as it is, as a whole, for now? In the first place, it seems quite clear that some elements of the ancient law will still remain in force when "all is accomplished" as a result of Jesus's exercise in "fulfill[ing]" the law. "You shall not murder" (Ex. 20:13, Deut. 5:17), an element of ancient law to which Jesus is about to turn his attention, is surely an injunction that will continue to hold sway when "all is accomplished." Some precepts contained in the ancient law will remain, even though the ancient law construed as an inviolable whole and as an end in itself will not.

Second, we can see that to Jesus, while the ancient law is not an end in itself (in the sense of permanent, divine commandment), it *serves a purpose* in the Jesusian teaching. He did not come to "abolish" it but to make use of it for his own, higher ends—"to fulfill." Jesus is a radical, but he is not reckless. Declaring at the beginning of his ministry that the ancient law is defective and has to go, even if that's what Jesus thought, would likely have led the authorities of his day to haul him in well before he finished the task of "fulfill[ing]" the law—telling people what they need to hear in order to understand and decide whether to follow his teaching. In addition, although he has come to teach people a new way to get along with one another in a community of goodwill that potentially includes everyone, if people get the erroneous impression that the old law is therefore null and void, the cost in short-term social disruption would be huge.

It is not as if Jesus imagines a transition from the world of the ancient law to a world in which "all is accomplished" in the blink of an eye. The world in which "all is accomplished," in accordance with Jesus's appearance on the scene "to fulfill," requires, precisely, *accomplishing*. A world in which the ancient law has been utterly cast aside *before* Jesus's teaching has taken root is a world in which it is unlikely that the Jesusian teaching *will* take root. Rather, the anarchic or lawless conditions are more likely to lead to Thomas Hobbes's "war of all against all" than to the triumph of righteousness. To "abolish" or "annul" the law would be to return to conditions prior to the law: One would first have to regain the essential elements of the law in order to arrive at the conditions in which Jesus propounds his teaching.

So it is that Jesus understands that his teaching *presupposes* the ancient law, the social order the law has built as it has come down to the time of Jesus. He means to transform the social order in a drastic, indeed elemental, way. But that does not mean he thinks he can do so by discarding the old law. Rather, he seeks to build on it. While Jesus indicates he thinks that *in time* elements of the ancient law must "pass," and therefore, that the law's current claim to status as a permanent whole cannot stand, there is no way to get to the point at which "all is accomplished" except with and through the law.

Most translations of Matthew 5:19 refer to someone who "breaks" even the least commandment. The NASB translation, on which we have been relying here, uses "annuls." Other translations give "relaxes" or "looses." The difference matters if there is a distinction to be made between simply "breaking" a law and more fundamentally "relaxing," "loosening," or "annulling" it. The Greek root is *luō*, which does indeed evoke this distinction.[1] Jesus's injunction seems to be aimed not at whoever *breaks* the least commandment but, less restrictively, at whoever seeks to *overthrow* the law, even its least element. Jesus thereby opens up the possibility that one might *rightly* break a commandment without in general seeking to annul it or to loosen its force. As we will see in the verses that immediately follow, Jesus directs people inside themselves in order to assess how to act toward others. Conforming

---

[1] See W.E. Vine, Merrill Unger, and William White Jr., *Vine's Complete Expository Dictionary of Old and New Testament Words* (Nashville, Tenn.: Thomas Nelson Publishers, 1984, 1996), p. 78.

outwardly to the letter of the law is not enough and may, in fact, be the wrong thing to do.

Jesus takes the ancient law as it is, enjoins people to obey it and teach it, allows for the possibility of exceptions to it, says his purpose is to fulfill it, and points to a time when his effort to fulfill the law will have succeeded (when "all is accomplished") and some of its elements will "pass" (about which we as yet know little). With this is mind, we can turn to the specific laws Jesus addresses in the Sermon.

THE ROOTS OF MURDER

Law regulates conduct. From Jesus's time down to our own, if you are rightly accused of breaking the law, it's because you have *done something* the law forbids or *failed to do* something the law requires. Although law sometimes purports to regulate your thoughts, feelings, and beliefs, its only instrument for assessing your compliance with such provisions is to consider what you do or don't do—including what you say. Now, in our day, especially in the part of the world where the Jesusian teaching is most deeply rooted, we tend to think law has no business holding people accountable for their private thoughts and, in most cases, even for giving voice to opinions that are unpopular. We view societies that want to inquire into what people think so they can enforce a specific orthodoxy as incompatible with the requirements of freedom. The totalitarian ideologies of the twentieth century, fascism and communism—along with any other ideology that seeks total control in the political sphere over the beliefs of those who fall under its sway—are recent examples of doctrines based on a wrong idea about what righteousness is and what the satisfaction of the desire for it entails. The easiest way to see this is to note that such ideologies, when they acquire political power, *must* engage in repression, for the simple reason that all people won't voluntarily subscribe to their tenets. Thus, they run afoul of the Jesusian teaching that all who desire true righteousness will be satisfied. The only way to a *universal* sense of righteousness is the creation of a world in which people *voluntarily* agree that the satisfaction of their individual desires for righteousness is dependent on the satisfaction of every member of the community's desire for righteousness.

So Jesus has already pointed to an important aspect of law: It's not just that the law must be laid down in some fashion; it's also a matter of whether people accept the law as it has been set forth. But how do we find out? Obviously, a problem arises if society seeks to resolve this difficulty by interrogating its members in an effort to enforce orthodoxy, since the end result is repression. Jesus has a different solution. He wants *each person* to inquire for himself or herself into the question of whether the law is something he or she agrees with upholding or something he or she wants to break. And then he wants us to ask ourselves whether that feeling is justifiable in the context of a world in which the satisfaction of all is the satisfaction of each. Therefore, the real test of law is indeed our own inner conviction, but it is not the role of the political authorities to examine such convictions. That is a task reserved for each of us alone.

Jesus starts his consideration of specific elements of the ancient law with the prohibition on murder and with what should happen to murderers: they "shall be liable to the court" (Mt. 5:21). Rather than continuing with a discussion of a different way to deal with murderers, Jesus changes the subject, addressing the question of *who else* deserves to be before the court. Jesus says that "everyone who is angry with his brother"[2] is due in court (Mt. 5:22). Further, those who call a brother "good-for-nothing" are due in the *high* court (the Sanhedrin), and those who call a brother "fool" have no less than hellfire coming to them. With this progression, Jesus describes a hierarchy of disdain, ranging from one's internal feeling of anger toward another, to the verbal expression of that anger in the form of a term of abuse ("good-for-nothing," or *Raca*), to the rejection of the other at a more fundamental level ("fool").

---

[2] Some manuscripts add "with no reason," but it seems to me that the sense is otherwise.

But what is the connection between disdain of the sort Jesus condemns here and the way in which Jesus opened the subject, namely, the crime of murder? What we can see is that murder would be the most extreme form of expression of the disdain that begins with anger in one's heart toward someone to whom one is ordinarily very close—one's own brother. Beyond the narrow sense of fraternal kinship, Jesus also seems to mean "brother" in a more general sense. Think of the term as designating your own people: your family, your kin, your neighbors, your fellow members of the tribe, your fellow citizens—all those with whom you feel a sense of bondedness, not necessarily based on personal acquaintance. To clarify further, think of "brother" as a category in contrast with the other Jesusian categories "stranger" (for example, see Mt. 25:35 and following) and "enemy," to which he will shortly turn (Mt. 5:44). Strangers are people toward whom we don't have a bond of fellow-feeling at all, and enemies are people who, by their own action, repudiate such a bond.

Jesus, for his part, will countenance no anger and insult among brothers. Abjuring such feelings is a fundamental obligation of community. A community as explicitly religious as Jesus's would see offering a sacrifice at the altar in the temple as the most solemn of all activity, taking precedence over any other. According to Jesus, however, this is not the case. He switches to a direct form of address, admonishing "you" who are about to present an offering but "remember that your brother has something against you" to put aside the offering until you are "reconciled to your brother" (Mt. 5:23–24). An offering to the divine is not appropriate from someone who is not yet reconciled with those on earth.

We have discussed the Jesusian typology of the "good person" along with its implicit opposite number, the typology of the "bad person." We have seen that in offering this description and in making certain claims about what is in store for those in each "good" category, as well as the implicit repercussions for those in the "bad" categories, Jesus's teaching has an unmistakable this-worldly element. He envisions a world in which the desire for righteousness is satisfied for all—which entails an end to persecution and to any and all assertions of superiority of one over another that frustrate the other's desire for satisfaction. We have seen his determination to get from here to there, so to speak, not by overthrowing the law but by building on it. This will entail listening to Jesus's guidance on how to fulfill the law and then choosing to act on that guidance until it is fully implemented ("all is accomplished").

But *what should we do*? How should we govern our own individual behavior? Jesus has given some indication of this in the Beatitudes by describing certain kinds of conduct and the states of mind that underlie them as "blessed," happy, or fortunate—and by implication, there are some things we might be doing that we should put a halt to, namely, any conduct inconsistent with the good conduct in a community of goodwill. Only at this point, having provided a general description of where we are going and a description of the procedure for getting there, does Jesus begin to get specific about people's conduct.

"You" should reconcile with your brother. Your offering will do you no good in the absence of reconciliation. The offering is no substitute for the effort to reconcile. And who is this brother with whom you must reconcile? None other than someone with "something against you." Where does the fault lie? In your conduct, such that your brother rightly has something against you? Or in your brother's, such that he is wrong to have something against you? Or in both in some measure? It doesn't matter. The first obligation, on "you," is to "be reconciled." We can add that the first obligation of your brother is no less to "be reconciled." But the other's obligation is not an obligation that comes before yours, and it will not do for you to proceed with your offering in a frame of mind holding self-righteously that the person with something against you is obliged to make the first move toward reconciliation. That obligation is yours, and it will not suffice to demand that reconciliation proceed on the basis of the other party's obligation to make amends to you, grant you concessions, or offer you apologies. The root of the Greek word translated as "reconciled" here, *diallassō*—the only occasion on which the word appears in the Gospels—denotes an exchange, mutual action.[3] If two people are reconciled, *neither* has anything against the other.

Reconciliation takes precedence over every other activity. Even when you are at the altar in the middle of making a sacrifice, if you recall that another person has "something against you," your obligation is to leave the temple and undertake reconciliation. If this obligation overrides even temple offerings, then whenever or wherever it comes to mind that "a brother" has a grievance with you, it is incumbent on you to set aside what you are doing and attend to reconciliation.

Does this in turn mean that whenever *anyone* has a grievance with you, you should drop everything to pursue reconciliation? That's not quite what Jesus says. The injunction pertains to your "brother." Jesus's instruction here arises out of a situation in which you and the person with something against you have a prior relationship: the condition of brotherhood. You already feel a sense of bondedness with the other person. Those ties form the basis of the obligation to reconcile. Given such ties of brotherhood, there is no justification for your failure to pursue and achieve reconciliation and no activity in this world that takes precedence: Reconciliation is fully and in all instances possible between "brothers" and is a matter of top priority.

The category of "brother" is an expanding one, not one whose membership is fixed. We can turn Jesus's instruction around in order to note that *if* you are reconciled with someone, you *achieve* the condition of brotherhood. You can create a tie where none existed before. Surely this is both advantageous and worth the attempt. Here again, the mutuality of the exercise is essential; reconciliation is not a matter of one party doing all the accommodating to the nonnegotiable demands of another, as a slave does to a master under penalty of death. Rather, the essence is the cultivation of the relationship between the two in such

---

[3] *Vine's Complete*, p. 514.

a fashion as to eliminate whatever each may have against the other. This aspect of brotherhood—the ability of nonbrothers to become brothers—is essential to the spread of the Jesusian teaching.

After delivering his message about the primary obligation of brothers to be reconciled, Jesus calls on his listeners to "[m]ake friends quickly with your opponent at law while you are with him on the way" to court, lest your opponent set in train a sequence of events that lands you in prison—because if he does, you won't get out until you pay him the last cent you owe him (Mt. 5:25–26). The relationship between adversaries at court is more antagonistic than that between brothers who have reconciled or even brothers who need to reconcile. Nevertheless, you do have a connection with "your opponent at law," and that is, precisely, the law you both live under. After all, you agree that a court is the place to settle your disagreement. You have not chosen to fight to the finish. Why not, then, take the next step: "Make friends." Once again, act to eliminate the point in dispute. Be reconciled. Reach a mutual accommodation.

If, rather, you insist on turning to the law to settle the matter between you, rather than taking it upon yourself to settle it, you will turn an obligation toward your opponent into an obligation before the law. Here, Jesus warns that the problem with making a dispute into a legal matter is that the law can be very rigidly applied, such that you will have to comply down to the last cent.

Jesus starts with the obvious and universally accepted necessity of calling murderers to account in court, and then extends the summons to all who have a grievance against a brother or a brother with a grievance against them. The purpose of this exercise is not, however, to clog the courts, but to get people to understand that the conditions in which they remain unreconciled with a brother do them no good. Jesus's instruction here to drop everything, pursue reconciliation, and do it first, may sound as a matter of first impression like a demand for altruistic conduct on the part of the person of whom the demand is made. But that's not quite right: There's something in it for that person. Both people are better off, mutually so, for working to eliminate the conditions that keep them apart. Their previously existing relationship of brotherhood or bondedness demonstrates that reconciliation is possible. Yet there is something incomplete about their brotherhood: what they have against each other. Where reconciliation is achieved, the condition of brotherhood as a mutual tie is, in a word, "fulfilled." And, at least in potential, it is susceptible to extension to others.

In calling all of us before the bar, Jesus means to advance a condition in which reconciliation diminishes the need of anyone to appear before the bar. So it is that Jesus provides a first indication of what will "pass" from the law when "all is accomplished": those aspects of the law delineated for the purpose of regulating the conduct and settling the disputes of those with "something against" each other.

Nor does this Jesusian fulfillment necessarily come into play only at some unspecified, distant future time. Unless everything Jesus refers to in the phrase "all is accomplished" takes place all at once, then before "all" is accomplished, *some* will be accomplished. When people are reconciled, then *all is accomplished* between the two of them. With respect to each other, they no longer need the law as it applies to the governance of their earthly conduct. Such law can accordingly "pass" without loss. The world of the law cannot effectively inquire into what we feel and believe, when it does, repression is the result. Yet when we ourselves look within, in the spirit of reconciliation, of removing the obstacles standing in the way of a community of goodwill, we can diminish the very need for law itself.

WOMEN AND MEN

Once he has completed discussing the conditions pertaining to brotherhood, Jesus turns to relations between the sexes. Here, we need to recall that his listeners, even those favorably disposed toward his message, would begin with the understanding that relations between men, including brothers, are and should be very different, even radically different, from relations between men and women. That men and women are different in certain respects is not in doubt, not even in our day. And in fact, in some parts of today's world, women enjoy little more in the way of equality with men than they did at the time of Jesus. However, in this section of the Sermon, Jesus does not set out to delineate differences and to lay down different rules for the regulation of the conduct of men with regard to men versus men with regard to women. Rather, his theme here is the one-sidedness of the law and conduct of his day and the ways in which these respective sets of regulations for man-to-man and man-to-woman should become more alike. It continues and extends his theme of reconciliation.

Jesus begins with the prohibition of adultery articulated in Exodus 20:14 and Deuteronomy 5:18. Under the ancient law, it is a very serious crime, punishable by death for both in the case of a man who commits adultery with another man's wife (Lev. 20:10). Jesus says, "I say to you that everyone who looks at a woman with lust for her has already committed adultery with her in his heart" (Mt. 5:27–28). Just as he presents murder as the most extreme expression of disdain, Jesus presents adultery here as the ultimate form that inner lust takes. Jesus seeks to go to the interior root of the problem that gave rise to the prohibition of certain conduct in the ancient law. In each case, if people manage to correct the problem at the root, then the law becomes unnecessary. Jesus emphasizes the point in the next two verses in some of the most florid language attributed to him in the Gospels: If your right eye or right hand causes you to stumble, rip it from your body and throw it away because it is better to lose an eye or a hand than to have your whole body condemned to hellfire (Mt. 5:29–30). The precise connection between "look[ing] at a woman with lust" and the "right eye" and "right hand" is not specified, and there is no mention of any other body part that might more routinely be associated with lust. But in any event, neither lust nor anger toward one's brother is really a matter of a body part, but of something intangible: a desire.

We might therefore take the two verses as a general exhortation to get rid of whatever lies within that is leading you astray. Jesus's point in mentioning acts of self-mutilation would seem to be, as in the case of the offering at the altar, to evoke the extreme instance in order to validate a general case. If, even at the altar, you realize someone has something against you, you should attend to it immediately, and the more so in cases involving less compelling uses of your time. If it would cost you an eye or a hand to get rid of what's causing you to stumble, that would be a price worth paying: the bargain is all the better if the price is cheaper—in this case, the expurgation of a desire.

Jesus continues on the subject of adultery with the question of divorce, which he opposes except in cases of infidelity. The reason he gives is that divorcing a woman "makes her commit adultery," and a man who "marries a divorced woman commits adultery" (Mt. 5:32). Divorce leads to adultery; lust leads to adultery in the heart: There would seem to be adultery going on all over the place, at least as Jesus sees it.

If the questions of anger and murder that Jesus raises seem not at all distant from the concerns of our times, the same cannot be said with regard to his injunctions on sexual morality. However, it's important to note that here Jesus is most concerned with the effect of divorce on the woman. It "*makes her commit adultery.*" A man can send her away, according to the ancient law Jesus cites (Deut. 24:1), with no more than a piece of paper. In doing so, he accomplishes his wish, but she, more than he, pays the price, in Jesus's telling. It is unfair to her, so long as she has been faithful to him. Moreover, under the ancient law, divorce is an option husbands enjoy with respect to wives (whenever he decides "he has found some indecency in her," Deut. 24:1), but it is not an option wives have with respect to husbands. One could say, with some fairness, that in relocating the crime of adultery into the heart of the man who is looking on a woman with lust, Jesus postulates a scenario in which a man commits adultery without implicating a woman in the crime. Given the stark power imbalance between men and women, Jesus's prescription has the effect of nudging relations in the direction of greater equality.

It is possible to imagine a "solution" to the problem of divorce law more in keeping with the equality of the sexes, such as has been devised in divorce law in the modern world. But such a world is a vast distance from the world in which Jesus lived. In the context of those times, it is no small blow for equality to reconceive adultery as a "crime" that arises in the first instance in the heart of a *man* and needs to be addressed at that level, as Jesus has done. Moreover, he also offers a more comprehensive solution to the problems of inequality in the adultery and divorce law of his time by, in essence, telling *husbands* that they should not exercise their power to divorce their wives.

Here again, if the relations between husband and wife are correct, let alone loving—if they remain reconciled (so to speak) with each other—then they have attained something like the ideal that "brothers" obtain when they are mutually reconciled. If she remains faithful to him, not only sexually but in a general sense, he should remain faithful to her. The marital bond is not solely a matter of legal obligation: When relations between husband and wife are right, the ancient and modern law that governs the conditions of marriage, adultery, and divorce no longer much matters to them. It, too, can pass.

Swearing to Tell the Truth

The movement of this section of the Sermon on the Mount has been from relations between brothers under law to relations between men and women under law and now turns directly to the question of what role the authorities should have in assessing people's compliance with the law. The issue arises in the context of oath swearing.

The next ancient law Jesus cites is "You shall not make false vows, but shall fulfill your vows to the Lord" (Mt. 5:33, referring to Lev. 19:12, Num. 30:2, Deut. 23:21, 23). Jesus offers the amendment,

THE ANCIENT LAW   51

"make no oath at all," neither by heaven, nor earth, nor by Jerusalem, nor by your own head; rather, "let your statement be 'Yes, yes' or 'No, no'" (Mt. 5:34–37).

In Jesus's time, the scribes and Pharisees had an elaborate set of rules regarding the swearing of oaths.[4] Many of the regulations had an arbitrary quality, and the cumulative impression of swearing oaths to God but failing to live up to them was the profanation of God's name. Jesus proposes a radical solution, to clear away all the underbrush at once by eliminating oaths. But it's not just against the contemporaneous backdrop that we should consider his injunction. The point is more profound than that. The real radicalism here lies in the Jesusian teaching that one should simply tell the truth. Not "Yes, by God," or "Yes, by Jerusalem," or "Yes, upon my head," but simply "Yes, yes."

Why would we think someone who swears an oath is more truthful than someone who simply says "yes" or "no"? Perhaps because of some specific fear on the part of the oath swearer of incurring the wrath of God, or of the city, or of forfeiting one's head. But in the first place, what God does is God's business, Jesus notes, and likewise the city the city's. And as for your own head, "you cannot make one hair white or black," so there is no use pretending that you have compelled some kind of punishment to befall you in the event you go back on your word. If people think they can trust you to tell the truth only when you swear, they think that in general, you're a liar. And if that's what they think of you, they would be naïve not to be suspicious of what you say even if you do swear to tell the truth.

The real effect of an oath is to turn ordinary discourse into a matter of law. If I say, "This is so," others will judge my truthfulness on the basis of whether they agree that "this is so." If, however, I *testify under oath* that "this is so," or if I swear by God in heaven that it is, then my statement is no longer merely a matter between me and my interlocutors.

---

[4] *Vine's Complete*, p. 438. Everett Ferguson, *Backgrounds of Early Christianity*, 3rd edition (Grand Rapids, Mich.: William B. Eerdmans Publishing Company, 2003), p. 495.

What once was a private matter, in the sense that the other parties to the conversation would decide for themselves what to make of my statement, becomes instead a matter in which the authority of the law has now been introduced as a third element in the interaction between me and the others.

This has two large consequences. The first is that when oaths are abundant, as evidently they were in the time of Jesus, the reach of law is accordingly extended too broadly; it ventures into places where it need not or should not try to go. If a matter can be settled perfectly satisfactorily by the two people it has come between, it should be so settled. In this respect, the implication here is similar to Jesus's plain instruction in the case of reconciling with your "brother:" You don't go to court to pursue this reconciliation; you mutually undertake it on your own initiative. Jesus seeks to limit the reach of the law by getting people to resolve their differences not under penalty of law but by prior agreement among themselves. So, too, Jesus seeks to diminish the role of the law in relations between husbands and wives by encouraging them to remain together and understand the benefits they receive from their relations.

The second consequence is that once the law is extended too broadly, it loses its force as law. If people swear oaths with reckless abandon, they invite the law to land upon their heads. But can it each and every time someone vows "by God" to do something but fails to perform? That is too much to expect of the law; the law cannot be called on to intervene in all such cases. If it is called, it will fail. And the result of its failure will be to lose the force the law requires. Some will escape the just punishment they themselves have invited by swearing an oath. More important, however, than the law's force in the sense of compulsion—the lawful authorities' ability or inability to mete out punishment—is the law's moral force.

The moral force of the law is its ability to make people comply voluntarily, either on the strength of the claim of the authority of the law (for example, law as God's will or the king's) or because they see the law as "right" for other reasons (or both). If the law is routinely flouted without consequence, however, it will lack moral force and fail to compel through fear of consequence. As a result, it will be undermined. Recall that Jesus has declared himself in support of the law. In these passages about oaths, he is showing one way in which that's true: Of course, it is necessary that the law prohibit false oaths, but such a law provides no guidance on the extent to which people should swear oaths in the first place. Jesus admonishes them simply to tell the truth, thereby keeping their truthfulness largely a private matter. In so doing, he rescues the law from the risk of the exposure of its irrelevance due to a foolish attempt to extend it where it does not belong.

But we should look a little further into the question of what happens when someone makes a statement without an oath and others come to question its truthfulness. If people don't agree with my declaration, they may ask whether I made my statement owing to a mistaken judgment on my part or whether I lied. If it's the latter, they will judge me a liar, and I will be obliged to suffer the consequences of their judgment. I will surely find it more difficult to get the same people to believe me again. To the degree that the story of my lying extends beyond the people originally involved, I may acquire a reputation as a liar that will cause others to doubt what I say before I utter a word. There is a social sanction, a price to be paid, for lying.

This in turn presents a reason for telling the truth beyond its own innate value. To be caught out in a lie by one's friend or perhaps one's "brother" is likely to ruin the friendship or the sense of bondedness underlying brotherliness. It is easier to lie to a stranger; the likelihood of ever having to face the music is lower. As in the previous cases, Jesus offers a moral injunction: You should tell the truth to others, as you should honor your commitment to your wife, as you should reconcile with your "brother" and make him your "friend." Your reason for doing so is not merely that these things are good in their own right and that they make you a moral person; in addition, you also get something out of it. As people reconcile and make friends, as they work to remain reconciled as husband and wife, as they envelope themselves in a reputation for truth-telling and find themselves encountering others who have the same reputation, there are political and social consequences. A society organized around these principles, what we have been calling a community of goodwill, is very different from a society in which they are matters of indifference—devalued, that is, in favor of conflict and contentiousness, of the view that others are merely a means to a desired end, and of mistrust and corruption.

More broadly, one could say that Jesus, given the conflict and contentiousness he saw around him at the time, had the temerity and vision to propose an alternative to that world on a scale that had never before been contemplated. After all, it is not as if reconciliation between "brothers" was unknown before Jesus presented it in the Sermon on the Mount as a universal imperative. Along the same lines, he did not invent there the idea of a happy marriage or that the bonds between people are based on their mutual sense of trust. All these elements of connection between people were out there, part of the human experience, but they were too small a part. Jesus wishes to see them extended as far as humanly possible.

To present his case for how to live in this world as persuasively as possible, Jesus does more than make a declaration of how people *ought to* live. In addition, he offers a plausible account of what life will be like in such a world, thus demonstrating to people that they would prefer such a world to the one in which they find themselves. He believes that what he says about people and how they can live together is both *true* and *beneficial*. His world speaks to people's sense of aspiration for themselves and those close to them, to the desire for righteousness that he described as the first outward stirring of the soul. The way he proposes for getting from the current state of affairs to the one he favors is entirely plausible: More people will decide to adhere more closely to his political teachings because of the benefits they bring.

FROM REVENGE TO RECONCILIATION

While Jesus has pointed the way toward setting matters right between people, brother to brother and man to woman, he has not addressed the matter of those who refuse reconciliation. Jesus will soon have something to say about those who are determined to be our enemy. First, however, he turns to the case of those who live among us but have done us wrong, from criminals to those who cause injury unintentionally.

Jesus here turns to the ancient principle of justice elaborated in Exodus (21:23–25), Leviticus (24:17–21), and Deuteronomy (19:21), "an eye for an eye." The principle, which is not unique to the Hebrew scripture, is generally regarded as one of the oldest legal doctrines. It's called the *lex talionis*, Latin for the "law of retaliation." In sum, if you have done someone harm, your punishment accords with the harm you have done. Take an eye, lose an eye; break a bone, have a bone broken; kill someone's animal, forfeit one of your own; kill, and you forfeit your life.

In response to this ancient doctrine, Jesus's "But I say to you . . ." is among the most famous and difficult instructions he gives on how to live in the world. He says, "Do not resist an evil person; but whoever slaps you on your right cheek, turn the other to him also. If anyone wants to sue you and take your shirt, let him have your coat also. Whoever forces you to go one mile, go with him two. Give to him who asks of you, and do not turn away from him who wants to borrow from you" (Mt. 5:39–42).

Before we take up Jesus's injunctions here, it's important to understand that while *lex talionis* sounds undeniably harsh in the modern world, it was actually an advance in the idea of justice, a moderating influence on the exaction of penalties and the imposition of punishment. In the mists of antiquity from which the *lex talionis* emerged, the punishment for having caused the loss of an eye was not a choice between suffering the loss of one's own eye and suffering some lesser retribution;

on the contrary, it was a substantially greater punishment, such as death, perhaps not only for you, but for your entire family.

Here, we need to return to Hobbes's famous description of the "war of all against all." How does an idea of justice emerge from such a world? The answer is with great difficulty. Perhaps the strongest person rules, imposing order among unruly subjects. But at the merest sign of disruptive influence or challenge to the order, the strongest must take action, either winning the submission of the challenger or killing the would-be usurper (or losing the status of ruler). This is a world without any law at all. The strongest possesses absolute authority, and others obey or face the consequences. There is no *justice* in such a world, nor does the concept of the *legitimacy* of the ruler arise. Neither is there any stability to the politics of such a world: At any moment, the strongest may find he is no longer the strongest, and his new successor will then face the same difficulty.

It is a cycle that's difficult to break. The only real way out is through the ruler himself: Will it be possible for such a ruler to devise arrangements that decrease the likelihood of challenges to his position? Can he manage to attain a degree of acceptance of his position of power, and if so, how? Here, the question switches back to his subjects. Although some would be too afraid to try to overthrow him, this is not true for all of them, so the question then becomes: What can the ruler give them that will cause them to refrain from challenging him?

The answer is law: He can settle their disputes for them, rather than merely leaving them to work out all the arrangements beneath him the same way he attained his position of primacy, by strength alone. All political decisions will still flow from the ruler, who will remain answerable to no one, but his decisions will hereafter be something other than merely ruthless calculation and protection of his own interests combined with an arbitrary indifference to all others. He will settle matters in accordance with general principles, or law.

This has two elements. First of all, at his discretion, he may decide to tell his subjects what they *must* do and what they *must not* do. He can also leave this matter for them to figure out on their own, agreeing to intervene only when a disagreement between two of them on what each of them must or must not do is brought to him by one of the parties. As a practical matter, we know down to our own day that even if he does lay down the law, there will still be disputes over its precise meaning and its applicability to a particular set of facts.

Second, he may decide to tell his subjects what consequences they face for failure to abide by the law he has set down. He may establish a code of punishments—or a principle for deciding how to punish.

Perhaps he will decide that even the smallest infraction by one of his subjects against another will warrant the penalty of death and the expunging of all the malefactors' male heirs and relations, as well as slavery for the women and children. But if this is his principle of justice, it is not necessarily one his subjects will regard as an improvement on arbitrary and lawless rule—which is to say, it is unlikely to do much to provide him the legitimacy he seeks.

He needs, perhaps, a principle of moderation as well as law: in short, an idea of justice that has the potential to be accepted, at least in principle, as fair by the people who come before him seeking his judgment in the controversy between them. One of the most basic of such principles available to him is the *lex talionis*, or proportionate retaliation for wrongdoing.

It might be helpful to distinguish between two kinds of possible infraction here: prohibited action against which the ruler or the authorities feel they *must* take action on their own initiative—in other words, a crime—and prohibited action in which the ruler takes action only at the behest of a party who believes he has been wronged by another—a tort in civil law. The *lex talionis* has potential to apply to both cases, but more broadly in the latter than the former. Historically, the criminal law has punished far in excess of the proportion of the offense: the death penalty for horse thieving, for example, or life in prison for even a starving man's theft of a loaf of bread. This is to say nothing of crimes directed against the state itself, such as treason or attempted regicide, for which certain legal codes specified not merely death but also a schedule of tortures to be inflicted prior to death.

But if you accidentally kill someone's horse, under the *lex talionis*, you owe him a horse, not your life. The principal of justice entailed in proportionate retaliation is accordingly especially useful to a ruler or a state in settling private disputes—in the administration of justice, where the state takes the role of a disinterested third party.

So when Jesus draws attention to "an eye for an eye," he establishes thereby a context in which there is a rule of law governed by a mutually agreed idea of justice; a moderating principle of proportionality is part of the bargain; and the enforcement of the *lex talionis* is in the hands of an authority acting as a disinterested third party, whether the king acting on his own wisdom or a court of law. This is the context in which Jesus offers his guidance on how to fulfill the law.

While the Jesusian teaching here has applications beyond the precise context in which it arises, Jesus did not preface his remarks about the other cheek, the cloak as well, and the extra mile with a description of a Hobbesian state of nature or a battlefield. The applicability of the statements he makes to such other contexts is something we will have to look into. But we need to begin where he does in order to see what he means in the context he has set.

Jesus began, precisely, with a world of law, the ancient law, in this case the *lex talionis*. He repudiates any attempt to "abolish" the ancient law, thereby rejecting the view that his teaching is only applicable on a clean slate. Once again, he is building on the ancient law, taking it as given, in order to "fulfill" it and bring about a world in which "all is accomplished."

What, then, should you do when an "evil one" slaps you on the cheek? Well, by the operation of the *lex talionis*, you might consider yourself enjoined or at least permitted to slap the "evil one" back. But that's not quite right: You are not the king or the court; you are a private person who has just been done an injury. It is not your place to invoke the principle of *lex talionis*. That power belongs to the legitimate authorities, those whose responsibility is to enforce the law. If you take this task on yourself, you in effect reconstitute yourself as the authority with respect to the situation at hand. It's not hard to see where this can lead. If everyone facing such a situation responded by slapping the "evil one" back, that would be the end of any claim to legitimate authority that the law has. We would be back in the world of all against all, in which the strongest emerges as ruler. It's a pretty good bet that the "evil one" would be a serious contender in such a struggle, uninhibited as he is now by the social and legal prohibitions of slapping you in the first place.

We need also to be mindful of the offense the "evil one" has committed. Jesus describes a slap on the cheek: A slap on the cheek is hardly a lethal blow. Jesus does not say here that if an "evil one" comes to kill you, tell him to kill the rest of your family as well. The slap on the cheek is an offense, yes. But how wounded are you really? And what, exactly, is wounded? Is it really your cheek that is at issue here?

The answer is obviously no. The redness of your cheek comes not merely from the contact with the hand of the "evil one" but also from your embarrassment. What a slap on the cheek really wounds is your pride. Who is this "evil one" to slap you? By what right? By no right! But what are the consequences of allowing him to slap you without retaliating? You will be exposed as someone who suffers the unjust insults of others without taking swift action to vindicate what you know is right, namely, that he should not slap you.

Jesus offers another way out. In advising you to offer the other cheek to the "evil one" for a second slap, he propounds other grounds for the vindication of your dignity as a person. You need not accept the slap as a blow to your pride of a sort that must be answered in kind in order to expunge the injury to you and reestablish your dignity in the eyes of others. Your dignity as a human being is not of a sort that requires its affirmation by one and all. Whether or not one and all should affirm your dignity is a different question—they should, but until they do, there will remain the problem of the "evil one," in this case someone who thinks so little of you as a human being that he is willing to slap you in the face. You are not obliged to respond to such a person in kind. Indeed, if you were *obliged* to respond in kind, then you could be compelled to slap someone on the cheek by virtue of his action in slapping you. What kind of freedom is that?

No, the point is precisely that you are a free person, in possession of the full measure of dignity. A slap cannot take that away from you. You already live in a world of law, according to which it is wrong for the "evil one" to slap you. Notwithstanding that the "evil one" fails to accord you your dignity, you have other ways to affirm it than by striking back.

Note that what Jesus counsels here is not really passivity. To be passive would be simply to await a second blow. On the contrary, Jesus advises the active step of offering the other cheek. To offer the other cheek is to deny that the "evil one" has the power to compel your action; it is an act not of passivity but of defiance. It is the free act of a free person who need not and will not give up the law in order to affirm freedom. Pride gets in the way of this understanding of the radical freedom and equal dignity of human beings by looking outward for an affirmation of that dignity. The Jesusian teaching is that freedom and dignity lie within and can never be obliterated by another.

We need to understand this because even in a world of law, we may yet come upon an "evil one." As the Jesusian teaching progresses, by "fulfill[ing]" the law so that "all is accomplished," no doubt there will be fewer such "evil ones." But even when "all is accomplished," we will need to be mindful of evil ones and what they seek. They want us to think they have the power to compel us. They do not. They only acquire such power if we ourselves grant it to them.

As for the "evil one," he belongs before the law and needs to answer for his criminal unwillingness to abide by it. The answer he owes is not to the particular party injured, but to the community of goodwill as a whole. His offense is against its laws and principles all in all, not just the individual he has directly harmed. We can see in Jesus's teaching here a compelling case against vigilante justice, which is the substitution of private action for what ought to be public accountability.

Jesus next says that if someone sues you for your shirt, you should give him not only that but also your coat. The question for the court is whether to order you to hand something over at the behest of another who desires it. In this case, because the object your legal adversary desires is the shirt off your back—an extreme demand—it seems obvious that the lawsuit Jesus is positing here is to some degree unjustified.

Again, the counsel Jesus offers is something other than passivity: He doesn't merely say "give up the shirt." He says to give up something else besides. Handing over the coat is like offering the other cheek: another way of affirming the essential freedom of the giver. As in the case of your red cheek, the essence of the matter at hand is not fundamentally about the disposition of an article of clothing. It is the self-vesting of some portion of one's dignity in the notion of one's ownership of things. But ownership is something that depends on others: They recognize something as rightfully yours, your property. What others grant in recognition is something others may take away, rightly or wrongly. They may wish to deprive you of something that is rightfully yours, but only if you see your freedom and dignity bound up with the possession of particular goods does their exercise in depriving you of those goods harm your freedom and dignity.

If someone forces you to walk a mile with him, Jesus next says, walk a second mile. (Some sources suggest that the origin of this specific injunction lies in Roman law, according to which a soldier on a march may require a passerby he comes upon to accompany him for a distance as long as a mile bearing his pack.) The point is the same, only this time it's directed at physical confinement under legal coercion. Freedom, once again, is not something of which you can be deprived against your will, but the attempt to deprive you of your freedom is no less wrong than suing people for the shirts off their backs or slapping them around. The response Jesus advocates serves as the most appropriate demonstration of freedom in response to bad conduct.

Jesus then moves outside the realm of coercion to say that if someone asks you for something, you should give it, and if someone wants to borrow from you, you should lend. He raises this matter in language that reflects the influence of Deuteronomy 15:7–11, which concerns an obligation to help the poor. It is thus clear from the context that the request at issue involves something like a hungry person asking for alms[5]—and not, for example, someone with a murderous glint in his eye asking to borrow your knife. Accordingly, we should understand the request to which Jesus refers as legitimate (or at least not illegitimate) in its purpose. But why should you grant such a request? You don't have to. You are free to keep what is yours. That's the point. One demonstrates one's freedom also by doing something one does not have to do—in this case, by one's act of generosity toward another.

With the examples he offers in these four verses, Jesus clearly means to remind us to look inside to find our freedom, but he also wants the activity of this inner freedom to have an effect on the world around us. First of all, there is the matter of exposing the bad behavior of others in the harshest light possible through the conspicuous refusal to sink to their level. Perhaps your mother told you that two wrongs don't make a right; if so, she was rejecting the *lex talionis* in favor of the Jesusian teaching. In a world of law, rising above retaliation in circumstances in which many if not most would feel in their gut the justification for retaliating, we offer a powerful example of right conduct. More than that, though, we have seen that in a world of law, turning the other cheek turns the power of coercion on its head. It exposes the "evil one" for precisely that quality, and all who believe in the law will see it the same way. To strike back is to invite an inquiry into who started the whole business, and the "evil one" will have no difficulty in lying enough to cause doubt, an awareness of which fact

---

[5] The Greek root of "asks" in the passage, *aiteō*, "suggests the attitude of a suppliant" as distinct from a request made by someone on "a footing of equality or familiarity" (*erōtaō*). *Vine's Complete*, p. 40.

has kept many a schoolyard bully in business. Suddenly, the world of law is at risk of losing clarity about who's right and who's wrong in the case at hand.

It is also possible, though not all that likely, that turning the other cheek will induce shame—not in the person being struck but in the person striking the blow. While such persons may be beyond the reach of shame, the effort to shock them out of their overweening self-regard by confronting them with a freedom they do not (yet) understand is perhaps worth a try. Beyond the possibility of reform, there is the sanction of law. So we can see here, perhaps, another reason Jesus is so emphatic in his reaffirmation of the law, even though he means to introduce modifications: Until everyone participates fully in the community of goodwill, the appearance of the figure of the "evil one" will require a response—but that response must be a response based in law, not in private retaliation.

Your Enemy

Having outlined new standards of conduct in the context of conditions of "brotherhood," marriage, and law more generally, Jesus turns to conditions in which none of those preexisting connections obtain—the case of your enemy. "You have heard that it was said, 'You shall love your neighbor and hate your enemy.' But I say to you, love your enemies and pray for those who persecute you, that you may be sons of your Father who is in heaven; for He causes His sun to shine on the evil and the good, and sends rain on the righteous and the unrighteous" (Mt. 5:43–44).

It is interesting that the textual foundation in the Hebrew scriptures is stronger for loving your neighbor than for hating your enemy. The most frequently cited reference to the latter is Deuteronomy 23:3–6, in which the Israelites are abjured from ever making peace with the Ammonites and the Moabites. Perhaps the reason the ancient law does not make more of the need to hate your enemies is that people at the time, Israelite and Ammonite both, and all others, required no special instruction to act fully in accordance with that principle. In this context, what is striking about the ancient law is, precisely, the admonition to "love your neighbor as yourself " found in Leviticus 19:18. Here, the call is to extend outward toward one's neighbor a regard of the sort one has for oneself.

Who is this "neighbor"? Jesus is later confronted with precisely that question, as we shall see (Lk. 10:29–37). For now, we note that the term is vague, and this is not accidental. We can perhaps begin with the other main term—"love"—by thinking about those whom we don't really need to be told to love: children, parents, one's spouse, relatives, friends. There is something ordinary and unforced, in most cases, in these intimate connections. Not so, perhaps, with your neighbor. The possibility of such feelings as suspicion, jealousy, and covetousness is present. Here, we may indeed need authoritative exhortation to get to "love," but following such an injunction entails no punishment or hardship for me, insofar as my neighbor, no less than myself, is enjoined to love me.

This is not, however, a contract whereby I agree to love my neighbor in exchange for his agreement to love me. Accordingly, I am not relieved of upholding my end of the bargain if my neighbor fails to uphold his end. We are both enjoined. If one of us fails to live by this principle, it's a violation of the law by which the community of goodwill lives—the law that makes the community what it is. There may be consequences for the failure to abide by it, sanctions imposed by the community against someone who refuses to act in accordance with its standards, perhaps ranging from opprobrium ("Mr. X is not very neighborly") to social ostracism to legal sanction to banishment to death—either as a result of a legal process or by the spontaneous action of a mob (the latter obviously being incompatible with the principles Jesus raised in response to the "evil one" who slaps you).

Importantly, the ancient law instructs me to love not merely my *next-door* neighbor but also to extend my "love" outward from my immediate proximity—beyond those at hand. How far? Well, throughout the neighborhood or, in other words, to the limit of those who live in the community of that very law which binds us to love of neighbor. This is not an easy law to follow, and no doubt it will be honored in the breach as well as the observance. Still, it has certain far-reaching, if not indeed revolutionary, implications. What it mandates is a certain form of *equality* among members of the community. If I love my neighbor as myself, I attach an equal value to the both of us. Now, we know already that this doctrine poses difficulties: While I know the value I place on myself, it is no small thing to try to attach that same value to another. The doctrine is in that sense aspirational, and it sets a very high standard. (Not necessarily the highest, though: One might, for example, place a higher value on the life of one's children than on one's own life, and so sacrifice one's life in order to save them. One might also be willing to undergo persecution for the sake of righteousness, where righteousness entails working for the good of others.)

What, then, does it really mean to "love your enemies," not just your neighbors? We might begin with what it means to have or be an enemy. Here, Jesus suggests that from the point of view of the old law, an enemy is someone you "hate," perhaps viscerally. We therefore have to begin with the notion of "enemy" as a relationship between two people, or two peoples, or two nations. What divides you from your enemy? And what do you have in common?

The easy answers are, respectively, "everything" and "nothing." To be in a relationship of enmity is to be in a relationship in which there are no ties of goodwill that bind you: no law, no "brotherhood," no neighborhood. There is accordingly no way you can agree on how to resolve the differences between the two of you. The only option each of you sees (assuming that both parties to the relationship of enmity are aware that they are enemies of each other) is to try to kill or force the submission of the other or to separate yourself by as much distance as possible if you fear the struggle that might ensue.

In truth, though, this is a misimpression, one that Jesus sets out to identify and correct. Note to begin with that, in most cases, enemies are aware of one another as such (and if not, one party will treat the other as something better than an enemy while the other pursues the relations between the two in accordance with the hidden or secret understanding of the other as enemy). But even a common understanding between two people that they are enemies *is* a common understanding between the two. They are not so radically apart as they might like to think.

Animals don't have enemies: The predator/prey relationship is different, even though we sometimes use terms like "natural enemies." To have an enemy is a matter of a person's *understanding* that someone is an enemy. We come back to that idea of "hate." The condition of enmity is precisely not "natural." If it were, how could we escape it? Generations of people would be doomed in perpetuity to a state of hostility.

Hobbes's "war of all against all" is one *possible* outcome, and it may be the initial state of relations between people and a "state of nature" in the sense of the human condition *before* we encounter people who are willing and able to forge different principles according to which they will live. Nevertheless the Hobbesian struggle remains *only one* possible outcome. Others are possible as well.

The paradox is that these other possibilities emerge from the very *mutuality* of the sense of enmity itself. Jesus, in instructing us to love our enemy, is seeking to extend the injunction to "love your neighbor" beyond the boundaries of the community in which it originally applied. Building on a relationship of enmity that is nevertheless the starting point of *mutual* relations, Jesus proposes to substitute love for hatred. Note that as in the case of the injunction to love your neighbor, the Jesusian injunction "love your enemies" goes out not just to one party, but also to all those who find themselves in a relationship of enemy to enemy. Upon their *mutual* substitution of love for hate, they will benefit from something akin to neighborly relations. The separate communities in which they find themselves will become joined by something. The

THE ANCIENT LAW   67

equality members of a community enjoy as a product of their shared sense of neighborly love thereby becomes, in potential, *universal* equality, applicable not just within a community but beyond its boundaries and beyond the boundaries of any and all particular communities. This possibility comes from the way in which people mutually relate to one another even when they are in conditions of enmity.

Jesus notes that the sun rises and sets on the good and the evil, the righteous and the unrighteous (Mt. 5:45). The point is to reach out, to attempt to turn evil into good and unrighteousness into righteousness through the mutual relationship of "love": to eliminate the "enemy" as a category by the substitution of brotherly or neighborly relations. Jesus asks, "If you love [only] those who love you, what reward do you have?" (Mt. 5:46). Jesus jokes that even tax collectors can say as much. Meanwhile, if you extend that love outward and it turns out to find reciprocation, the reward can be great: It is accordingly worth the effort, so much so that Jesus identifies it as a general obligation. The Jews and the Gentiles, he says, are alike in greeting their own kind as brothers— no small achievement in its own right, for reasons we have seen, but itself no cause for a member of either group to regard himself as superior to members of the other.

The real challenge comes from reaching beyond one's own kind, to others—all others. "Therefore, you are to be perfect, as your heavenly Father is perfect" (Mt. 5:48). This is not merely an injunction about what you "should" do: Jesus is not just pointing to a gap between how people should act and how they do act. He is saying that human beings *are*—that is to say, people *exist*—in order to be perfect. The end, purpose, or fulfillment of the human condition as we find it in this world is the perfection of the sort Jesus describes: each person's extension of the equality that is neighborly love to all others.

Although the Sermon on the Mount addresses a wide variety of relations between people, Jesus has chosen not to address the question of what to do when someone spurns your offer of friendship and replies instead by seeking your destruction. His choice here does not mean that he is unaware of the importance of the question or fails to address it, as we shall see in chapter 10. But for now he chooses to retain his focus on the immense possibility that inheres in the idea of a community of goodwill constantly reaching out to include others.

3.

SELF AND OTHERS

Jesus has been talking a great deal so far in the Sermon on the Mount about the importance of others—the need to reach out to them, to extend brotherly relations to an expanding neighborhood, to get beyond the world of law to mutual reconciliation wherever possible. Others matter. It is unacceptable, in Jesus's view, to look around you at those to whom you already feel connected and be satisfied. The importance of this theme of the Jesusian teaching is no less today than in his day: To take a couple of obvious examples from recent memory, it would have been entirely un-Jesusian to hear of genocide unfolding in Bosnia in the 1990s and feel nothing toward the people who were its victims. The same with the disaster scene in Indonesia following the tsunami in December 2004. Yet in ancient times, or by certain other codes, greeted with similar circumstances befalling another people or tribe, one might feel indifference at best and glee at the misfortune of one's rival at worst. This tendency, then, is what Jesus has set out to correct.

But there is a right and a wrong way of valuing other people. The first twenty-four verses of the sixth chapter of Matthew constitute an extended critique of the most common form the wrong way takes: the tendency to do things in order to win approval and praise from others. When we do this, Jesus holds, we only *seem* to value others; actually, we are using others as an instrument in the service of our own selfish desires. We value them only for what they can do for us.

Jesus notes this tendency in areas from almsgiving to religious observance to the accumulation of wealth. He begins this section of the Sermon by saying, "Beware of practicing your righteousness before men to be noticed by them . . ." (Mt. 6:1). Likewise, you should not trumpet your giving to the poor in order to be "honored by men" (Mt. 6:2), nor should you put on a public show of piety in order to be "seen by men" (Mt. 6:5), nor should you make a big deal out of fasting in order to be "noticed by men" (Mt. 6:16).

Jesus castigates those who engage in such conduct as "hypocrites." He uses the term in its classic Greek sense, that of playing a role on a stage: representing oneself as something other than what one really is. A true almsgiver is someone who gives alms because it's the right thing to do. A hypocrite, by contrast, is merely playing the part of an almsgiver in order to be applauded for excellence in that role—to be "honored by men."

This section builds on the previous discussion of law in that all the subject areas Jesus deals with here pertain to obligations under the law. In the course of his endeavor to "fulfill" the law, Jesus has sought to push people out from themselves and to get them to think more deeply about the needs of others. Jesus has thereby *personalized* the law. He has made sure his listeners understand that in complying with the law, the purpose is not merely obedience to the law for its own sake, as an end in itself, but also improvement in the way people get along with each other. He points his listeners in the direction of brotherhood, a universal sense of fellow-feeling and accordingly a kind of equality. (As to what kind, what constitutes the flesh on the bones of this doctrine of equality, we will soon see.) Now, having broadened his listeners' understanding of the purpose of the law through his injunctions to reach out, Jesus directs his listeners back within themselves to a consideration of the *reasons* for obeying the law.

The purpose of obeying the law is not to win praise. One must not act *for* others as a way of acting *for oneself*. To obey the law is to do one's duty toward one's fellows. These other people are not means to an end, namely, the satisfaction of one's own desires—for example, the desire for praise from others. Other people are ends in themselves, and only in treating them that way is it possible to act in accordance with the true potential of the law.

Jesus has a very good reason for rejecting the point of view that sees no problem in doing well (for oneself) by doing good (for others): If your top priority is winning praise, you have in effect placed your sense of self-worth in the hands of others. For if you happen not to be winning the praise of others, as you think you deserve, you will feel yourself to be somehow unsatisfied or incompletely fulfilled. Then what happens? You might become sullen—or morose, bitter, or resentful. You might cultivate a sense of grievance against those whom you believe are failing to praise you properly or a sense of envy toward those who *are* winning the praise you think you should be winning. Or both. Needless to say, none of that is conducive to Jesus's program of reaching out to others.

Similarly, you might also decide to adjust your conduct, to do things differently, in order to get the praise you want, but what would that say about your own freedom and integrity? If the crowd can make you do what it wants by withholding its praise from you until you conform, then the actions you take will begin not with the knowledge you have of what is right—perhaps as reflected in the obligations imposed upon you by law and perhaps further as those obligations have been clarified, corrected, or "fulfilled" through the teaching of Jesus—but by what the crowd tells you to do. This severs the connection of law and what's right. If praise is your aim, then the standard you apply to your conduct is that it should be of the sort that leads people to praise you. The "law" for you is simply what wins you praise. In exchange for the freedom you have within you to know what's right and to act in accordance with it—the "fulfilled" law in the Jesusian sense—you substitute the "law" of the crowd. And, of course, it is all too easy to imagine circumstances in which what will win you praise from the crowd is truly monstrous.

We should understand Jesus's use of the terms "noticed," "honored," and "seen" in the broadest sense. By speaking in such general terms, he clearly means to encompass all the forms praise may take, all the awards available from others—from the development of a good reputation in the community, to fame, to riches, to power. But as we can readily see, those in the best position to shower you with riches are the rich themselves since they have the means. Likewise, those with the capability to elevate you to the ranks of the powerful are those who are powerful already. The risk here is that the pursuit of "notice" and "honor" will cause one to show special favor to those best positioned to give the best rewards.

This vision of earthly success invites an outlook that's very different from the one with which Jesus began the Sermon on the Mount, in the Beatitudes. Instead of uplifting those less fortunate, from the poor in spirit to the mourners to the meek, the temptation underlying the pursuit of honor and notice is precisely a sense of solidarity with those who themselves already enjoy honor, wealth, and fame. If you are not yet among their ranks, you aspire to join them, and so you emulate them. If you have been admitted to their club, your first priority will be to behave in a way that enables you to retain their praise and good opinion. What becomes, then, of the hunger and thirst for righteousness? The relief of this primordial desire would come from the false satisfaction that privilege elicits at the expense of others. This end result would deny to others the satisfaction of the same elemental stirring toward righteousness.

Note that Jesus is not saying a good reputation among one's fellows is a bad thing. He is instead explaining that the right way to acquire a good reputation is not to do so by using other people as a means to that end. One's almsgiving should be for the benefit of the person to whom one gives alms, not for one's own benefit. If its real purpose is the benefit that comes from honor, then it is susceptible to distortion even into its opposite if that is the swiftest path to praise.

For Jesus, a good reputation is a by-product of right conduct. It is not axiomatic, however, that right conduct will produce a good reputation, in the sense of popular acclaim. As Jesus has explained, for at least some period of time, some people will be persecuted for righteousness's sake and for the sake of Jesus's teaching. In that case, the most righteous of conduct yields not the highest reputation but, in the short run, the opposite.

The longer-term question of reputation is a different matter, however. Here, from the Jesusian perspective, the question is this: Whose side were you on, that of the righteous or the persecutors? Here, we have the preeminent example of Jesus himself. He did the right thing and suggested that others do the same, showing them that no matter how hemmed in by circumstance they felt, they were free to do so. In addition, he did and taught the right thing not in order to win the praise of listeners, but to offer them guidance by which they might benefit. He went on to pay the most terrible earthly price, his life, for the extent to which he refused to conform his conduct to that which would win him honor and praise—a risk, as we have seen, he was perfectly well aware he was running yet freely chose. Nevertheless, for this determination, he was eventually honored on a global scale unequaled by anyone before or since.

THE LORD'S PRAYER

At the center of this section of the Sermon on the Mount, indeed of the Sermon on the Mount as a whole, Jesus gives the words that have come down to us as the Lord's Prayer (Mt. 6:9–13). These are, of course, the most famous and oft-recited words of the most famous book in the world. Yet perhaps surprisingly, there is an aspect of them that has gone underappreciated over the intervening two millennia, even by those who have repeated them time and again. "Your kingdom come," says the prayer, "Your will be done. . . ." Where? "On earth . . ." (Mt. 6:10).

Now, one could certainly construe this statement as the invocation of the arrival at some future time of a kingly figure embodying and dispensing perfect justice, which perhaps reflects Jesus's listeners' sense of "Our Father, who is in heaven" (Mt. 6:9).[1] The language Jesus uses, however, does not explicitly refer to the arrival of a king but a kingdom. A kingdom is a place where the king's will is sovereign, or law. And it is this "will" that is to "be done, On earth." Jesus is therefore talking about the arrival of the law on earth.

As we have seen, this law has to be construed as distinct in certain respects from the ancient law. We cannot take the existing ancient law at the time Jesus is speaking as the last word on law: a complete and unchanging whole. We can, however, take what Jesus says as the *fulfillment* of the law, the release in the world of the teaching whereby "all [will be] accomplished." It is accordingly the Jesusian teaching about how to live in the world that will result, in time, in the arrival of the "kingdom." This kingdom cannot be characterized as a place where the merely arbitrary will of a capricious king holds sway. Rather, knowledge of the will that is to govern "on earth"—in other words, how one should behave on earth—is fully accessible to people through the teaching of Jesus in "fulfill[ment]" of the law. The extent to which people implement this teaching is up to them.

Recall that Jesus's purpose here is to tell people how to pray. He begins by disclaiming the "meaningless repetitions" (Mt. 6:7) to be found in Gentile prayers. For what, then, should one pray? The list is remarkably short: for the arrival of the "kingdom" on earth; for food each day; to be forgiven for what we have done wrong in connection with our forgiveness of the wrongdoing of others (the context here, therefore, is once again a social order based on law, not the law of the jungle); not to be tempted to behave badly and to be rescued from or preserved against evildoers. Of the things specifically mentioned, all but one specify obvious elements of the political and social teaching Jesus has already propounded—the exception being the case of bread.

---

[1] See, for example, Isaiah 2:2–4. The Lord establishes his house in the highest mountain, "and all the nations will stream to it." People seek the Lord's guidance, and "the law will go forth from Zion / And the word of the Lord from Jerusalem. / And He will judge between the nations."

As a matter of first impression, the prayer for food is a bit of an outlier. The beseeching here is for the arrival of conditions in which people generally act rightly, forgive each other and are forgiven when they act wrongly, and don't fall prey to evildoers, perhaps because daily life no longer generally exposes them to evildoers—at least not of a kind whose evil is more obnoxious than a slap on the cheek and granting that they will have to remain vigilant for evil of a worse sort. Where does bread fit in?

In the first place, we need to understand the use of *artos* (bread) broadly, in the sense of the "necessities for the sustenance of life."[2] We might then ask: What would happen to a social order based on the other qualities outlined in the Lord's Prayer (the themes of which Jesus has been advancing in the Sermon), if, all of a sudden, there was no bread to eat the next day? In other words, what would be the chance of realizing a social order based on these principles—the "kingdom com[ing]," that is—if people were literally starving? It seems clear that a political and social order based on the Jesusian teaching—demanding as it does a high level of ethical conduct and restraint from the exercise of what would seem to be all-too-human passions, all for the sake of a greater degree of brotherhood and the outward expansion of neighborly relations—is facilitated by a certain degree of freedom from want.

As Jesus is well aware, it is obviously not true that the only way to obtain one's daily bread is through divine intervention (except, perhaps, in the sense that the ability to earn enough to buy one's bread or the ability to make it for oneself can be described as God's will or the gift of God). In any event, there is nothing here to suggest that Jesus's meaning is that one shouldn't have to do anything in order to secure one's bread (or livelihood) except pray. If possible, one should go to work. It would be a strange doctrine indeed that demanded from a divine being the delivery by divine means of what it is perfectly possible for people to obtain through their own effort.

---

[2] *Vine's Complete*, p. 77.

So it seems safe to conclude that Jesus is not envisioning a land of lotus-eaters, to whom all "necessities for the sustenance of life" are given without effort. That Jesus expects most people to work for their livelihood will also come through clearly in various parables, as we shall see.

But should those who have already earned their bread for today and tomorrow continue to pray for it? There are two reasons why one must answer "yes" to this question. The first is simply that life is full of uncertainty, and even if you've got bread stored up for a lifetime, there is no sure sense in which you can say that you have fully met your coming needs beyond the possibility of circumstance to change things. Someone might come in with a conquering army and take it all away from you: the best laid plans of mice and men. At best, one may take prudent measures to prepare for various possibilities ahead. But it would be arrogant to suppose that your preparations place you in a position beyond challenge.

More important than that, however, is the answer that comes from the language of the Lord's Prayer itself. Jesus frames the prayer not as an individual but as a corporate entreaty. He does not tell people to say: give *me* my daily bread, forgive *me* my misdeeds, protect *me* from falling prey to evil. The prayer is, rather, on behalf of *us*.

So, who is this "us"? At a minimum, it seems to be all who say the prayer. This is true whether or not they are themselves in possession of life's necessities. In this sense, one's personal situation is irrelevant. The request in the prayer is a request for *all* to receive their daily bread. Until *everyone* has the necessities of life provided for, the request remains valid on behalf of all of "us." It would probably not go too far to observe that once I provide (to the extent possible) the "necessities for the sustenance" of my own life through my own effort, so I am enjoined to assist others in the provision of what *they* need. If someone else is unable to provide for life's necessities, and I am obliged to take action on my own to obtain life's necessities for me, and if my prayer concerns not merely *me* but *us*, then I am likewise obliged to take action for *us*. This prefigures a Jesusian teaching that will come out more fully later, namely, the special responsibility of those with *more* of the good things of the world toward those with fewer. Our obligations do not end when we have provided merely for our personal needs. Again, consider natural disasters, such as an earthquake or tsunami: When we hear of such terrible events, our impulse, in accordance with the Jesusian teaching, is not to laugh at the misfortune of others or to take the story merely as a reminder to hoard stores of food for ourselves in case something similar should befall us. It's to send help to those in dire need.

The sense in which Jesus uses "us," however, is not actually confined to those saying the prayer he specifies. Before presenting the Lord's Prayer, Jesus says something that seems slightly odd in the context of what follows: "[Y]our Father knows what you need before you ask him" (Mt. 6:8). Yet if that's true, clearly it is true of those who go to the trouble of reciting the Lord's Prayer as well as those who do not. People, insofar as they are human, have certain necessities of life in common. They are universal necessities, whether or not one says the prayer. Jesus is not suggesting that *only* those who say the prayer should have their needs fulfilled; he has already acknowledged the needs as universal. Consider the case of the "poor in spirit," those so downtrodden they are unable even to pray for themselves. Jesus is not seeking to exclude such people from the benefit sought in this prayer. Rather, he has emphatically spoken up for the needs of such people—indeed, all people. In the ultimate sense, the "us" to whom he refers is *all of us*, all people.

In Jesus's telling, it's not just that human needs are universal, but also that the "Father knows what you need before you ask him." This raises the question of why one should pray for daily bread at all. Perhaps if one has one's bread at hand, one should offer a prayer of gratitude. But this prayer isn't exactly framed in those terms, like grace before a meal: Its purpose is to beseech. Moreover, if one still lacks bread for tomorrow, then by Jesus's own terms, it cannot be necessary to specify that fact. It's *already* known.

The specific elements Jesus directs people to pray for, beginning with daily bread, reinforce the cooperative element of the prayer. The essential point of saying the Lord's Prayer is not to remind the Father of what I need (which, Jesus says, the Father already knows). The prayer's point in this world is to remind those who recite it that *others* have the same needs: "I" am part of "us." *We* are the ones who need reminding.

Viewed through this prism, the purpose of the other specific petitions of the Lord's Prayer becomes clearer: As we all desire to have our own shortcomings forgiven, we must remind ourselves to forgive others theirs. Temptation will always be before all of us, and we must remind ourselves not to yield to it. When others slip, we may find ourselves faced with the need to forgive them. We have a collective stake in deliverance from evildoers, both in keeping them away from us and in evading their clutches. And so we should work together and help one another to those ends.

Furthermore, the social importance of this prayer begs the additional question: What will the status of the Lord's Prayer be when Jesus's petition that "all [will be] accomplished" comes to pass on earth? Would that make the Lord's Prayer obsolete? There are two issues at stake in these questions. First, we would need to be certain that "all [has been] accomplished" in terms of the fulfilled law everywhere on earth, for all people. Until we achieve this certainty, if ever we do, we should be wary of complacency. The starkest reminder of this will be our failure to solve the problem of want: an insufficiency of the "necessities for the sustenance of life," that is, "our" daily bread. There is much starvation and want in the world today, and we should not be satisfied with our own prosperity.

Second, even in the event that one day we are sure that "all [has been] accomplished" for everyone, we are not quite finished. We have to ask: What about the future? Here Jesus directs us to face up to a hard truth: Insofar as this world is concerned, his is a political and social teaching that can guide us to the arrangement of worldly affairs so that the desire for righteousness, the primal desire, is satisfied for all. Unfortunately, that's not the end of the matter. Otherwise, there would be no further need for the Lord's Prayer. There is, for example, still the prospect of contingency disrupting the provision of the necessities for life: famine, natural disaster. A bigger problem than that, however, lies within us. As long as we are who we are, Jesus reminds us, we will be inclined, however infrequently, to commit slights against others (probably because we are thinking in terms of ourselves—of "me" rather than the "us" of the prayer). We will want to be forgiven, and so we had better remember that we need to forgive. There will always be temptation before us. Because some of us may succumb to it, there will always be the risk of running into evil. This will also hold true even when "all is accomplished." So the prayer by which we remind ourselves of what we owe one another will remain necessary for *us*.

The mention of bread in the Lord's Prayer is Jesus's first foray, however tentative, into the question of political economy. Jesus underscores the social dimension by instructing each of us to seek the necessities of life not only for oneself but also for all of us. Each of us has it within our own capacity, beyond the ability of others to take away, to act freely, but we do not exercise this freedom properly if we understand it simply as doing what we please. We need to act in a way that's grants the equal freedom of others and for the others to do the same. This is not a matter merely of moral philosophy, of what we "should" do because it is right; instead, Jesus teaches us that we gain by doing what's right when others also do what's right.

However, this is not quite a matter of *individual* gain. If it were, each person would be in a position to enjoy the benefit of others doing what's right while remaining personally indifferent to doing what's right with regard to others. The problem here is obvious: If we each think we can profit from the right conduct of others without conducting ourselves rightly, then the net effect is a group of people in which no one acts rightly. There is no benefit for anyone. If such a group is lucky, the rule of law may yet hold sway, preventing people from acting too badly because of fear of the consequences. Such a rule, based on authority backed up by force, might well turn out to be iron and unforgiving. Even so, matters can get worse: deterioration into an altogether lawless struggle of all against all. Recall that Jesus means to preserve the law. He steps in with his teaching at a point far above the struggle of all against all and even above the purely force-based rule of an iron will. He starts with a group of people who have already been admonished to love their neighbors—and to the extent that they have done so, they have already begun to benefit from the collective advantage of right conduct toward one another. Jesus, in coming to "fulfill" the law, seeks to spread this mutual advantage outward, to more and more people, crowding out the land of "enemies" by expanding the neighborhood of brotherly relations.

The gains people thereby enjoy are corporate, or social or collective. Such gains are realized and felt by individuals, but only in groups. And indeed, Jesus understands and consistently warns that a great peril to the adoption and spread of his teaching is the tendency to view the world only through the prism of one's own needs, desires, and advantage. He admonishes people, "Do not store up for yourselves treasures on earth, where moth and rust destroy, and where thieves break in" (Mt. 6:19). Here is, precisely, the gain from selfishness. It is subject to decay by natural processes, as well as to the selfish whims of others, perhaps a thief. Rather, he directs people to store treasures for themselves in heaven. "[F]or where your treasure is, there your heart will be also" (Mt. 6:21).

Here, Jesus uses the word "treasure" to refer to two different things: first, worldly possessions, then in a higher sense. To Jesus, true wealth is not a matter of material possessions, and while he describes this in relation to heaven, as always it also has an earthly application. In this world, the higher treasure, and therefore the place the "heart will be," is the expanding neighborhood of brotherhood. The qualities of such a world are of such great value as to dwarf worldly riches. The poorest poor person in a world built on the Jesusian teaching, the community of goodwill, will be better off than the richest rich person in a world in which the Jesusian principles are unknown. That poor person in the Jesusian world will benefit from the felt commitment of those dwelling alongside her to see to the needs of others, whereas that rich person will be forever at the mercy of decay and the capricious will of others.

Jesus follows this point with an analogy similar to the ones he has already proffered about salt and light. Here, he describes the eye as the "the lamp of the body" (Mt. 6:22). So long as the eye is clear, the body will have light, but if the eye is bad or evil, then the deepest darkness will take over within. The passage becomes clear and its place in the sequence here apparent when we think about the traditional idiomatic usage of "evil eye" as a synonym for covetousness or greed, for example in Proverbs: "Eat thou not the bread of him that hath an evil eye" (Prov. 23:6 KJV), and more directly in relation to what Jesus has just said about the perishability of earthly treasure, "He that hasteth to be rich hath an evil eye, and considereth not that poverty shall come upon him" (Prov. 28:22 KJV). Once again, the warning against undue attachment to the material comforts of this world could not be clearer. The covetous eye spoils the one who covets, spreading darkness from the eye inward; but the clear eye draws the light inside, which in turn makes one *shine*: The inner light not only illuminates you, but also allows you to illuminate others. As in the case of saltiness and shininess at the end of the Beatitudes, the genius of the light of the Jesusian teaching is that in lighting the way for others, the light source itself is in no way diminished. On the contrary, the brighter it is, the more illumination it can bring to others. The torch, once burning, can light other torches without diminishing itself.

Jesus says that it is impossible to serve two masters, God and mammon, at the same time. It is striking that he chooses to personify wealth as "mammon" (Greek *mamona*), an object of worship, thereby establishing a kind of negative parallel between (proper) worship of God and (improper) worship of earthly riches and comforts. Of course, it is not merely the act of worship about which Jesus is speaking in either

case. Once again, he is also addressing himself to this-worldly considerations; people don't really bow down and pray before their money.
Nevertheless, some do make it the most important thing in their lives,
more important than their relations with other people. The worldly
component of serving God is to live with others in accordance with the
Jesusian teaching. To do so is to put material goods in their place.

Over the next few passages, Jesus pushes this doctrine to the limit:
His message is that there is no reason to worry about what you will eat
or drink or the clothes on your back. He asks, "Is not life more than
food, and the body more than clothing?" (Mt. 6:25). He cites as evidence the birds in the air, who find what they need to eat, and the lilies
in the field, whose beauty is finer than any garment. He notes that people are worth inestimably more than birds and lilies. People should
have faith that God will provide for them as for the birds and the lilies.
Jesus calls on his listeners to worry not about material things: "Who of
you by being worried can add a single hour to his life?" (Mt. 6:27). In
a direct parallel to the passage that introduced the Lord's Prayer, he
notes that the Gentiles seek food, drink, and clothing, reminding his
listeners that the Father already knows what people need. Jesus tells
them instead to seek the kingdom and righteousness of which he has
been speaking, and everything else will follow.

Jesus's language is at its most poetic in this passage. Yet in saying
that God will provide, he clearly means something other than there will
be no more famine or other scarcity of any of the material necessities
of life, that people will always find what they need to keep the body going with or without effort on their part. In the first place, that would
contradict his plain meaning in the Lord's Prayer in relation to one's
daily bread, since it's not passivity he counsels. Second, it's simply not
true that everything lies effortlessly at hand: Jesus does not proclaim
the end of famine and cold, and, indeed, all too many people since his
day have died of hunger or of exposure to the elements. The benevo-
lent view of mankind Jesus ascribes to God is not proof against such
scourges. If we insist on understanding Jesus in this way, we reduce his

statements to nonsense or false promises—a species of the hypocrisy he is denouncing.

Let's try a different, more plausible approach. For starters, birds don't just perch in the tree branches all day in the expectation that someone or something is going to come along to give them food. The lilies don't blossom without the right mix of soil, sunlight, and water. They are provided for in the sense that the natural environment gives them the "necessities for the sustenance of life," to return to that very useful phrase. It's easy to assign a little more volition to the actions of a bird than to a lily bulb: We see the bird actually flying around and picking up scraps for a nest, pecking at worms and other insects, and so on. Bulbs seem merely to subsist in the ground. But Jesus's use of the two together is especially illuminating in reminding us that birds and bulbs have in common the sufficiency of the natural environment in sustaining them. The apparently more active bird is, no less than the bulb or lily, a creature entirely dependent on and integrated into that environment. There is nothing about the bird or the bulb that transcends the merely natural.

Now, we could say that people, at least in principle, also live in an environment that is capable of providing them what they need for survival. To the extent that people are like birds and bulbs, one could say that they have been provided for, one way or the other, no less satisfactorily. However, one would also have to accept the consequences: As some birds break their wings and accordingly can't gather food, they die; as drought befalls the lily bulbs, they don't bloom. Some people will manage to acquire the "necessities for the sustenance of life," but some will not and will therefore perish.

Clearly, abandonment of people to their fate in the natural world is not what Jesus is getting at, and the reason is that unlike birds and bulbs, people can and do transcend the limits of the natural environment. There is something about people that goes beyond the merely physical world of life in nature. In fact, one might say that what makes people people—and not creatures analogous to birds or lilies—is exactly that element which transcends the physical. This is what Jesus means when he asks, rhetorically, "Is not life more than food, and the body more than clothing?" Surely, the answer to this question cannot be: "Yes, more than food and clothing—water, too, and shelter, and air to breathe, and the activities of procreation." That just doesn't go to the essence of Jesus's objection. The point is that attending to "the necessities for the sustenance of [merely bodily] life" doesn't fully address the needs of people, who are more than merely bodily.

As far as this world is concerned, people are more than merely bodily and natural, first and foremost, in their relations with one another. No one would bother wasting breath exhorting the birds and the bulbs to organize their affairs with their fellow birds or bulbs in a different way. Everything about such interactions has already been provided, so to speak, by the physical environment. But no one would say the same about people. For them, how they relate to one another can be no less powerful a determinant of their well-being than the playing out of natural processes around them. And in relating to one another, people, unlike birds, have choices.

When Jesus says to seek the kingdom and righteousness first and let the rest follow from it, he is asserting that the top priority for people is to act in a certain way in relation to one another. He has already provided a rich account of what he has in mind (though he is not yet finished): He wants people to act in such a way that their common desire for righteousness, properly understood, is satisfied; he wants them to develop "brotherly" relations more fully and to reach out and extend brotherly relations beyond merely their neighborhood, to include their old enemies—an obligation he wants both sides to embrace. They should do this not merely because it's right, but also because the world they thereby create will be the most satisfying possible world for all those who live in it.

He has also hinted at one of the astounding consequences of living in such a world: People will take an interest not only in winning their own daily bread but also in obtaining daily bread for their neighbors as well—for "us." Jesus is therefore speaking not solely in a metaphorical sense when he says that if we seek the kingdom and righteousness, "all these [material] things will be added to you." In this "kingdom," people, even the least able among them, have the best chance of seeing to their bodily needs as well.

Before the kingdom arrives, it is therefore a misplaced priority to look first to the needs of the body and only secondarily to the state of one's relations with others. Jesus tells people not to waste their time worrying about the needs of the body. This is, of course, different from saying that one *should not attend* to the needs of the body. Clearly, in most cases, one should, while also attending to the needs of one's neighbor. To spend one's time worrying, though, is to spend one's time *not* attending to what one ought to. Worry is a substitute for efficacious action, and it won't add so much as an hour to your life, as Jesus pointedly observes. Worry is a waste of time. Instead, people need to devote their time to the realization of the highest aspiration of this world: the kingdom and righteousness. This, they pursue in their relations with one another.

"Worry" is in some respects a bit of a luxury good: After all, if you are busy seeing to your needs, you probably don't have much time to spend worrying. In fact, it is probably fair to say that unless you are especially heedless and unfocused, you have time to worry only once you have already attended to your needs. Jesus says not to indulge yourself this way—to give in to indolence in the guise of thinking about the troubles tomorrow may bring. For now, Jesus says, people should be too busy for the lazy leisure of worry—busy building the kingdom.

I have said that "in most cases" people should indeed attend to the needs of the body. Why not all? Quite simply because there are profound exceptions, and in some respects, it is the existence of this category of exceptions that differentiates people from the birds and bulbs. People are capable of extraordinary things: They will sometimes risk death for glory. They will go to war to vindicate a principle. Mothers will starve themselves so their children can eat. Some will enter a burning building in order to pull out a stranger. Some will accept death rather than recant their beliefs. And some will endure persecution for the sake of righteousness.

Some of these behaviors have parallels or perhaps antecedents in the world of mere animals, but animals cannot give an account of what they are doing. People, however, have the capacity to freely choose actions that may jeopardize their survival—in the knowledge that that's exactly what they are doing. It's not recklessness we're talking about here: a failure to calculate accurately the possibility of harm coming one's way if one pursues a particular course of action. It's the conscious willingness to risk one's life for the sake of something one deems more important. Needless to say, no one better embodied that quality than Jesus. But, in principle, such a course of action is available to all people, and it is one of the signal things that separates people from animals.

Jesus tells his listeners not to worry about tomorrow because "Each day has enough trouble of its own" (Mt. 6:34). By this, he means we should spend our time getting busy working on the "trouble" we have today. Even in our latter-day community of goodwill, no member of it will have to look too far or hard to find something or someone in need of immediate attention.

4.

JUDGMENT AND THE GOLDEN RULE

The political teachings of Jesus direct us outward, from ourselves to others. As a matter of the human race's history and of human inclination down to our day, the first stirring of desire with regard to others is the desire for righteousness, which can easily get stuck in its selfish aspect, as a desire to be satisfied at the expense of others. Jesus seeks to channel this primal desire into the recognition that we can only truly satisfy ourselves when we recognize that the same desire in others can and must be satisfied as well.

Nevertheless, we all know selfish people. The spread of the Jesusian teaching has not eliminated this quality from people's makeup. The question of what to *do* about such people is a difficult one. One approach would be to denounce them and write them out of polite society. For relatively mild cases of selfishness, this might take the form of social ostracism. For more severe cases, such as those who wish to impose their selfish will on others by violence or to advance an agenda at the expense of the equality Jesus is promoting, the sanction might also be more severe.

But not so fast. At the beginning of the seventh chapter of Matthew, about two-thirds of the way through the Sermon on the Mount, Jesus proffers the famous admonition: "Do not judge so that you will not be judged" (Mt. 7:1). Eleven lines later, he offers his most famous saying on how each of us should get along with others: "In everything, therefore, treat people the same way you want them to treat you . . ." (Mt. 7:12). The relationship of the two statements is important. The first tells you what you need to put behind you in order to implement the principle set forth in the second.

What does Jesus mean by that first injunction? Is he saying that we should not form opinions about others, so that no one will form an opinion about us in turn? That doesn't make sense. In the first place, Jesus has been issuing judgments right and left since the beginning of the Sermon on the Mount. Perhaps he is reserving a right of judgment for himself that he is unwilling to grant to others. If so, however, that would seem at odds with one of the main themes of his Sermon: the denunciation of hypocrisy. Now, one could avoid this problem by arguing that Jesus's status is different from that of the people he addresses, except that in general, he seeks to exemplify that which he espouses. Nowhere in the Sermon does he claim special status for himself; there is no "do as I say, not as I do" element to his message.

We shouldn't be too casual in our approach to the language here, importing from our time and seeking to impose on Jesus's language the proposition that, for example, one should not be "judgmental." Rather, what Jesus warns against here, as will become clearer in the following passages expanding and clarifying this message, is to "judge" in a very distinctive way: to let the past conduct of a person form the basis of how we approach our relations with him or her.

To judge is to examine and find fault and condemn (or not to find fault). The importance of Jesus's statement is to urge people to put aside consideration of what is past when they think about what to do in the future. Here, Jesus poses the issue as follows: Don't begin with your finding that the person with whom you are interacting has been at fault, even—in fact, especially—if it's true. To do so is to trap yourself and society in a vicious circle. How are you going to love your brother if your brother doesn't deserve love? What if he once did something that offended you? Is it your position that he has to make amends before you can love him? If that's the case, then you have exempted yourself from the injunction to love your brother, since your brother would first have to demonstrate that he deserves your affection and brotherly treatment. Without such a demonstration, you will be unable to extend your brotherly relations outward to your neighbors in an ever-expanding neighborhood, let alone to your enemies. You will commence proclaiming your good and just reasons for disregarding the Jesusian teaching more or less upon hearing it.

Of course, you are unlikely to be alone. Maybe you think you will get away with your refusal to reach out because others won't hold *your* past actions against *you*. Such an assertion of special privilege in the satisfaction of your desire for righteousness, however, is something Jesus has already ruled out. The greater likelihood is that the Jesusian teaching will have no social impact whatsoever, as everyone asserts a right not to implement it on the basis of claims of past injustice. In a world where the temptation toward selfish conduct is always with us (and in which we can expect many if not most—if not all—people to act selfishly at least at some times) the cumulative judgment and condemnation that individuals might heap upon one another to dispel any sense of mutual obligation would quickly harden into a most un-Jesusian world of retribution and recrimination.

Jesus is not denying that injustices have been committed. On the contrary, what he seeks to do with this injunction is to render past injustices irrelevant to the possibility of moving forward.

Jesus goes on to say (Mt. 7:2–5) that each person will see applied to his own case the standards of judgment he brings to bear on others. He articulates a principle of reciprocity, and at a minimum, it holds that one should not accuse someone else of something that one has done oneself. More broadly, what Jesus warns against is not just accusing someone of X when you yourself practice X—the essence of hypocrisy in the modern sense of the term—but of accusing someone of X when you yourself have done Y, which is just as bad as X. Here, reciprocity joins with proportionality. If you pick a nit with others, expect others to do the same to you, though the nits may be different.

In fact, if you insist on pointing out the faults of others, you should first ensure that you do not have greater faults of your own. Before you speak out, you should examine yourself carefully and take action as required to rid yourself of the flaws you have. Jesus's evocative language—he refers here to the speck in the other's eye but the log in one's own—seems to evoke a kind of self-inspection before a mirror. Once you have removed the log from your own eye, if you still find fault in your "brother," then you will at last be able to see clearly enough to approach him in the same spirit in which you just reviewed and improved your own conduct: You should be thinking about helping him rid himself of the fault in question, not condemning him for it.

Throughout, Jesus tells his listeners to avoid any sense of moral superiority that might attach itself to the perception of faults in others. The danger here is clear: If you are using the weaknesses, foibles, flaws, and infelicities of others as reason to feel better about yourself or as a source for your own validation, then you have every incentive to allow the one to whom you now feel superior to persist in those very shortcomings. This runs directly contrary to two essential Jesusian teachings. The first is the one we have just been reviewing, the obligation to help others rather than merely to remonstrate with them or to condemn them. Second, this sense of superiority is the opposite side of the coin of the sense of self-regard that comes from being concerned to win the praise of other people. It's no accident that Jesus returns to the term "hypocrite" here. As Jesus warned against drawing one's own sense of self-worth from the acclaim of others, so he warns against boosting one's sense of self-worth by pointing out the faults of others.[1]

Following this discussion of judgment, Jesus then abruptly switches metaphors and emphasis, saying, "Do not give what is holy to dogs, and do not throw your pearls before swine, or they will trample them under their feet, and turn and tear you to pieces" (Mt. 7:6). Having dwelt on the rather demanding conditions that people need to fulfill before they turn their attention to helping others get rid of their flaws, Jesus then goes on to urge caution about offering such help at all. He turns from the worthiness of a person to offer others guidance to the worthiness of others to receive it. It won't do the dogs and pigs any good, he says. On the contrary, it's likely to inflame them and cause them to turn against you.

While at first glance it may appear that Jesus is contradicting his earlier message about the need to reach out to and on behalf of others, this is not the case. He warns against reaching out to animals *as if* they were people. As we have seen, Jesus distinguishes the merely animal in man from the human in man on the basis of the relations people (but not animals) are capable of forming with one another: in his "fulfilled" law, relations based on freedom and equality. But to say that human beings *are capable* of such relations is not to say that human beings are *already in* such relations. Once again, running through the Sermon on

---

[1] There is also the question of whether you know what you're talking about. I, a proud almsgiver, see someone else walking past people begging alms without giving them anything. I therefore judge that person to be stingy and therefore my lesser. But how much do I really know about the person toward whom I have assigned myself the role of superior? Specifically, what do I know for sure about how much she gives in alms and under what circumstances? Perhaps she has walked by those seeking alms because she has no alms left to give, having given away everything she has but the clothes on her back just before coming into my field of vision. Perhaps she is the living embodiment of the teaching of Jesus—unbeknownst to me. I have no right to assign myself a sense of superiority not only because it is wrong to seek this form of superiority, but also because I have no basis for knowledge of any such superiority. Indeed, there is no such "superiority" of this sort.

Now, extend the lesson outward a hundredfold, to all the opportunities that present themselves in the course of a day to find fault with others and superiority in one's own eyes, barely any of which provide anything close to full and sufficient context necessary to understand, let alone pass judgment on, the conduct of which you have just caught a glimpse. That would be the log in your own eye, indeed.

the Mount and underlying Jesus's teaching for this world is the law. Jesus starts with people who are in possession of the law amongst themselves. He seeks to enrich their understanding of the advances that are possible from that starting point. But not everyone has the law. Some are lawless. And unlike the naturally beautiful lilies of the field, some of what persists naturally is rather ugly. The spectacle of the dogs fighting among themselves for a scrap of meat or of the pigs (unclean animals) scuffling in the muck is an unattractive one, and it turns downright menacing with the thought that they might turn on those who first stirred them up by tossing in front of them something for which they scramble but ultimately discover they have no use. That could be you.

The way, then, to reconcile this passage with the instruction Jesus proffers to love your enemy is simply by recognizing that to love one's enemy is to invite a reciprocal relationship where none existed before. If it is fulfilled, it supplies the essential precondition of the more advanced state of relations between people that Jesus is propounding. It becomes the basis, then, of helping your brother remove the speck from his eye, once you have made sure you have removed the log from your own. If it is not fulfilled, however, then you are stuck in a lawless set of relations, and you would be ill-advised to sally forth with projects whose essential preconditions have not been met. In such circumstances, you place yourself needlessly at risk by jumping the gun. The first step is to achieve a basis in freedom and equality, and it is toward this that your attention should be directed.

Though Jesus has an extraordinarily ambitious program for human relations over time, here we see the "realism" that underlies it: You must not skip steps—or if you can, it will be because you have found others alike in their desire to skip steps. The latter point turns out to be highly significant, in that it paves the way for people to engage fully in relations with one another that are completely Jesusian but without first going back and learning the ancient law, thereby recapitulating in person the evolution that society as a whole has undergone up to the time of Jesus. The importance of this down to our day is unmistakable. It points to the possibility that the community of goodwill will spread rapidly—though this possibility is not a certainty. Skipping what's essential—whether out of excessively idealistic motives or imprudent calculation—will only imperil the desired end. Those who maintain that the Jesusian teaching is too soft-hearted for the real world need to try to understand what he has to say here more fully.

Before the Golden Rule

The next sequence in the Sermon on the Mount serves as a preamble to the single most important precept of the Jesusian teaching, offering an organizing principle for all interaction in a world characterized by law: what has come down to us as the Golden Rule, "In everything, therefore, treat people the same way you want them to treat you . . ." (Mt. 7:12).

Moving on from the "realistic" passage about the perils of throwing pearls before swine to the Golden Rule, Jesus offers the following observations, whose language comes in a form that seems to echo the promissory or predictive character of the Beatitudes. Jesus says: "Ask, and it will be given to you; seek, and you will find; knock, and it will be opened to you. For everyone who asks receives, and he who seeks finds, and to him who knocks it will be opened" (Mt. 7:7–8).

Using language that is frustratingly vague, Jesus does not tell his listeners what they should ask for, what they seek, or whose house they should seek admission to by knocking on the door. It seems clear that Jesus is offering a gesture, like those we find in many of his parables, to the reward people will enjoy for seeking God—or, in the case of this world, for seeking and acting on guidance into how to conduct themselves in relation to others. This does not answer the riddle, however. One must know *which* question to ask, what to seek, which door to knock on; otherwise, one might not get the right answer. Jesus seems to be suggesting that we already somehow know what the right question is.

We do know the right question. We learn it from the law itself—from the fact that we live in a world in which the law is a fact of life for us.

We have seen that Jesus came not to "abolish" the law but to "fulfill" it such that "all is accomplished" at some point in the future. Here, Jesus indicates that the law, as it is, contains within it the seed of its own fulfillment, in the sense that law is continuous, developing step by step by step, from the dawn of the first law to the fulfilled law Jesus promises in accordance with which "all is accomplished."

Now, we must beware: The fulfillment of the law is not a predetermined outcome. The seed of law may or may not grow on its own; that's up to people. They may develop the law and seek to expand its reach, or, on the contrary, they may lose it altogether, slipping back into anarchy or barbarity. They may seek an ever-stronger connection between the law and an idea of righteousness or justice for their fellow human beings, or, on the contrary, they may push the law in the opposite direction, toward official enactment of the perpetuation of the privileges of a few, up to the extreme case of Nazi Germany's laws on Aryan racial supremacy. Jesus's own arrival on the scene bespeaks his intention to explain how the law can be fulfilled, in a way that no one before has ever proffered, with the purpose of making clear to people what they must do to fulfill it. He seeks thereby to hasten the arrival of the day when "all is accomplished."

Nevertheless, the question of how to fulfill the law—what to ask, what to seek, where to knock—is already present whenever people mutually possess an idea of what law is and adopt among themselves legal relations for governing their affairs. From that moment, they begin a sequence of events that may, under proper conditions, lead to the fulfillment of the law. The ancient law already points people in the direction of asking themselves what the limit of the law is, how much the law can achieve. Starting from the most basic of legal relations governing people, what can people build from there?

For the purpose of our discussion, we have so far just taken the term "law" in the ordinary sense in which Jesus uses it and in which his listeners presumably had no trouble understanding what he meant. But some aspects of his meaning will become clearer if we delve a little more deeply into the question of what the law is. A law is a rule governing human conduct, a specification of how to conduct oneself correctly. How does it govern? In two ways: by its coercive power or the fear thereof (do this or face punishment, up to the penalty of death) and by its voluntary acceptance (the extent to which people comply with the law because they believe it is good, either in itself or because of the effects it produces, or both).

There is little doubt that earthly law has its origin in coercive authority: A strong ruler lays down what he expects of his subjects. But voluntary acceptance is a different matter. Here, the coercive power of law runs up against what Jesus has described as the "hunger and thirst for righteousness." In saying that this desire "will be satisfied" for all people, Jesus is claiming that the coercive power of law will (in time— when "all is accomplished") be in harmony with what people voluntarily accept as right.

This balance between coercive power and voluntary acceptance may take the form of people's acknowledgment that the law must retain a coercive element for our own good, so that we continue to abide by the law even if it works against us in the particular circumstance at hand. For example, we have courts to settle disputes that arise over contracts between two parties, and the two parties enter into the contract knowing that if a dispute arises, the matter will be settled in court. That's where the dispute gets settled even if one of the parties, when the moment arrives, decides that his chances would be better if he could settle the matter by force.

A condition of harmony between coercive power and voluntary acceptance may also be reflected in our ability to get along with less severe punishments than our forebears: The more people voluntarily abide by the law, the less it is necessary to frighten them into doing so with the prospect of terrible punishments.

In addition, harmony between coercive power and voluntary acceptance may manifest itself in the ability of people to get along with, so to speak, less law: If they have a shared idea of the conduct expected of them in given situations, then they will act in accordance with their shared expectations. They won't have to go to court to seek the enforcement of their rights because others will understand and comply with their duty not to infringe on those rights. Their shared understanding of what is right will be their "law" or rule in a way that is more real and alive to them than the laws on the books.

So what begins with coercive power ends—or at least may end—in the voluntary acceptance that takes place when the content of the law matches up with everyone's desire for righteousness. Of course, not just any desire calling itself by the name "righteousness" will suffice. If, by righteousness, I mean that which is to my advantage, then as we have seen, this desire of mine will run afoul of the desire of others for righteousness. My sense of righteousness must be compatible with yours. We must have a common idea of righteousness and what that entails in terms of our conduct in order for the desire for righteousness to be "satisfied" for all of us, as Jesus says it will be.

So what, then, shall we ask, shall we seek, shall we knock on the door of? What is the question? How do we move from law in the coercive sense to law that is voluntarily accepted?

The way to do so is to ask: What can I do *next* to contribute to the satisfaction of the desire for righteousness that all of us feel?

Of course, if only *I* ask this question, *we* get nowhere. While my asking might contribute to the perfection of my own morals, as far as the organization of this world is concerned, the critical Jesuian point is the *shared* sense of righteousness. That's what enables us to enrich our "brotherly" relations with one another as we seek to extend our "neighborly" relations outward, even to the point at which old "enemies" put their enmity aside. The social and political benefits "we" will enjoy the more often *each* of us asks this question, and the more *of us* who ask it, will be vast and beyond riches. This question has locomotive force for the propulsion of social relations in the direction of the satisfaction of our common and primordial desire for righteousness.

Strikingly, the question is not that difficult to answer. Now, if we begin with a grand abstraction—What is happiness? What is justice? What is the purpose of human life?—we may find ourselves somewhat flummoxed, or we may not have the slightest idea. Some will find the answer in faith in God, and others may give up in despair. But according to the Jesusian teaching, as far as what to do in this world with respect to our relations with others is concerned, we need not feel obliged to find within ourselves an answer to the largest questions in order to know what to do next. The answer to that question is immediately at hand.

It is: "In everything, therefore, treat people the same way you want them to treat you. . . ."

This Golden Rule is the single most succinct and precise summary of the Jesusian teaching,[2] the distillation to purest essence of his guidance for people about how to live in the world. It is noteworthy not only for its conciseness, but also for its accessibility: Most any adult, and for that matter most any child past a certain developmental stage, can not only grasp the instruction Jesus offers, but also understand at once how to apply it in daily life.

The Golden Rule is profound in its simplicity. And, of course, to modern ears, like many other sayings of Jesus, it rings so familiar as to risk seeming trite—like the sound of the first four notes of Beethoven's Fifth Symphony or Hamlet's "To be or not to be" soliloquy, only more so. To try to appreciate it afresh, let's look at it back to front.

Ending with the line, "the same way you want them to treat you,"

---

[2] Some claim for the Golden Rule a broader pedigree. One finds in Confucius's *Analects* the precept, "Do not do to others what you do not want them to do to you" (15:23), and in the *Mahabharata*, "This is the sum of duty: do nothing to others that would cause you pain if done to you" (5:1517). Both of these sources predate Jesus. They also, in my view, say less than Jesus did, restricted as they are to the negative element: "do not"; "do nothing." Jesus's formulation encompasses the negative element but envisions a range of possibility for mutually beneficial interaction that goes much farther, with vastly greater social and political consequences.

the Golden Rule offers the question: How is that, exactly? Do we want what we deserve? Is this a formula that calls for the neutral administration of justice according to the rule of law, according to which we are fairly rewarded for our good behavior and fairly punished for our bad behavior? Well, no, not exactly. Of course, I do not want to be treated unjustly, in the sense of persecution, but neither do I quite want to be treated only in accordance with the neutral application of the law. I would like, perhaps, a little more sympathy than that.

This is an important point about the law, one that Jesus was driving at in his injunction to "make friends" with your "opponent" on your way to court—thus settling matters between you, lest the law keep you locked up until you have fully discharged whatever debt you owe (Mt. 5:25–26). The law grants no mercy and expresses no sympathy: That is not the role of law. Rather, the law sets forth general rules to cope with the widest possible variety of circumstances—and accordingly, the law will shoehorn your particular circumstances into its confines. Though we need general rules, we also need to be attentive to particular circumstances, or at least I would like to have my particular circumstances attended to, and so would you. The idea Jesus expresses here is to direct us beyond simply the rule of law and into consideration of these very human particulars. It is a further illustration of the way in which Jesus seeks to personalize the law in order to "fulfill" it.

In the Lord's Prayer, we ask to be forgiven "our debts" as we "have forgiven our debtors." We certainly have no claim to be forgiven for what we have done wrong in the absence of our own willingness to forgive others for what they do wrong. The spirit of this request in the Lord's Prayer is similar to the spirit of the Golden Rule: If we owe a debt, then we can be made to pay, by the full force of the law if need be. However, we would prefer to have forgiveness directed toward us in a spirit of mercy or sympathy.

Here, Jesus points to an interesting problem: It is impossible to live in this world in such a fashion as to incur *no debt*, and therefore to have no need, ever, of the sympathy or mercy or forgiveness at issue here. It is not simply a question of people being, somehow, after all is said and done, sinners. It's also a product of the inability to live a life on this earth in which one's obligations never come into conflict. For a very basic illustration of this problem, consider the question of how the Golden Rule applies to a parent's dealings with a child. Clearly, the test a parent applies is not to ask, "How would I like to be treated?" as if the parent and the child were already fully equals in the Jesusian sense. The child is in need of instruction, and the parents have to provide it. As we have seen, Jesus is firm in his condemnation of those who "teach" others to break the law (Mt. 5:19), and his special concern for the education of children is a point to which he will return. Nevertheless, one does not raise a child into a full and equal adult in the manner of flipping a switch: The process is gradual, and to some degree, it is a matter of trial and error, as one begins to extend the privileges and responsibilities of adulthood to the growing young person. The point being that one will *make mistakes*: you in granting privileges perhaps prematurely and the young person in acting irresponsibly with the privileges granted. One will not want to be judged too harshly for those mistakes, nor to judge the young person too harshly. Surely, this is one important reason for the ancient law's injunction to honor your parents. Likewise, systems of justice have long treated juveniles as a separate category, not fully accountable as adults are.

The middle portion of the Golden Rule says, "Treat people the same way," This, too, raises a question: Why should anyone catch such a break as to be treated the way he or she would like to be? What entitles any of us to anything more than treatment in accordance with the law in all its majesty? Well, because if we ourselves are following the Jesusian teaching, we have already been treating people with the sympathy we would like for ourselves. We have a track record we can point to. We are not asking anything on our own behalf that we would be unwilling to extend to others, which we prove by treating them with sympathy even before we are in need of sympathy ourselves.

The essence of the Jesusian teaching here serves as a corrective to another possible doctrine for the guidance of human conduct: Treat people the way they have treated you. Jesus enjoins us to turn away from this point of view. It's not good enough. As a principle of social organization, it drives people into a least-common-denominator cycle of action and reaction that has as its starkest expression the *lex talionis*, an eye for an eye. The way to break this cycle is to go first: Rather than treating someone the way you have been treated, treat them the way you'd like them to treat you, regardless of what they do next. Oh, there are limits, of course. Jesus, let us recall, is at pains throughout the Sermon on the Mount to explain that he is talking about the *next steps* for people to take once they live, as his listeners do, in a world of law—shared general precepts. The fact that in some instances there are complexities to the implementation of the Golden Rule principle must not obscure the simple fact that in *most* instances there are *no* complexities in living by it fully. Certainly, there is no excuse for the failure to do so in a world of law, where the greatest risk you might routinely run would be for an evildoer to slap you on the cheek. You'll survive with your freedom and dignity as a human being intact if in response you turn the other cheek.

But by going first, by actively treating with sympathy and fellow-feeling someone with no special claim on your sympathy, you can be co-engineer of a breakthrough to a very different world from one organized around retribution for wrongdoers. To do this, you must set aside the past. You must declare the slights you have suffered beforehand irrelevant to the problems of the present moment and instead introduce the forward-thinking principle Jesus has set out in the Golden Rule.

The Golden Rule begins, "In everything. . . ." That simplifies matters. No, this is not a rule of sympathy or mercy applicable only in special cases, maybe when somebody else really needs a break. It is a general rule, and it applies in all your relations with other people, every last interaction with every last one. If you are selling something, you must put yourself in the place of the buyer and ask how you would want to be treated in *that very transaction*. You would want to receive fair value for the price you paid, and so you should give fair value for the money you receive. Because you want the other party to comply with the terms of a contract you have signed, you comply with the terms you have agreed to. Because you would not want someone spreading false rumors about you or scandalizing your name, you refrain from spreading false rumors and scandalizing others.

All of the situations discussed in the previous paragraph are subject to legal regulation, a subject Jesus has been exploring throughout the Sermon on the Mount: fraud in business transactions, breach of contract, slander, and defamation. But if we are able to liberate business transactions, contracts, and matters of reputation from the legal system by virtue of our own good conduct—by dealing honestly with one another, by keeping to our agreements, by telling the truth about others— then we will be better off. The law, as Jesus has suggested, can be a blunt instrument. Better to "make friends."

However, the Jesusian teaching cuts more deeply than that. Because you know that in all circumstances you would like to be treated courteously by others, in all circumstances you treat others with courtesy. Common courtesy isn't something that can typically be regulated in a courtroom. And yet its political and social meaning are in certain respects every bit as profound as the things that can be. Discourtesy is often nothing more than the manifestation of one's sense of superior status with regard to another. It is an offense against the proposition that the desire each person feels for justice or righteousness can be met for all. To "lord it over" someone speaks for itself as an offense: No one has a justifiable claim to do so.

This helps clarify another aspect of the Golden Rule: What if I would like to be treated in a *superior* fashion? Of course, if my desire for sympathetic treatment, not simply legal or just treatment, comes at the expense of someone else, then for reasons Jesus has already explained—the need for all to "be satisfied"—my desire is an unreasonable one, and I should not expect anyone to act in fulfillment of it. Moreover, the Golden Rule is a two-part proposition: If I would really like to be treated in superior fashion, then I am obliged to treat others in superior fashion. In doing so, I am not really establishing a claim to *superiority* but to *equality*. If all goes well, we will be equal in treating each other as superior.

While it sounds paradoxical, it is actually the essence of the Jesusian teaching: Social and political relations are not a zero-sum game in which more for one necessarily means less for another. We can settle for a world in which equality means no more than that the unforgiving judgment of the law comes down equally on everyone. Indeed, we should acknowledge that getting to the point of living in such a world is no small achievement, as we can readily appreciate by thinking about what a world with no law is like: a struggle of all against all. Such a world does not, however, exhaust the possibility that inheres in relations that begin in the law. Such a world does not represent the fulfillment of the law. The latter, the product of the Jesusian teaching, raises all of those living by it to a higher level. Indeed, by the terms of the Golden Rule, we are limited in our aspiration for how well we will treat one another only by our imagination—how we wish to be treated. If you wish to live like a king, what you need to do is treat others like kings, and they you.

But what happens if you are *alone* in embracing the Jesusian teaching of the Golden Rule? If it goes unreciprocated by others, isn't the Golden Rule a recipe for servility? Well, in the first place, you won't be entirely alone. You've already got family, "brothers" in the broader sense, neighbors, with whom you enjoy Golden Rule–type relations. It's important to remember that Jesus did not *invent* the possibility of treating someone the way you want to be treated. The conduct he proposes he knows to be possible on the basis of his own observation of people. He is not asking for a leap into the unknown, in the manner of a utopian dreamer. Rather, he seeks the extension and deepening of these relationships of mutuality to the limit of what's possible.

In the second place, it may not be so difficult to find others willing to act in this fashion. After all, this is no mere idle moralizing on Jesus's part: articulation of a doctrine of what we "should" do because of some abstract principle that has little discernible connection to our happiness and well-being in this world. There's something in it for us. Quite simply, that's the ability to live in the world Jesus has described: a world in which the law is in the process of being fulfilled. We will find such a world more to our liking than one in which the law is static or in decline.

If we concern ourselves with the question of who goes first as if it were a matter of who has the right to go second—to wait for someone else to make the first move—then collectively, we stay where we are. If, however, we embrace the Jesusian principle and act on it, the leap we take is not simply one of faith, but of expectation that people, knowing themselves how they want to be treated, will come to understand that the only plausible way to guarantee such treatment for themselves is to treat others the same way. We find here the underpinning of the idea of mutually beneficial contracts and of the "win-win" transaction.

The Golden Rule verse in Matthew says in its entirety, "In everything, therefore, treat people the same way you want them to treat you, for this is the Law and the Prophets." The concluding words come because, with respect to how people should live in this world, the Golden Rule *is* the fulfillment of law and accordingly everything the prophets foretold. It is the end toward which the law points and of which the prophets promised.

5.

THE PATH AND
THE FOUNDATION

Rather than telling people *what to do*, Jesus has told people *how to know* what to do: The Golden Rule is the distilled essence of his teaching, a principle for conduct that encompasses all interaction between any two people. He then proceeds in the final passages of the Sermon on the Mount to discuss the future of his teaching, how it will spread in the world.

To begin this discussion, Jesus turns to a metaphor similar to the "ask . . . seek . . . knock" with which he preceded his discussion of the Golden Rule. Now he tells his listeners, in what could easily be an answer about where to knock in order to seek entry into the Jesusian teaching, that they should enter through the narrow gate, not the wide gate (Mt. 7:13–14). He says, "For the gate is wide and the way is broad that leads to destruction, and there are many who enter through it. For the gate is small and the way is narrow that leads to life, and there are few who find it." The easy thing to do is to go along with the crowd. But surely the crowd doesn't select the wide gate in the expectation that by going that way, they will be walking into their own destruction. In some cases, perhaps, people as individuals may be willing to strike out for their own doom in full knowledge that that's what they are doing. When it's large numbers of people flowing through a wide gate, however, they probably have something else in mind.

Jesus reminds us that at the most basic level people are social and political creatures who seek relations with one another that progress beyond a war of all against all or the rule of the strong over the weak. They have a view of their common good. In describing large numbers of people passing through the wide gate to their destruction, he reminds us again that the political and social relations people come up with don't always work out. Sometimes, people agree to act together in perpetuation of what's wrong, not necessarily realizing that it is wrong. They see everybody heading for the wide gate, and they join the throng, perhaps without bothering to ask whether what's beyond the gate is good for them or even whether it's what they want. They want what's beyond the gate merely because others want what's beyond; that's good enough for them. They take their measure as individuals by their conformity to the crowd. They find their validation in moving in the same direction the crowd is.

Moreover, the gate is, after all, wide. It's inviting. It says, "Use me!" It's not human caprice or ill will alone that sends people down the wrong track. The world puts before them certain enticements they will surely notice. There is nothing the least bit remarkable about this fact. It's the origin of our need from time to time for the forgiveness of others: the temptation that we ask not to be led into, lest we yield to it. The Lord's Prayer asks God not to lead people into temptation; here, we get a much clearer picture of how temptation works in human terms: It's a nice, wide gate, easy to pass through, and everybody else is going that way.

Here, Jesus sharpens his earlier point about doing things in order to win the approval of others: This can be the route to destruction. Furthermore, it's not just the individual who is at risk. Whole societies can collectively make bad judgments, sometimes by doing no more than what's easy and validating one another's choice of what's easy.

This discussion is not only a warning against taking one's compass from the judgment of the crowd but also against being too much in one's own time and place, too caught up in what others are doing and thinking or doing without thinking. Sometimes it may seem to us that the only decision we face is whether to go along with the spirit of our times or to seek some form of escape from it. It's as if we see the world as a path that leads only through the wide gate ahead. We either go through it or we are lost, purposeless, directionless. But that denies our ability to consider matters outside the frame of reference the crowd imposes—to look for another way. Needless to say, Jesus's essential point is to remind people that they have the freedom to seek within themselves the truth about what they should do in their relations with others. And Jesus has strong claims about what that truth holds.

The point is that there's more than one path and more than one gate. In addition to a broad one on a wide path, there is a small one on a narrow path—one that cannot be passed through in a throng. Getting through the small gate entails a sequence of steps: first, considering the possibility that there may be a different gate from the wide one; next, finding the small gate; third, recognizing that the small gate is a better choice; fourth, rejecting the pull of the crowd toward the other, wider gate; finally, Jesus's language suggests that one may have to pass through the small gate all by oneself. That may be a hard thing to do.

Jesus says that "few . . . find" the small gate. That may be true. But he doesn't say that if you do happen to find it, what you should do is clamber through and quickly shut it behind you, so that "few" others will "find" it. Nor does he say you should camouflage the entrance to the narrow path so that others will mostly miss the turnoff on their way to the broad gate. Jesus is not insisting that everyone else looking for the right thing to do go through a process of finding the small gate every bit as difficult as the first one to find it.

Instead, the idea underlying Jesus's metaphor is that those "few" who find the small gate will want to help others take the path they have pioneered. The point is not that only a few *should* go through the narrow gate but that only a few manage to *find* that gate. Once someone has found it, that person can show the way to others, and the others won't need to find it on their own. Indeed, only if someone who finds it *fails* to show the way to others does it become necessary for anyone else to "find" it all over again.

Nevertheless, the path remains narrow and the gate small. It will indeed likely be necessary to go through one person at a time. And, of course, this makes sense in two ways: First, in effect, because no one can make you go through the gate, nor go through the gate for you: It's a free choice, the product of your freedom. Second, we shouldn't allow ourselves to become confused by Jesus's warning about the crowd going through the broad gate by jumping to the erroneous conclusion that Jesus wants or expects only a few people to make it down the narrow path. Jesus doesn't have anything against large numbers of people doing something when it is the *right* thing. What comes first is the question of what's right, and the more people who reach the correct conclusion, the better. Ultimately, the hope is for people to get to the right answer on their own, not solely because others have reached that conclusion; that would be just another way of following the crowd and taking your sense of worth from others. If the crowd is right, you may not do much harm (and this fact is relevant to the spread of the Jesusian teaching). But a compelling answer to the question of what is the right thing to do can only come from within.

Jesus has not proffered his teaching about how to live in the world in order to be ignored or to reach only a small number of people, although he suggests here and elsewhere that the Jesusian teaching about how people should organize their worldly affairs will spread through the world not suddenly but gradually, in the time it takes until "all is accomplished." In contrast to how the crowd of his day may be tempted to go, he has pointed out that there is a better way. He has shown his listeners the narrow path, and he has articulated what lies beyond this world in terms of the ability of people to live in expanding and deepening brotherly and neighborly relations. It's up to each person to decide whether or not to follow the path he describes—single file, through the small gate.

The next passages of the Sermon on the Mount raise the problem of those who, knowing better themselves, beckon to the broad gate anyway, trying to lead people astray. Never mind whether the once-popular broad gate is still drawing the crowds it used to. Quite possibly it will not be, to the extent that Jesus's teachings about how to live in the world are taking hold: People will know about and seek to enter via the small gate. But Jesus has warned throughout about the ongoing presence of evildoers and temptation. Here, he reminds us that those bad tendencies come in two different packages. The first sort we have already seen—the evildoer who is quite blatant about it: someone who would slap you in the face. But there is another kind, too, and a trickier one: someone whose evil comes cloaked in the trappings of what's good.

Jesus famously warns here against wolves in sheep's clothing (Mt. 7:15). We have already seen how Jesus connects his fulfillment of the ancient law with the prophets: The Golden Rule, he says, is "the Law and the Prophets," what each is meant to be when understood and embraced by people. So, here, Jesus issues a warning against "false prophets": those who claim to be acting in the name of fulfilling the law in the Jesusian sense, but who actually strive to subvert it to their own ends.

How do you tell the two apart? Apart from divine sorting out of the lawful from the lawless to which he refers in the last passage of this section (Mt. 7:21–23), he offers some very practical guidance for this world: "You will know them by their fruits" (Mt. 7:16, 20). He says that "every good tree bears good fruit, but the bad tree bears bad fruit"; it's impossible to get bad fruit from a good tree or good fruit from a bad tree, the latter being useful only for firewood (Mt. 7:17–19).

So, in the first place, a tree looks like a tree: It may not be a simple matter to tell by mere outward appearance the distinction between someone who is prophesying in an effort to further the Jesusian teaching and someone who only seems to be doing so. In using the term "prophets" here, Jesus connects the past, present, and future. He is clearly speaking in this passage of those who will come after him, but he reinforces the claims of continuity he has made with respect to the past. The true message of the ancient prophets is to foretell and anticipate the fulfilled law of the Golden Rule and the Jesusian teaching more broadly. The prophecy of ancient times was an incomplete description of what was to come, or else it would have constituted all by itself the fulfillment of the law, and the teaching of Jesus would have been superfluous. Nevertheless, the fact that the ancient prophecy was incomplete does not mean that the ancient prophecy didn't point toward its own completion. It began the process that culminates in Jesus's "fulfill[ing]" the law.

The task of the "prophets" to come, if they are true prophets, will be to learn the fulfilled law Jesus taught and spread it, teaching it to others. We have seen how Jesus uses the metaphors of saltiness and shininess: In learning the Jesusian teaching from Jesus or from someone who follows it—to whom Jesus here gives the designation "prophet"— the student deprives the teacher of nothing: The teacher is neither less salty nor less shiny on account of having enlightened the pupil; on the contrary, the act of enlightening others is essential to the development of one's own saltiness and shininess.

But all those to come who purport to be prophets may not be true prophets, and we may not be able to tell from appearances a true prophet in the Jesusian sense from a false one. Apparently, they may say many of the same things. Jesus here indicates that he expects some people to repeat his words but to reject his teaching.

His expectation is well-founded. In the first place, it is a product of his self-assurance about the truth of what he is saying: In the future, many will repeat what he says, though some will not mean it. He anticipates that his teaching will achieve a certain rhetorical dominance, in that even its enemies will find it convenient or necessary to present themselves as part of the tradition he established with his language and principles, if only to try to subvert the Jesusian teaching. Once again this is hypocrisy, but we should be mindful of the adage about hypocrisy as the tribute that vice pays to virtue. After Jesus has promulgated his teaching in fulfillment of the law and people begin to understand it, accept its implications, and take it personally with regard to their own sense of freedom and equality—the proper route to satisfaction of their "hunger and thirst for righteousness"—it becomes difficult (though not impossible[1]) for others to advocate some contrary principle for the organization of human affairs. In many cases, those who would like to establish or entrench a political and social order that works to their own advantage at the expense of others will nevertheless feel obliged to cloak their wishes in words that seem to embrace the Jesusian teaching. They find themselves unable to advance their interests except under a false flag. In our time, think of the number of autocrats and tyrants who somehow feel obliged to say they believe in democracy and to put on a show of (rigged) elections to prove it.

A second reason for Jesus to anticipate the appearance of false prophets on the scene—those who repeat what he said in order to further aims that are different from his—is the element of time, which Jesus thinks is on his side. He has pointed to a moment at which "all is accomplished" in accordance with the law he has come "to fulfill." Beginning with the listeners to his Sermon on the Mount and continuing to our day, people have found themselves somewhere between the point of fulfillment and the point at which "all is accomplished." Another way of saying this is that the Jesusian teaching must *spread*. According to Jesus's own terms, its advance will not be characterized by its sudden,

---

[1] One such contrary principle would be the Nazi doctrine of Aryan racial supremacy, especially emerging as it did in a society that was in many respects liberal. Nazism was not a vestige of the past, as, for example, slavery in America was, but a new doctrine based on inequality. Interestingly, Marxism-Leninism or communism, the other grotesquely disfiguring ideology of the twentieth century, while rejecting a so-called bourgeois false consciousness of equality, nevertheless trafficked in its own doctrine of equality. In practice (and also in theory), the latter doctrine is very different from the universal equality Jesus propounds, but one still finds people who view it as a kind of "fulfillment" of the Jesusian teaching about equality. Such devotees would benefit from a consideration of the "fruits" of Marxist ideology, namely, communist regimes now universally understood to have been tyrannical.

universal acceptance, but by its promulgation from person to person, bringing in its wake the earthly satisfaction of the desire for righteousness for those who live by it. It turns out to be a matter of great utility to the spread of the Jesusian teaching that even many of those who oppose it inwardly feel they have to pretend they support its principles (see chapter 10). In addition, the Jesusian principles can (and have) spread genuinely even through the agency of those who propound them falsely, or understand them imperfectly, or fail to live up to them fully.

Meanwhile, it can be hard to tell the true proponents of the teaching from the false ones. Jesus says that to do so we need to examine "the fruits."

There are two senses of the term at play here. In a figurative sense, the "fruit" of something is that which follows from it. So we can think of Jesus as referring to *what follows* from the teaching of latter-day prophets, both the true and the false kind. If the doctrine they espouse sounds attractive but turns out in practice to be pernicious or otherwise deficient, then we need to revisit the attraction. If, on the other hand, their words result in outcomes that are recognizably positive, then chances are good that those propounding them are the genuine article.

We do need to be wary on one additional point, however: The full "fruit" may not be apparent from the first fruit that appears to us. The outcome may look good at first but turn out to be questionable or worse as we see more or as time passes. There is also the possibility that we will be too hasty in our condemnation, a problem Jesus warns against, as we have seen.

But the occasional challenge or difficulty of rendering an accurate judgment does not excuse us from our obligation to scrutinize the "fruit" and determine whether it is good or bad. What Jesus proposes here is, in effect, a reality check. This is important because fine-sounding words are relatively easy to devise compared to outcomes that are genuinely fruitful. The words themselves, if they are consistent with the Jesusian teaching, are not irrelevant in their own right: They can have a positive influence even if they are insincerely intended. But words alone are insufficient.

An important purpose of Jesus's teaching is to have an effect in the world, to change it for the better. His teaching is not meant to be *merely* words. It is directed not only toward the improvement of our understanding of how people should live together but also toward *changing* the way people live together in accordance with this understanding. Its fruit is accordingly accessible not only to those who do understand the teaching but also to those who may not understand it but whose lives have been touched and improved by encountering its fruits in the real world.

Jesus says you can't get bad fruit from a good tree or good fruit from a bad tree. It certainly seems right that you can't get good fruit from a bad tree, but it's not so clear that all the fruit from a good tree will be good fruit. Some of it may rot from within for causes initially unapparent to the observer and unrelated to the goodness of the tree. Which is exactly the point: In such a case, it's not the tree's fault. There is a reason or cause outside the tree for the badness of the fruit. Jesus thereby reminds his listeners of an additional element of complexity in considering the case at hand. The integrity of the Jesusian teaching—the good tree—is not proof against subsequent malign influences having nothing to do with the teaching.

What we really have here is a simple real-world test for the value of the teaching of a latter-day prophet: If the effect is good, then the teaching is good, and if the effect is bad, then the teaching is bad. This is important because judgment accordingly does not stand or fall on our ability to assess the teaching in question according to our understanding. We can be clever if that's who we are and the faculty we possess, but we don't have to be, because everyone can easily tell good fruit from bad. No one would eat bad fruit. Proper judgment of the question is accordingly available to each and every person, not just to those with the ability to scrutinize the inner workings of the tree.

In fact, the real-world test, as Jesus presents it, occupies a higher place than judgment based on understanding alone. Jesus is warning here against the danger of misplaced judgment based on misunderstanding. Since it can be difficult to tell a true prophet from a false one on the basis of the prophet's words alone, Jesus puts those who pride themselves on the ability to see through the words, to penetrate to their true meaning by means of superior understanding, on notice: They may be mistaken. The reliable test is the one that looks at outcomes—the fruit.

There is, however, an additional sense of "fruit" in relation to the tree. It's that the fruit, in addition to being something tasty that people enjoy eating, is also the means by which the tree reproduces. The fruit in this sense refers to generational transfer: how a tree produces more trees.

In this sense, to examine the fruit is to examine the offspring. We may take this to invite scrutiny not only of the teacher or latter-day prophet, but also of the students or listeners. The question for us here is the extent to which the students or auditors themselves come to exemplify the Jesusian teaching about how to live in the world. Or rather, Jesus's suggestion is that students will reflect the truth or falsity of the message of the teacher or prophet, thereby clarifying the validity of that message in a way that words alone could not. A decent crop of followers is an indication of something of value in the message of the teacher. A dissolute and feckless entourage or school is an indication of deficiency in the teacher, and that's so no matter how fine sounding the message.

Throughout history many thinkers have been at pains to keep a certain distance between themselves and their students; they would be reluctant to accept responsibility for what their students do with the insights they as teacher have provided. Jesus takes a radically different view. In telling us to judge the tree by the fruit, he invites the application of the same standard of judgment to his own teaching. Yes, we can look at what he says, scrutinizing it to extract the full measure of his meaning, as we have been trying to do here. But that's not all we have to go on. Jesus also invites the consideration of his teaching in the light of its effect on people: his fruit. Far from distancing himself from the real-world consequences of his words, he fully embraces the idea that his words will have consequences. They are meant to change people, and it is on the basis of the change he brings about in them, not the fineness of his thought and sentiment alone, that he wishes to have his teaching considered.

Put another way, Jesus is the original shiny and salty one, the pathfinder. And it is relevant to the fulfillment of his teaching that others in turn, under his influence, become shiny and salty themselves and are able to show an even greater number the narrow path to the small gate. His teaching was not meant to lay dormant for two thousand years, or even two years, until some high-minded philosopher came along and discovered that in his words was something of latter-day interest. On the contrary, it was meant to have an effect on its initial hearers, who in turn would repeat it in such a fashion that their hearers would be affected by it.

It is interesting, in this context, to recall that Jesus never wrote anything down. From the beginning, the spread of his teaching in this world was dependent on word-of-mouth. His listeners, affected and impressed, spread what he had to say to others, and the others did the same, and so on. It is because of word-of-mouth in the early days that we have access to Jesus's teaching in the form of the Gospels. Such was his faith in the efficacy of his teaching that he entrusted it entirely to those who heard him. He not only said that you could judge a prophet by his fruits; he subjected his own teaching to the same test.

BUILDING A GOOD HOUSE

At the conclusion of the Sermon on the Mount, Jesus offers a final metaphor for our consideration. It concerns the proper construction of a house (Mt. 7:24–27).

"Therefore," he says, "everyone who hears these words of mine and acts on them, may be compared to a wise man who built his house on the rock" (Mt. 7:24). Though the rains came and the winds blew, yet the house still stood because of the soundness of the foundation. Those who hear Jesus but do not act on his words are like someone who built his house on the sand; this foolish builder's house was swept away by the wind, rain, and flood, "and great was its fall" (Mt. 7:27).

Once again, Jesus emphasizes the connection between his words and the action taken by his listeners. The words are not meant merely to be contemplated; they are meant to change people's behavior in this world. To hear *and to act* on what one hears is the sound foundation. To hear without acting is to remain in danger.

Jesus begins with the image of a house, a place where people live. The this-worldly implication of what he is saying could not be clearer: His teaching is intended to have an effect on how people live their lives. Here, he offers them guidance on what action to take to secure themselves against the elements (a point to which we will shortly return). The house is not a found object, like, for example, the caves in which some of our ancestors might have taken shelter. It is a built thing, an act of construction. Most houses, especially ones that are destined to last, entail construction by more than one person. House building is a cooperative venture.

As such, we are invited to consider the house figuratively as well. The implication for Jesus's political and social teaching is clear: The house, broadly construed, is the place people make for themselves to live in: their social and political world, the one governed by their interaction with one another. To hear and then act accordingly is to take Jesus's guidance on how to live in such a world. The result will be a structure that can lay claim to permanence: It is secure against the elements. By contrast, to hear and to fail to act on the Jesusian teaching is to risk that the social and political world thereby constructed will lack a secure foundation and will therefore be vulnerable.

Jesus speaks prospectively: He addresses himself to what will take place as a result of acting on or failing to act on his teaching. In this sense, going forward, those who have heard what he has to say about how people should relate to one another in this world are on notice: To reject the insights of the Jesusian teaching about how to live in the world is to remain at risk.

Prior to Jesus, there was the ancient law and the prophets. As we have seen, the fulfillment of the law, which Jesus claims as his purpose, is not the importation of something alien into the law, but rather the development of the law to the limit of the possibilities inherent to the very idea of law. Thus, we wouldn't be quite right to think that when Jesus talks about a house swept away and "a mighty fall," his meaning is that the old world—the world of the ancient law—will be swept away. Some things will, however, change. We might think of the ancient law as pointing to two possible sites for the construction of a house: one atop stone and one atop sand.

The ancient law is akin to the path down which people have been traveling. Now, with the arrival on the scene of Jesus's guidance on how to live in the world, people face a choice: a wide gate at the end of a broad, long trodden path that leads to a building site on sand or a small gate on a narrow offshoot of the path, which Jesus has found, this one leading to a building site on stone. You can't do without the path—the law. It took you to where you are, and this was no small thing, as one can see by comparing the world in which Jesus speaks with the world of those who lack the law and live their lives as a struggle of all against all. It would be a big mistake to minimize the importance of what people have achieved up to the point of Jesus's arrival on the scene. As we have noted, it would not have made sense for him to propound his demanding guidance in a world that was altogether lacking in the law, nor should we fail to take him seriously when he says that he did not come to abolish the law: The Jesusian teaching begins with the law.

But now, with the arrival of Jesus and the articulation of his teaching, we have reached a new moment, a turning point. It is time to make a choice: to accept Jesus's guidance about how to live in the world or not. The people to whom he was delivering the Sermon on the Mount knew perfectly well that you don't build a house on sand, not if you want it to withstand the elements. Knowing this, they might nevertheless reject the applicability of the metaphor to the Jesusian teaching. There is always a choice.

On what basis, then, should people make their choice? Interestingly—though perhaps by now, unsurprisingly—Jesus anchors his claim not in an abstract vision of the good or in an appeal to people to improve themselves simply because they *should* do so, but in a description of what they will gain for themselves in this world if they live by his teaching. This is not to deny the divine element of Jesus's appeal, but the appeal is not *merely* based on a heavenly reward. It also promises advantage in this world to those who embrace it: The house we are building is where we will live, and the question at issue is whether we build it on a secure foundation. By Jesus's own description, his teaching is not divorced from consideration of his listeners' own wishes and desires—what we might nowadays call their self-interest—but actually is based on granting those wishes and satisfying those desires.

However, in the Jesusian teaching, it is not just individual self-interest that needs to be attended to. There is self-interest, and then there is something like what we have come to know as *enlightened* self-interest: a self-interest based on more than merely the swift gratification of any personal desire. Although certain modern thinkers have invited us to try to develop an enlightened sense of our self-interest by looking within ourselves, Jesus enjoins us to think about the question in relation to our dealings with others. The most reliable guidance on how to treat others is to put ourselves in their place and ask how we would like to be treated: the Golden Rule. This is a standard within reach of everyone. If we build our society and politics—the house in which we live—on that foundation, then we will have created something that endures.

To show what we are up against, Jesus uses the metaphor of a storm: rain, flood, winds—an example of the worst that nature can throw against a house. Jesus's language is evocative and memorable, and his point is clear: His goal here is to demonstrate the trials to which the real world will subject our house and the people who dwell in it. To answer the question of what perils we face, we first have to know what we want and whether it is really possible to have it. What we desire, Jesus says, is righteousness, and we can have it—but only on certain conditions. We cannot call any old yearning we feel by the name of the desire for righteousness. Righteousness is not synonymous with "what's good for me." If it were, then there would be no satisfying it: Everyone's sense of self-righteousness would come into conflict. The only way to settle matters, to decide who gets the pleasure of satisfaction, would be a test of strength, and the outcome even for the winner would be at best temporary, since the winner would be subject to future challenge.

Out of the first serious attempt to solve this problem and advance past the point of constant struggle—to recognize in enmity, in other words, a problem that actually can have a solution—the law was born. As people embraced the law, perhaps because they had come to see its wisdom in regulating human affairs, perhaps merely because they feared the consequences of breaking it, they began to discover the further possibility of law and learned the advantages that living under law could bring. Now comes Jesus to fulfill the ancient law by refining it and distilling it to its purest essence—the last word, so to speak, in human relations, in how people should get along with one another: the Golden Rule.

So, the only way to satisfy *anyone's* desire for righteousness is to satisfy *everyone's* desire for righteousness.

PART II

PARABLES, SCENES, AND SAYINGS

6.

PROPAGATION

Jesus was a storyteller and aphorist *par excellence*. Considered in relation to the question of how people should live in the world, his stories and sayings fall into two broad categories. One group consists of stories that speak to the substance of the Jesusian teaching, in which Jesus elaborates on some of the themes we encountered in the Sermon on the Mount about *what* people should do and how they should act in relation to one another. In this group, we will also find illustrations of the human propensities that get in the way of people's embracing the Jesusian teaching as well as certain pragmatic advice for coping with such difficult characters, including even sworn enemies of everything in the way of freedom and equality that he stands for. We will take up these parables in the next chapters.

The other, our topic here, pertains to the propagation of the Jesusian teaching itself: how it spreads, by what human action, and the resistance it encounters. In the religious context, this is, of course, the question of evangelization and proselytism, and it remains about as controversial nowadays as it was in the beginning. In some parts of the world, preaching the Christian gospel is illegal and punishable by death, and practicing Christians are subject to persecution for their beliefs.

In the spirit of removing the log in one's own eye, however, Christians recall that Christian believers have engaged in religious persecution themselves. To the extent that modern-day Christians reject the spread of the faith by coercive means, they themselves generally see this as spiritual progress, a product of a deeper understanding of the teaching of Jesus.

And not just the religious teaching. The insight that one must not take up the sword in order to coerce others to confess that "Jesus is the Christ" is a *political* insight. And it has its origins not in some outsider's critique of the Christian religion as practiced, but in the political teaching of Jesus itself. Indeed, it is a distinctly Jesusian insight that faith cannot be compelled. At worst, a theocrat of whatever hue may obtain outward compliance from those unwilling to die rather than go along; but a critical element of Jesus's focus on what goes on within a person's heart, as we have seen in the Sermon on the Mount, is to demonstrate the freedom that inheres there.

It makes no sense to try to compel what cannot be compelled. Jesus did not gather an army, conquer a territory, and impose his teaching on those living there. We have seen how contrary any such enterprise would have been to themes he explored in the Sermon on the Mount with regard to the voluntary establishment of a community of goodwill.

But if not by force, then how? Very simply, by persuasion. By setting out a case, in words and by example, and letting people respond to it as the free persons they are according to the terms of the case itself. Jesus is perfectly well aware that others hold views different from his, often addressing himself directly to such competing views. The point is that on questions of how worldly affairs should be organized, he contests other views in the realm of speech, not power. He does not seek to deprive those who hold different views of the ability to voice them. On the contrary, he meets their arguments with arguments of his own. In doing so, he sets an example from which we still profit, even though some cling tenaciously to the belief that force, even terror, is an appropriate instrument of persuasion, either in compelling others, in demonstrating the zealousness or righteousness of one's cause, or simply to exterminate those unwilling to comply.

Because the spread of Jesus's teaching is intimately connected to its substance, he devoted a great many of his public statements, especially in the form of parables, to the question of the spread of his teaching. Its spread, as any other, entails its transfer from one person to another, through space (from here to there throughout the world) and time (from generation to generation). What we will see is that the propagation of the Jesusian teaching is rather different from learning your ABCs, or for that matter, an academic discipline or a craft. The point of the Jesusian teaching is to *change* the person who is taught, to bring about a new approach to the question of how to live in the world. These parables show how that happens.

The First Parable

The very first story explicitly identified as a parable in what is generally regarded as the oldest Gospel, Mark, is about the relationship between what Jesus says and what people hear. It is the parable of the sower and the seed (Mk. 4:3–9).[1] In six sentences numbering little over a hundred words in English translation, Jesus tells a story that conveys startling insights into the universality of his message; the way people will come to understand the principles he advocates and upholds; and a first glimpse of what the world looks like when ordered according to those principles. Of course, he says none of this directly, in so many words; that is exactly the point. His message is at its most powerful when people are able to discover it for themselves. His stories are mysteries to be solved using the clues Jesus himself provides.

A man was sowing seeds, Jesus says. Some fell on the roadside "and

---

[1] The parable of the sower and the seed is also the first parable explicitly identified as such in Matthew, 13:1–15. It also appears (though not first) in Luke, 8:4–10. Numerous scholars have argued that Mark, or a lost book prior to Mark, is a source for material in the other Gospels.

the birds came and ate it up." Some landed on rocky ground, with little soil to take root, and after each sprouted, the sun scorched it, "and because it had no root, it withered away." Some fell among thorn bushes, "and the thorns came up and choked it, and it yielded no crop." But some seeds fell in fallow earth, "and as they grew up and increased, they yielded a crop and produced thirty, sixty and a hundredfold." Jesus concludes this message to his large audience (Mk. 4:9), "He who has ears to hear, let him hear."

How would the people gathered on the shore of the Sea of Galilee that day have understood the parable of the sower as it came, word by word, from Jesus's mouth? The picture he paints is vividly precise: birds pecking at seeds; scorched shoots; a thorny thicket; finally, a field abundantly full of crops for harvest. But, surely, as they heard these word portraits, his listeners knew that something was missing, that whatever the point Jesus was making, it was not simply farming that he had on his mind. The story of the sower is marked by what is missing from it, and this absence builds and heightens tension even over the course of a few simple sentences. What is he talking about? What does this story *mean*?

It's the admonition he delivers to the crowd at the very end that provides the key to the story: "He who has ears to hear, let him hear."

It is one thing to have ears, as do all those in the crowd, and it is something else really to hear—to get the message, to understand and fully appreciate what has been said. There is a difference between the faculty of hearing and the ability to put that faculty to use. Truly hearing is not just a matter of receiving the words spoken in accordance with the language skills at one's disposal, the basic knowledge of vocabulary, grammar, and usage most all children pick up by age five or so. Truly hearing is a matter of the effect the words spoken have on the mind of the person whose ears they have entered—the processing of the spoken word into an understanding of its meaning at its fullest. Truly hearing involves judgment. It is an interaction between the speaker and the listener.

By example, the first parable of Jesus thus demonstrates the way in which Jesus got people to listen to him. With artful language, he conjures a vivid image in the minds of his listeners, but they know the image is incomplete. Something is missing from it that is not yet clear. At the end of the story, Jesus's words provide the decisive key. But it is only a *clue*. Now it is up to the listeners. If the story is to yield its meaning in the fullest, those who have heard it will have to go back and reflect on what they have just listened to—those precisely conjured images—and understand them in the light of the clue the speaker has provided.

How successful they will be at deciphering the message is an open question. Perhaps they will indeed be able to go back to the beginning and think afresh about what they have heard, at last able to take it all in. Or perhaps they will make use of the clue and get the message, but then quickly forget it. Perhaps they will understand they have been given a clue, but conclude that they have better things to do than go back and think about the story again. Perhaps they will fail to apprehend the clue at all and give up, reaching instead the conclusion that the speaker, though charismatic, was a purveyor of nonsense, a spellbinding teller of tales signifying nothing.

And this is the first meaning of the parable itself. Some seeds grow into mature crops; some grow but are scorched; some are choked out; some get eaten by the birds. Some people hear and understand; some hear and understand but turn away; some have ears and begin to hear but give up before they understand; and some have ears but hear nothing: "He who has ears to hear, let him hear."

The parable of the sower is first a description of Jesus telling his listeners the parable of the sower: A speaker tells a story to an audience. The story is a mystery, but the speaker gives a clue. Some in the audience are able to use the clue to solve the mystery. What they find is that the story is a description of exactly what has taken place, except now they know what the speaker knew from the outset. They have, in essence, used the words of the speaker to become like the speaker. They now know that by learning what the speaker says, they acquire the ability to *be* as the speaker *is* and to *do* as the speaker *does*.

The importance of this mechanism—hearing, knowing, becoming—to the spread of the teaching of Jesus simply cannot be overstated. Elsewhere in the Gospels, Jesus will discuss it more thematically, for example: "If you continue in my word, then you are truly disciples of mine; and you will know the truth, and the truth will make you free" (Jn. 8:31–32). Jesus says "continue *in* my word" rather than "continue *to follow* my word" or "*heed* my word." You come to inhabit the teaching, "my word," in the same manner as one who has come to understand the parable of the sower and the seeds—you realize that you, the listener, are in the story. First, one hears the word; then, one understands the word; then, the word is "in" one at the same time one is "in" the word. The teacher understands the parable he tells in the way he wants those who hear the parable to come to understand it themselves, and he provides them the means to understand it in the course of telling the story.

We turn, then, to the "seed" in the parable. People often think of it simply as the word of Jesus, his message to his listeners. From there, it is a short jump to the conclusion that people are represented in the story by the terrain: some fallow (ready to get the message); some shallow (in whom the message won't take); some prickly (overwhelmed by distractions and temptations); some rocky (altogether unreachable). But that is not quite right.

A seed is something that contains within it the potential for a mature plant, provided the growing conditions are right. In this parable, people are not merely the growing conditions, whether favorable or unfavorable, in which the seed grows or not while remaining apart and distinct from the environment in which it is sown. The point of the story is that those with ears—at least some of them—*hear*. They change from a condition of ignorance as the story unfolds to a condition of awareness upon reflection at its end.

In a word, they *grow*, and in this sense, they are not merely the environment for the seed but the combination of the seed *and* its environment. The sower sets in motion the process by which the seeds grow into their full potential. Of course, what grows here is not insensate plant life; rather, it's people who are capable of hearing and of judgment. As those who hear the parable of the sower come to understand that the story is about those who listen to it, they come to a new awareness of themselves. The "growth" here entails a process of self-understanding, an awareness of one's own potential.

Jesus would seem to be the one who has done the sowing: The sower is someone with seeds who knows what happens to seeds when you plant them and care for them and why it is accordingly worthwhile to do so. The sower knows what the *potential* of the seeds is and wants them to grow. When the seeds find a proper environment and grow in accordance with their potential, Jesus says, they produce crops "thirty, sixty, and a hundredfold." The sower desires and benefits from an abundant harvest. We might think about harvesting the crop and eating the produce, and while that is certainly relevant here, there is also more to the metaphor.

Mature crops themselves produce *seeds*—a second generation of seeds that, cultivated properly, will in turn yield another crop and yet more seeds. This in turn is the transmission belt for the regeneration of the teaching of Jesus—the way in which seeds, and by extension people who have grown to their potential, produce more seeds—more potential.

There is nothing automatic about this process of regeneration, however. Left untended, a field whose crops are allowed to go to seed will soon revert to a wild or natural state. The process requires a sower, someone who *understands* what the seeds can become. Here again, the essential element of the parable of the sower comes into play: Those who truly hear it come to understand that it is about *them*. The surest way (if not the only way) to come to this understanding is to work out the meaning for yourself, to hear truly. In this way, people come to inhabit the teaching of Jesus. It becomes a part of them and is itself inseparable from its embodiment in people.

People become, in short, sowers themselves. The parable is an invitation to a new sense of self-awareness, which in turn serves as the key to the regeneration of the teaching. This self-awareness is not, in the end, the product of didactic instruction according to a fixed canon or creed; it is the product of truly hearing, working through the problem for oneself. The ability to work through the problem individually, in turn, makes it possible for a generation to grow from seed to sower. To sow is to embody human potential at its fullest because it is the combination of personal knowledge of human potential with the ability to cultivate it in others.

Unfortunately, not everyone hears. For one reason or another, some fail to capitalize on their full potential. And as a matter of first impression, the parable indicates that they come to a bad end: Some seeds are eaten by birds, some shoots are scorched, and some are choked by weeds. This does not, however, mean that in the absence of an ability to understand this parable, to place yourself in its teller's shoes and become a sower of seeds, your alternative is being eaten, burned, or choked. Here, it's important to recall that the analogue of the human being is the *combination* of the seed and its growing conditions. There is no need to be bloody-minded about the outcome. Jesus issues no threat here, only a promise: When conditions are right, the seed the sower sows will reach its true potential.

The critical point is that the sower sows *all* the seeds: True, in the course of his sowing, some "fell beside the road," some "fell on the rocky ground," and some "fell among the thorns," but this did not happen on purpose, since a sower would not deliberately try to plant along the road or in the rocks. He would look for the best soil—in fact, he would cultivate the soil to make it as fertile as possible, and he would plant as carefully as possible. Some of the seed, however, would inevitably be lost, falling on the rocks or in the thorns. That is not the intention, but it is an outcome. The hope is that all of the seed should grow into an abundant crop. The reality is that all of the seeds will not grow.

Ultimately, the goal of the parable is for everyone to understand its teaching in order to be able to carry the teaching forward: hearing, knowing, becoming. The parable contains a universal message, a teaching for everyone. The reality is that not everyone will understand it, but that does not mean one shouldn't *try* to reach everyone. To try to do so is the first obligation. We will have to read on to find further guidance on how to deal with those whom the teaching does not reach—those who, though they have ears, do not hear.

In the meantime, note that for our purposes here, the political teaching of Jesus, his guidance for life in this world, is readily discernible from the parable of the sower, the first parable recorded in the oldest Gospel—and it is a coherent whole apart from (if encompassed by) a religious teaching on questions pertaining to the immortal soul and salvation. It is a kind of Jesusian "discourse on method": an explanation of how his teaching works, how to learn from what he says. We don't "learn" the parable of the sower by memorizing it so that we can repeat it back on command. We learn it by figuring it out and living in it: hearing, knowing, becoming. And even if we hear the parable for the first time from someone who is *merely* reciting it from memory—without truly having heard, known, become—we can still take away from it exactly what Jesus intended. The Jesusian teaching cannot be obliterated by a human transmission belt that is at times faulty; so long as we still have access to his words, we have access to their transformative potential.

We know that the teaching is for all people, so that they can realize their full potential as persons whose desire for righteousness is capable of being satisfied. We also know that the teller of the parable sets an example that listeners will be able to follow once they understand the parable itself. And we know that in comparison with what we find growing on the side of the road, or in rocky ground, or among the thorns, there is something *orderly* about crops.

We can expect, then, to find something orderly about people who have developed in accordance with their full potential. The ordering principle is equality, according to which the satisfaction of the desire for righteousness, that primordial human desire, is indeed possible, but not for only one or a few. It's all of us or none of us—those who live in accordance with Jesus's political and social teaching about the arrangement of the affairs of this world will share the benefits of living in such a world equally. In order to join that world, they will have to appreciate the truth of the Jesusian teaching, whether they call it by that name or some other.

But people, unlike seeds, have to sow themselves.

THE "KINGDOM OF HEAVEN"

Many of the parables Jesus tells come to us in the form of similes, beginning along the lines of, "The kingdom of heaven is like . . ." We need to take a moment to be clear about the relationship of those words (and what follows them) to the this-worldly prospects for the spread of the Jesusian teaching. Where, or what, is this "kingdom of heaven"? And what, if any, is its relation to the world in which we live?

As a matter of first impression, it may seem as if Jesus is talking about something entirely other-worldly—a kingdom that is precisely not in or of this world. If that's so, then the kingdom of heaven will be of supreme interest to those who aspire to it in the afterlife, but will have little practical application to this world.

To reformulate the issue in such terms, however, is to see the self-evident absurdity in supposing that the words of Jesus have application only in a world to come—either in a heavenly beyond or in this world when and only when, by divine action, a heavenly order arrives here. As we have seen and will continue to see, Jesus is keenly interested in how people should act toward one another in this world. He is interested in this question not because human life on earth is nothing more than a proving ground for one's worthiness to enter heaven, but because he expects his teaching to change people's relations in this world for the better, which is valuable in itself. After all, as we have seen in the Beatitudes, Jesus maintains that the first stirring a person feels beyond passive acquiescence in the circumstances the world imposes is the desire for righteousness. This is a desire felt by people in this world and a satisfaction they seek, if they can get it, in this world. Jesus avers that they will be satisfied—pointing toward a way in which the universal desire for righteousness can be satisfied for all people. As such, it's clear that Jesus is not simply speaking about the next world in his parables. Moreover, all of the parables are in some sense tales of *becoming*. They all entail action in one form or another, the movement from one state to another. Sometimes it's people who act, sometimes the metaphor pertains to plant life; but these stories, as befits the fact that they *are* little stories, are in no case merely static descriptions or vignettes. Jesus does not present "the kingdom of heaven" as a fixed point somewhere beyond. As we will see, this "kingdom" is unique in that it reaches out to people and beckons to them, inviting them to join it where they are, not necessarily to cross a border (such as that between this world and the next) in order to be part of it. The *becoming* here entails a becoming in this world.

In this sense, we can see that the "kingdom of heaven" is not merely a model of perfection; rather, in Jesus's usage, this "kingdom" is something we can take part in building here and now. In fact, he says it is our obligation to do so, not merely because of aspirations we may feel with regard to the next world, but because in so doing, we act to fulfill the potential for righteousness we all possess. We want to be moving in that direction for the sake of our lives in this world and our relations with other people in the here and now, whatever benefits may ensue in the next.

As to whether the this-worldly accomplishments people are able to achieve in line with their embrace of the Jesusian teaching will ever make this world indistinguishable from the "kingdom of heaven," we are right to be dubious. Absolute perfection is an attribute of the divine.

Nevertheless, we should be careful with our doubt. In particular, we must not allow skepticism about the ultimate this-worldly outcome to become an excuse for the failure to act rightly in the here and now. What to do is not, after all, a great mystery, something up in the sky. Jesus has made it clear with his political teaching: his instruction about how to live on earth.

When Jesus speaks about what "the kingdom of heaven is like," his purpose is not to draw a radical distinction between this world and that "kingdom," but to set us on the path of ordering human affairs in accordance with the principles of the "kingdom." That's the Jesusian teaching. As he notes, "where two or three have gathered together in my name, I am there in their midst" (Mt. 18:20).

SPREADING THE WORDS

Jesus offers a number of metaphorical illustrations of the power of his teaching to spread and grow. In several Gospels, he likens the teaching to a tiny mustard seed that grows into a huge plant (Mk. 4:30–32; Mt. 13:31–32; Lk. 13:18–19). He also likens the kingdom of heaven to a small amount of yeast capable of leavening a large amount of flour (Mt. 13:33; Lk. 13:20–21).

In these examples, we have the case of a little that does a lot. A diminutive seed turns into the largest plant in the garden; a pinch of leaven a woman hides in three pecks of flour leavens all the flour. What begins with a few words from the mouth of Jesus grows over space and time into something vast in its reach, importance, and implications.

First and foremost, Jesus tells these stories to indicate the potential to spread his teaching. In these few words, however, he offers far more than merely a prophecy of the success of what he has set out to explain to people. He means to offer a more detailed account of how his instructions can propagate even among those who have understood him only partly, or only barely.

In the Luke version of the mustard seed story, there is a notably casual element to the planting of the seed. It is not so much sown, as in the other two Gospel versions, but *tossed* into a garden. We are left with the same big plant in the end, but in the Luke version, the process described takes place not as a deliberate act of cultivation but perhaps even despite the intention of the one who threw the seed. In either case, what we have in the end is a hearty plant. The Matthew and Mark versions invite us to think about the deliberate act of propagation of Jesus's teaching, the Luke version its ability to propagate almost accidentally.

The Luke version presents a slightly more complex notion. While an element of this metaphor is, of course, the dropping of a seed that has the potential to become a giant plant in a place where it can grow, it's not obvious that the person who drops it understands its full potential or even understands that it has potential. The implication is that a full appreciation of the potential for the Jesusian teaching to grow is unnecessary for its growth. Indeed, the extent of the growth may come as something of a surprise.

There is likewise an additional element to the story of the woman and the leaven. It's not just that a small amount of yeast (or other leaven) can wreak great change on a large amount of flour, perhaps a bushel. It's also that the woman in Jesus's story hid it in the flour. We don't know why she did that. Perhaps someone else wanted to take it. In any case, the hiding place was in some sense a foolish choice, in that the leaven will not remain what it is for long, nor will the medium of flour in which it is hidden. Instead, the leaven and the flour interact. The former transforms the latter, and in this case, it seems almost obvious that the process described is taking place without the intention of the human agent involved (unless, of course, the woman hid the leaven in the flour in order to ensure the ensuing interaction, another possible interpretation). Once again, as in the augmented element of the story of the mustard seed in Luke, there is an indication of how powerful a process the propagation of the Jesusian teaching is, how receptive the world is to it—perhaps well beyond the expectation even of those who take a part in spreading it. Perhaps, in some cases, whether they know they are spreading it or not. Perhaps, likewise, irrespective of an intention on their part.

Jesus, for his part, is clearly on the side of the mustard seed's growth into a big plant and the leavening of the three pecks of flour. By the terms of his similes here, his intention will prevail. The seed *will* turn into a plant, and the leaven *will* cause the flour to rise. The outcome of the process is not in doubt. It's organic: A seed in a garden (a fertile environment) will grow. The plant is the fulfillment of the combined potential of seed and garden, the end to which the combination points. Likewise, the organic interaction of yeast and flour is dough that rises through the process of fermentation; that, too, is the corresponding end.

Interestingly, you could cut off a small portion of the now-fermented dough and use it to leaven yet more flour—and the same ad infinitum, a metaphor for the spread of Jesus's teaching reminiscent, as we have seen, of his description of how the "saltiness" or "shininess" of one in whom his teaching lives can salt or illuminate others. We have seen in the parable of the sower and the seeds how the crop that is cultivated also in turn produces seeds for the next season's sowing; the same is true in the case of the mustard plant in this story: Though any given plant will die, the species lives on. The same with the progress of the Jesusian teaching in the world.

Had he wished to, Jesus could have said that *the kingdom of heaven is like a tiny mustard seed that grows into a giant plant.* Or, *the kingdom of heaven is like a small portion of leaven that leavens three pecks of flour.* Instead, however, he chose to add an act of human agency to his simile. In doing so, he has deliberately introduced an element of ambiguity and assigned it to the human role in the propagation of his teaching. Did the man in the garden intend to grow a giant mustard plant, or was he just tossing aside a superfluous seed? Did the woman who hid the leaven mean to leaven all the flour or not?

Despite the uncertain aspect of the human element, the teaching still flourishes. In dropping the seed, the man in the garden was true enough to the end of the propagation of the Jesusian teaching to ensure that it would take place, whether the man was aware of it or not. This would not have been true had he thrown the seed into the sea. The same with the woman hiding the leaven in the flour: Intention aside, that was enough, and hiding it in salt would not have been. Each character acts *as if* intending to propagate the teaching, but it is not a requirement of *acting as if* intending to do so that one be fully conscious of the final end of the process and willfully approach it with the intention of achieving such an end. Here, we have a powerful account of how a process of propagation that can only be called imperfect—all too human—can nevertheless be expected to yield results in fulfillment of the end envisioned by the one who set it in motion.

Another illustration of this uncertain element to the propagation of Jesus's teaching is the parable of the harvest (Mk. 4:26–29). In this instance, Jesus likens the kingdom to a man who plants seed: "He goes to bed at night and gets up by day, and the seed sprouts and grows—how, he himself does not know" (Mk. 4:27). Jesus notes that the soil does the work, readying a crop for harvest.

Here, the pivotal element to the story is the ignorance of the sower. The biology of plant life is beyond him. In terms of the comparison here, someone seeking to spread the Jesusian teaching doesn't necessarily have to understand the inner workings of its propagation.

While the man in this story doesn't exactly know how this process works, he is not entirely ignorant. He knows what to do with seed, and he knows when to take the harvest. Planting and harvesting his crop are precisely his intentions, and he knows enough to make good on them. If we have reason to doubt that we know the true volition of the man with the mustard seed and the woman with the leaven, we have no doubt about the intention of the man in this parable. He knows what he wants, and he knows when he gets it, even if he cannot say exactly how it comes about. In attributing the growth of the seed to the soil, Jesus points not

only to the robust character of the teaching but also to people's receptivity to it. Nevertheless, the process is not automatic. Someone must
plant the seed.

So we have three illustrations of the way in which the teaching of
Jesus can spread notwithstanding the imperfections of the agents of its
propagation. They need not possess wisdom and insight on the scale
of Jesus himself in order to effectively advance the teaching Jesus ini-
tiated.

The parable of the fig tree shoots (Mt. 24:32–33; Mk. 13:28–29;
Lk. 21:29–31) reminds us to be on the lookout for the early signs of
the receptivity of others to the Jesusian teaching. Jesus tells his listeners
to look at the fig tree and the other trees around them; when they "put
forth leaves, you see it and know for yourselves that summer is now
near. So you also, when you see these things happening, know that the
kingdom of God is near" (Lk. 21:30–31). Jesus associates the spread of
his teaching with the arrival of summer. The meaning of the story has,
then, three elements. The first is that his teaching will indeed spread,
and this is a situation that he likens to the uncontestable expectation of
the seasons' turning. Again, this image of transition reinforces his contention that he has the right answer, the one that is both true and beneficial, the one people will respond to on account of who they are in the
most basic sense, their primordial desire for righteousness. Summer is
coming.

Second, summer does not arrive, so to speak, unannounced. There
are early signs: spring shoots. There would seem to be two elements to
this temporal metaphor, one with respect to the propagation of the Jesusian teaching from person to person—the "micro" level—and the
other with respect to its spread throughout this world—"macro" considerations. In the case of the former, Jesus instructs us to be on the
lookout for indications that a person or people are beginning to act in
accordance with what he has said. In this metaphor, the process
through which his teaching takes hold is not sudden but gradual. We

might look to see whether someone treats *any other person* the way he or she would want to be treated. That might serve as an indication of the possibility of a further willingness to treat *everyone* in that fashion.

On the global scale, we should not expect the sudden arrival of summer without a preceding spring: The "kingdom," Jesus says, is not going to break out all over spontaneously and fully complete. Before "all is accomplished," we should expect *some part* to be accomplished, including even the most minute, barely perceptible part.

This leads to the third element of the parable: The arrival of the "kingdom" is indeed perceptible to people even at its earliest stages. Jesus casts his listeners as characters in the parable he is telling. They can tell when spring arrives and therefore when summer is coming. They already know, on the basis of their own experience, what to look for. But what experience can these people, the folks who were on hand when Jesus told this very story the very first time, have had of the coming of the "kingdom" Jesus is announcing and promoting? The circumstances of listeners hearing his message for the first time, by analogy, would seem to be those of people suddenly transported to a new planet: They would have no idea what its seasons are and how they begin to show themselves.

The answer is that the analogy is wrong. We return to Jesus's stated intention, namely, to "fulfill" the law, not to overthrow all law in order to obtain a blank slate on which to write a new law. People already know what brotherly relations are like. They have already been enjoined to love their neighbor, and moreover, they understand the benefits that come from loving their neighbor—how much better off they are in a political and social setting in which people see one another as affiliated with one another and not locked in a struggle of all against all. Jesus has told them to extend this principle outward: to take the knowledge they each can find within themselves about how they would like to be treated and to treat others accordingly. Common human experience has therefore already provided people with what they need to know in order to recognize the signs of spring, which point to the abundant spread of the Jesusian teaching.

THE NEW MESSAGE AND THE OLD LAW

The manner in which the old law influences the propagation of the Jesusian teaching is the theme of the parable of patches and wineskins—which, like the previous parable, is noteworthy for its presence in three of the Gospels (Mk. 2:21–22; Mt. 9:16–17; Lk. 5:36–39). First, Jesus observes that you don't patch an old garment with a new, unshrunken piece of cloth. If you do, when you wash the garment, the new piece will shrink while the rest of the fabric does not, and the patch will tear away, resulting in a tear worse than the one with which you began. Second, Jesus observes that you don't put new wine in an old wineskin because if you do, the maturation process of the wine will burst the skin. You will be out both wine and wineskin. Instead, you have to put new wine in new wineskins.

These passages are as well known as they are famously elusive. Let's start with Jesus's reference to something "new." Presumably, for our this-worldly purposes, he is talking about his instruction about how human affairs can and should be arranged for the benefit of each and all. But, as he notes, there's a potential problem his "new" thing faces. The problem arises in relation to what came before it. We'll take the two examples separately.

First of all, there's a tear in an old garment, probably caused by wear in the course of the passage of time. What in its day was a new garment, perhaps very well made indeed, is now a bit frayed. It can't simply be sewn together as is or it won't fit its owner. Something new has to be added to the garment. Jesus has the cloth to fix it.

Thus, we arrive at something analogous to Jesus's view of the ancient law. He hasn't come to "annul" it but to "fulfill" it: in this metaphor, to apply a patch. In order to do so without damage to the garment—the world of law—he must first shrink the cloth he will use for the patch. There is no suggestion that shrinking harms cloth. On the contrary, to the extent that it remains unshrunken, it is unready or unprepared for the task to which it is going to be put. In shrinking the cloth for the patch, Jesus is adapting it to the specific requirements of the task at hand. The ancient law, as we have seen, is a thing of incalculable value to those who possess it. Jesus takes the old law as his starting point, using it as the foundation for his new teaching, which completes or fulfills it.

The second example in the parable is similar, but with an added element. To pour the new wine into old wineskins is to ruin both: The skins will burst, and the wine will spill. That's quite similar to the problem of the new patch on the old garment. But Jesus then switches the emphasis, from the accommodation of new to old (as in the case of the garment) to the maturation of the new. Here, Jesus observes that the new wine has to go into new skins in order to age. In the Luke version, Jesus then makes a point about the superior quality of mature wine: No one wants to drink the new stuff after having drunk the old.

Is something wrong with the new wine, a dubious element with regard to what's "new" in the Jesusian teaching of which Jesus himself is warning here? The answer is both no and yes. No, there is nothing dubious with regard to Jesus's teaching about how to live in this world in terms of its internal cohesion or its perception of the problems of the human condition. There is nothing improper about its conviction that these problems are susceptible to solution, its proposal along those lines for a politics based on freedom and equality, or its awareness of the difficulties of the implementation of the proposal. But yes, there is something quite dubious about the Jesusian teaching, of which Jesus is fully aware and against which he does warn. In a word, it can be summed up as the *radicalism* of his views.

If you pour that radical stuff straight into the world of the ancient law—if, that is, your proposal is to take the Jesusian teaching and implement it at once, everywhere, permanently—then the result is going to be catastrophic for both the Jesusian teaching and the world subject to this misbegotten exercise. The only way the Jesusian teaching can spread is voluntarily, through its free acceptance by free people.[2] It is the worst sort of folly to think that the frame of mind required for the reign of the ethical principle that has come down to us as the Golden Rule can be arrived at any way but voluntarily, in a free act of a free person cognizant of the freedom of others.

To seek to conquer in the name of Jesus is to miss the essence of the Jesusian teaching about as flamboyantly as possible. It would not go too far to suggest that such attempts from the history of Christianity ran afoul of precisely this parable. Such errors are not confined to the propagation of the explicitly religious element, of course. The excesses of the thoroughly secular French Revolution, which entailed the wholesale chucking of the ways of the *ancien regime* to the extent of re-naming the months and renumbering years, were undertaken in the name of liberty, equality, and fraternity. It is no disparagement of the genuine achievement of the French Revolution in the extension of "the rights of man" to point out that the Jesusian approach to the spread of freedom and equality disavows the Terror as a means to that end. An even more egregious incidence of the disparagement of and at-tempt to nullify the old order was that of the genocidal dictator Pol Pot, whose pursuit of a communist agrarian paradise led him to empty the cities of Cambodia and condemn to death all remaining bourgeois elements, such as those who wore eyeglasses.

Again, Jesus is at pains to "mature" his teaching, to let it work itself out over time as the fulfillment of the ancient law in the direction

---

[2] Again, the context of our discussion is how people, responding to Jesus's teaching, may seek to spread it to other people. Needless to say, this precludes investigation here of the question of how the teaching might spread through divine intervention. Many Christians believe that the universal embrace of the teaching of Jesus (not limited to but including his teaching about how to live in this world) will arrive only with the Second Coming. This would also be consistent, for example, with the universal reign of God described in Isaiah 2. It is no criticism of the view an-ticipating future divine intervention on, so to speak, a global scale to note that Jesus also antici-pates the spread of his teaching among people to *a considerable degree* as a result of what he said during his time on earth. The question for us, then, becomes: What is the limit?

of "all" becoming "accomplished." As we have also seen, only at that time—which is to say, only in good time—will it be possible to see exactly which elements of the ancient law "pass."

In other words, it's not that the new wine cannot be drunk at all or that one needs to use one's bolt of new cloth solely for the purpose of patching old garments: One could make new ones. These parables contain a lesson for the propagation of the Jesusian teaching not only among those who have a strong tradition of law of their own, especially the ancient law of the Hebrew scriptures, but also among those who are coming to it from other personal origins that perhaps will readily accommodate the teaching in its more immediately radical form. There is, in principle, enough "order" in the doctrine of the Sermon on the Mount and as further elaborated in the rest of the Jesusian teaching to allow for self-sustaining implementation solely on its own terms, without reliance on the ancient law. However, this can be dangerous, not because of a deficiency of the teaching, but because of the lack of clarity about what the teaching requires and the larger reality of human frailty. In some instances, it may be possible to start with the Sermon on the Mount, but in others, and in the main, it is better to begin with the law you have and inquire what needs to be done to "fulfill" it—to make the crossing from the very first earthly idea of law to the final content of the supreme law, namely, to treat others as you yourself would like to be treated.

The Problem of Rejection

While the parable of the net and fish (Mt. 13:47–48) has the element of a bountiful result in common with some of the others we have been discussing, it also has an element not present in the others. Upon pulling the net up on shore, the fishermen sit down and sort the good fish from the bad, putting the former into containers and throwing the latter out. The action here is not only the fishing, but also classifying the fish.

It's difficult to read this passage without thinking of an earlier passage in Matthew, when Jesus recruits Peter and Andrew, two fishermen, as disciples, telling them, "Follow me, and I will make you fishers of men" (Mt. 4:19). The point here is that the casting of the net—the pitching of the Jesus teaching to others—brings in many good fish, but not good fish only. Some are bad. They need to be separated one from the other and processed accordingly.

Jesus is extraordinarily spare in his description of who is doing this sorting. He doesn't even refer directly to the fishermen. (The Matthew version of the mustard seed parable similarly omits reference to "a man," which we find in Luke.) We might think Jesus is referring to divine or final judgment passed on those caught up in the net, with the fish representing people of both the good and bad sort. But there are earthly implications as well. Those with the net would seem to be those casting the net of the Jesusian teaching: people in possession of the teaching who seek to propagate it. They are human, but likewise human are the fish in the net, some good, some bad. Some have responded to the Jesusian teaching by adopting it as their own, while others have failed to do so for one reason or another (and once again, we can return to the parable of the sower and the seed for possible reasons why not).

The destiny of the good fish in the net is transformation: A good fish *becomes* a fisherman when it is next time to cast the net. Having embraced the Jesusian teaching, the *fish themselves*, now transformed, will seek to spread it. When Jesus told Peter and Andrew that if they followed him, they would become fishers of men, he *fished* them.

We return, then, to the question of sorting. The earthly point here is that it is not especially difficult to tell a good fish from a bad fish. Jesus presents that aspect of the task as straightforward: Those who have imbued his teaching and fished for men will know who among those in the net have embraced it and who have not. The test would have something to do with the willingness of the fish in turn to go fishing.

Still, there remains the problem of the bad fish. In the parable we have just been considering, they get thrown out. Many if not most of the bad fish will have the defect only of being too small; if the fishermen throw them back into the water, they may yet grow to a size at which they will become good fish.

Which takes us to the parable of the barren fig tree (Lk. 13:6–9). Here, Jesus tells a story about a man who came to look for fruit on a tree he planted in his vineyard. "And he said to the vineyard-keeper, 'Behold, for three years I have come looking for fruit on this fig tree without finding any. Cut it down! Why does it even use up the ground?' And he answered and said to him, 'Let it alone, sir, for this year too, until I dig around it and put in fertilizer; and if it bears fruit next year, fine; but if not, cut it down'" (Lk. 13:7–9).

This story is a minor masterpiece of the importance of persistence in the spread of the Jesusian teaching. The fig tree is three years old and hasn't borne fruit, and the vineyard owner has had enough. His complaint about the tree using up valuable vineyard ground is not idle: Fig trees grow tall and throw a lot of shade. Nevertheless, the vineyard-keeper proposes to give the tree another year, with special attention to its nurture.

We have two immediate lessons for the propagation of the teaching of Jesus in the world: The first, of course, is that it does not always immediately "take" with everyone who hears it. The propagation parables we have so far considered have turned on what happens in a single episode: one season of sowing to cultivation, one cast of the net in the water, the effect of leaven on a single bushel of flour. In all of these parables, we have found reason to look forward, asking what might happen next, and that has pointed us to consideration of what happens from generation to generation. Though he did this in a more circuitous fashion with the parable of the net and fish, in the case of the barren fig tree, he is more overt, inviting us to think about the temporal element as it applies to individuals. Some, clearly, embrace his teaching right away. Others, however, do not.

So persist. It would be a gross misreading of the parable of the net and fish to suggest that with the depiction of the fishermen throwing out the bad fish, Jesus is proposing that all those who initially fail to take up his teaching should be cast aside. If so, the story of the barren fig tree would be entirely in contradiction. The intention of the latter is clearly to suggest that more labor in the task of spreading the teaching may pay off and is worthwhile in the case of even a recalcitrant individual. There is a chance that the person in question will come around. It is an imperative of the Jesusian teaching that one not give up.

We don't know how the story of the barren fig tree comes out. The first thing that is striking in that regard is that Jesus does not tell us how the vineyard owner answered the vineyard-keeper—whether the owner acceded to the keeper's proposal to try for another year. We do, however, know who outranks whom, and there is a strong message in this element of the story. Jesus is clearly on the side of the vineyard-keeper and not, else the story makes no sense, on the side of the impetuous owner. The best course of action here is to be determined not on the basis of the rank of the proponents of the contending views but on the merits. This standard may, indeed, give the decision to the lower in rank. The vineyard-keeper, though he may well be a slave of the owner and certainly sees fit to call him "sir," may nevertheless know more about the workings of the vineyard than the owner. In fact, he ought to, since that is his specialty, and the owner ought to respect that greater knowledge, rather than merely assert his prerogative. The owner should hear the keeper out and consider the latter's advice carefully. The owner should not be doing this out of some sense of *noblesse oblige* or in order to humor his servant, but because the keeper may be right.

In addition to the lesson about the propagation of the Jesusian teaching in this story, there is also a lesson about the *substance* of that teaching and instruction about how people should live. It's the way in which power (in the form of the owner) benefits from truth (in the words of the keeper). The owner *need not* pay attention; yet he may *choose* to pay attention, and he may find himself rewarded by making that choice. The only means at the disposal of the keeper for attaining the course of action he favors is *persuasion*. His persuasive power is based on his experience working in the vineyard; his work makes him more expert on this question, perhaps, than the owner, who also has other things to worry about.

This expertise, in turn, changes the relations between the owner and the keeper: The keeper is no longer merely doing the bidding of the owner on the strength of the owner's authority over him. *If the owner chooses to listen*, and *if the keeper chooses to speak up*, then insofar as they have the same end, namely, the improvement of the vineyard, they will both be better off. The discussion of the matter at hand becomes a deliberative process between equals, if only briefly. This has broader application: In listening, the owner treats the keeper in the manner in which the owner would wish to be treated if the situations were reversed. In speaking up, the keeper treats the owner in the way he, the keeper, would wish to be treated were their positions reversed.

By omitting the conclusion to the deliberations between the two, Jesus draws attention to the process—what is really going on with them. They are acting here in accordance with the Golden Rule, and at the moment depicted, the imperative of equality inherent in the Golden Rule trumps the authority relation of owner to keeper, or master to slave. Moreover, this process does not arise in the form of a (forgive the expression) *deus ex machina*. They do not act in accordance with the Golden Rule because someone in authority has ordered them to do so, or even because some teacher has told them it will be good for them. They "find" the Golden Rule, so to speak, in the situation, in that following it is best for both of them.

There is another possibility, of course. The vineyard-keeper could let the vineyard go to pot, all the while plotting a slave rebellion against the owner. Perhaps the keeper could indeed overthrow the owner and become the new owner—and perhaps he could remake his old master into a slave to serve him. But the former keeper, now owner, would be subject to the rebellious tendency of the new slave—and so the cycle continues. At some point, if it is to be broken, the two parties need to see that the moment of honest and equal deliberation Jesus depicts here is the model for the satisfaction of both of them: that the solution to the "hunger and thirst for righteousness" each feels must be mutual and can be mutual.

The second thing we don't know is whether, if the owner heeded the advice of the keeper, it worked out for them: whether the tree bore fruit the next year. Because of this omission, it's clear that Jesus is not trying to put a happy face on his tale. The imperative is to try again, but he offers no assurances that the effort will succeed. We can hope so, and try our best, but success is never guaranteed. And here, perhaps, we must face up to an aspect of the Jesusian teaching present not only in this parable but in the parable of the net and fish, as well as in the parable of the wheat and weeds discussed below, and elsewhere: The vineyard keeper says to try for another year, and if it fails to bear fruit by then, "cut it down" (Lk. 13:9). Likewise, some fish are simply inedible and need to be thrown back not because they will turn into something else but because otherwise they will rot uselessly on the beach.

There is, in some sense, always an imperative within the Jesusian teaching to try again with someone, to be open to the possibility that an "enemy" will return the love offered. But as far as the this-worldly implications of the Jesusian teaching go, there is also a somewhat pragmatic awareness of the possibility that one's outreach will be in vain. In the parable of the net and fish, the bad fish are useless for human consumption, so they are discarded. In this parable, the situation is worse: A barren tree cannot be allowed to use up precious ground in the vineyard. Insofar as the vineyard is a place of orderly cultivation, it brings to mind the law, as we have seen Jesus discuss it and build on it in the Sermon on the Mount. We come, then, to the question of the place in the world of the fulfilled law for something not in accordance with it.

There will be no person or class of persons enjoying an exemption that enables them to pursue the satisfaction of their misplaced desire for righteousness—to pursue an advantage—at the expense of others, rather than in accordance with the proper desire for righteousness they can share with others. The "kingdom," for earthly purposes the world of the Jesusian teaching as embraced by people, is an infinitely inclusive one; all are welcome to join.

A problem arises, however, from the case of those who spurn the political and social satisfaction of equal freedom. At first, this is a bigger problem for the adherents of the Jesusian teaching than for their opponents. The latter possess power that they may not wish to relinquish. But as the fulfilled law spreads by voluntary accession and we move farther toward "all" being "accomplished," it may turn out that those who insist on a different vision have a bigger problem. They refuse to be neighbors or brothers. They set themselves apart in opposition; they insist on perpetuating the role of "enemy." We will have no difficulty recognizing some of the great villains of modern times in this category, including the figure of the terrorist.

There is no place for them in the vineyard. Nevertheless, there remains an obligation on the part of adherents of the Jesusian teaching to continue to try to reach out in the hope that they will change.

THE WORK OF THE ENEMY

The "kingdom" in which people adhere to the Jesusian teaching has no place for an enemy, someone determined to overthrow or destroy the principles on which the community of goodwill is based. Yet an enemy may gain access and try to use the values that define the community of goodwill to undermine the community itself. The question seems quite contemporary, insofar as it might pertain to those who use the protections accorded to free speech, for example, to advocate the overthrow of the very political and social order that protects free speech. It also goes way back.

Jesus tells a story likening the kingdom of heaven (Mt. 13:24–30) to a landowner who sowed his field with wheat seed, but whose enemy came by at night and sowed the field with grass. When his slaves inform the landowner that both wheat and grass have sprouted, he realizes what has happened. The slaves ask if they should pull up the grass, but he tells them, " 'No, for while you are gathering up the tares, you may uproot the wheat with them' " (Mt. 13:29). He tells the slaves to let the wheat and the grass grow together until the harvest, at which time the reapers will cut them both down and separate them, burning the grass and storing the wheat in the barn.

This parable is perhaps the most evocative of the aspirations Jesus has for the spread of the "kingdom of heaven" in this world. Here, we see a direct conflict between the followers of the Jesusian teaching and those who do not adhere to it. And we hear Jesus explain how to deal with the conflict: by patience aimed at allowing the Jesusian teaching to grow.

In the terms of the parable, we see first of all the promise: a fertile field sown with good seed. With proper tending, there is reason to expect an abundant crop. We can see this happy prospect as people's unadulterated embrace of the Jesusian teaching: Again, as in the case of the parable of the sower, the human element is more than simply the seed: It is the potential of the seed to grow into a proper plant, a plant that not only nourishes but also reproduces itself in the form of more seed that can be sown the following season. To think in terms of a single crop is to miss the richer point about the spread of the Jesusian teaching.

Then something bad happens: Rather than a field full solely of budding wheat, useless grass turns up as well. The appearance of the grass baffles the slaves of the landowner, who even go so far as to ask the landowner how it could be that if good seed was sown, grass now grows as well. The landowner arrives by deduction at the answer Jesus has already provided: "An enemy has done this!" (Mt. 13:28).

The slaves ask whether, since an enemy has planted the grass, they should rip it out, undoing the work of the enemy. No, the landowner says, the price would be too high: Pulling up the grass so early in the season will imperil the wheat. Better to let them grow together and then separate them when they are mature.

It is as if the landowner has realized exactly what the enemy is up to, what strategy the enemy has adopted to undermine him: Whether out of anger at the enemy's handiwork—and the landowner seems clearly angry when he realizes what has happened—or out of a misguided sense of how to deal with the problem at hand, if the landowner pulls up the grass, as the slaves suggest, he will do so at risk of uprooting the wheat.

If the wheat is something akin to the teaching of Jesus as embodied in those who follow it, then the grass is an element alien to it. The critical question then goes to the landowner and the slaves operating in accordance with Jesusian principles: what to do. The answer is that the value of the Jesusian teaching in the hearts and minds of people—the crops growing up from the good seed—is so high that it must not be put in jeopardy. The slaves think they can pull up the grass and leave the wheat behind to grow to maturity; the landowner is not so sure. He doesn't assert that pulling up the grass would *necessarily* result in the destruction of the wheat, but he is unwilling to risk the wheat by adopting that course of action.

We need to keep our priorities straight: What's important is the wheat growing in the field—the Jesusian teaching in the world. The appearance of the grass is indeed vexing. No doubt, its presence will reduce the harvest of wheat not only in relative terms—how much wheat versus how much grass—but also in absolute terms, as the grass impinges upon the wheat, to some degree reducing its ability to thrive as it might in the absence of the grass. Though the wheat crop will be smaller, the solution to this problem cannot be simply to get rid of the grass. That might result in a field barren of wheat as well. We mustn't throw away what is most precious in order to rid ourselves of what opposes us. To do so gives the victory to the "enemy."

The landowner and his slaves, in this metaphor, are people who know something about the tending of wheat: They know how seeds grow into crops, how to nurture them, why it is useful to do so, what end they serve. Wheat seed and wheat crops are plants; they don't "know" what they are or why they grow. Wheat can't sow itself as a field of wheat. At best, noncultivable strains grow wild amid the grass. In order for wheat seed to be sown, a human agent is necessary. As a metaphor for the propagation of the Jesusian teaching, wheat requires a sower, and the sown seed requires attention in the field.

In the parable, the slaves know many things about sowing and tending the wheat, but the landowner seems to know more. The latter is at special pains: He perceives a risk the slaves do not. They are rasher than he. They are eager to deal with the problem at once. They understand that as the wheat and grass continue to grow, there will be no separating the two in the field, no way to undo what the enemy has done. Still, the landowner sees a bigger picture.

We can think about the wheat, owner, and slaves as a unity, the components of a single endeavor. The relationship of a teacher and student, with the sense that the teacher expects the students to learn their lessons well enough to teach them in turn, begins to capture the matter. At first, the students are ignorant, undeveloped: They are all potential, no actuality. Then their teacher goes to work on them, cultivating their potential, drawing on what is already in them—what they are capable of—in order to dispel their ignorance and impart the teacher's knowledge. In the fullness of time, the students have matured to such a degree that they are able to become teachers themselves. What the teacher knows, the teacher has transmitted to them without loss, and they in turn can transmit it to others without loss, from generation to generation: seed to plant to seed.

Taking the wheat, the landowner and the slaves as a unity, we can see the problem the grass poses more clearly: Adherents to the Jesusian teaching have to face the fact that they are not alone in the world, that they find themselves among others who do not share their views, and that the proponents of the Jesusian teaching, and therefore the teaching itself—to the extent that its this-worldly continuation and propagation requires its embodiment in people—are accordingly at risk.

The way to minimize this risk is not, however, to seek to expunge the nonadherents from the world—to pluck them out by the root while they are at their most vulnerable. To do so would place the adherents of the Jesusian teaching themselves at risk. The adherents may find themselves so damaged by the act of getting rid of the others that they will not survive.

Instead, they should be allowed to grow up side by side. The adherents of the Jesusian teaching are better off, on net, taking their nurture alongside the nonadherents than they would be if they tried to get rid of the nonadherents. True, the adherents will not be as abundant and will not grow to the same extent that they would if they had the field to themselves, but that is not the choice at hand. The practical choice as Jesus presents it is between allowing each type to reach maturity side by side with the other, on the one hand, and a procedure that gets rid of one type but puts the other at mortal peril on the other.

The reason pulling up the grass threatens the wheat is the possibility of damage to the roots. The roots are intertwined. We should always be wary of torturing Jesus's metaphors by pushing them to the point where the *differences* between the metaphorical situation described and the human circumstances meant to be illuminated come to the forefront. But in this case, the presence of the wheat and the grass in the same soil and the intermingling of the roots seem to evoke a sense of commonality between the wheat and the grass. It's not hard to see this as illustrative of a common condition of humanity. What the terms of the metaphor preclude is the possibility that the grass will decide to turn itself into wheat (or vice versa). Jesus's metaphor leaves out the element of human agency, the freedom people have at any time to accept or reject the elements of his teaching.

The omission of freedom is worth exploring. It seems clear that Jesus is placing special emphasis on those charged with caring for the field. The landowner hoped for and intended his field to be full of wheat only. As it happens, grass sprouts as well. The freedom at issue is that of the farmer: He has the power to expunge his field of grass, yet he does not exercise that power. It would be dangerous in the extreme,

possibly utterly self-defeating, to proceed with a program of cultivation of the wheat along with destruction of the grass. The effect might
well be the destruction of the wheat.

This illuminates a central aspect of the political teaching of Jesus:
the problem of power and how to deal with it. Power, in this metaphor,
takes the form of the option to take action against the intrusion of that
which impinges on your wishes. But the exercise of that option may
lead to a Pyrrhic victory. Power, exercised without due consideration of
the sort the landowner gives here, has the potential to destroy what it
sets out to protect. In this case, restraint is the better course.

Note that nothing in the metaphor Jesus presents suggests that the
landowner is any less the master of his field for his unwillingness to
take immediate action to undo what he sees as the work of an enemy.
His slaves think otherwise: They are angered by what has occurred and
seek to lash out: They provide the passion in the story. The central
conflict of the story is not between the landowner and the enemy but
between the passion of the slaves and the cool-headed reason of the
landowner, who can see past the anger to what best serves his true aims.

Jesus doesn't tell us who sowed the grass seed, and though the
landowner has figured out that an enemy has done it, he doesn't know
and may never know who was responsible.

What the landowner understands is that the enemy's purpose could
only have been to ruin his crop. The landowner's purpose, however, remains the same as it was when he planted: to harvest as abundant a crop
as possible. By keeping his focus on that objective and not allowing himself to become distracted by the actions of his enemy, which could result
in taking action that undermines his real purpose, he prevails over his
enemy. At the end of the season, he still has wheat to put in his barn.
While it's not as much as he would have had and there's also the trouble
of sorting the wheat from the grass, a crop still remains. The Jesusian
teaching, properly nurtured, can grow to maturity notwithstanding
adverse circumstances. One form of peril it faces is a misguided effort
to protect it. The landowner must not allow himself to become rash and

impetuous as a result of his indignation: He must remain Jesusian in his cultivation of the Jesusian teaching.

RESILIENCE AGAINST ADVERSITY

The ability of the wheat to grow even though grass is growing alongside it speaks to the resilience of the Jesusian teaching. Another example of the power of the Jesusian teaching to spread against resistance comes through in the short parable of the strong man (Lk. 11:21–22; Mt. 12:29). Here, Jesus tells of a strong, well-armed man who guards his house. Then someone stronger arrives, overwhelms him, takes away the armor he thought would keep him safe, and "distributes his plunder." We may take it from the conclusion of the parable that the strong man's gains are ill-gotten. He has taken what he has from those weaker than he.

The scene described evokes a world without law. This is also reflected in the backdrop against which the story occurs, the accusation (by the Pharisees, in the Matthew version) that Jesus casts out demons through the agency of Beelzebul, the king of demons—which is to say, lawlessly. The strong man evokes the contemporary figure of the war lord. He believes might makes right. Yet he turns out to be no match for the Jesusian teaching when it comes along.

This mismatch is not merely a matter of the greater might of the Jesusian teaching. Upon its success, its principles call for the distribution of the "plunder" accumulated under the old regime. We may take this as a reference to distribution of goods, but it is far more than that. The chief good of the Jesusian teaching in this world is the way it helps people organize their relations with one another. The strong man represents "righteousness" misconstrued as the advantage of the strong in a lawless world; he has plundered righteousness or the idea of justice for himself. It is the redistribution of justice by the new, stronger, Jesusian teaching that ensues: the satisfaction of the desire for righteousness of all.

Another illustration of resilience against adversity comes in Jesus's story of the sheep and shepherd (Jn. 10:1–5). He begins by noting that a thief will climb over the fence where the sheep are penned in order to get to them, but the shepherd will go through the door. When the shepherd calls out to the sheep, they will follow him out to the pasture because they know his voice, but they won't follow a stranger (such as the aforementioned thief) because they don't know his voice.

The Gospel according to John continues with Jesus's explanation of this story (Jn. 10:6–18). He explains that he is both the door and the shepherd, and the flock of sheep represents his followers. This explanation still leaves much for listeners to work out for themselves.

The sheep came into the pen through the door—in accordance, that is, with what Jesus had to say. When they leave the pen to go out to pasture, they do so at the command of the shepherd. Their leader is someone familiar to them. They know his voice, or they are familiar with what he has to say. They recognize it as that which unites them: They are a flock, in human terms a community, because they have in common the Jesusian teaching—a community of goodwill. Their adherence to it is what makes them who they are.

Despite their unity, others may have designs on them. Someone whose purposes are distinctly un-Jesusian may wish to convert this community to some other idea about how human affairs should be organized or to try to lure its adherents away, one at a time. Such a thief doesn't try to go in through the door, though. He has to sneak in.

The thief tries to beckon the sheep. There is an element of false pretense here, since the thief wants the sheep to take him for their leader. But the sheep don't listen. In fact, they run away from the thief. People who adhere to the Jesusian teaching know what they believe in: They understand it and have internalized it through the process of *hearing, knowing, becoming*: It is in them, and they are "in" it. A community organized according to Jesusian principles has robust defenses at its disposal. It is unlikely to be reconverted into something else. Its members know what is good for them because the Jesusian teaching responds to the primordial desire for righteousness in each of them with a program for satisfaction for all of them. Whatever the thief proposes, whoever he is, he cannot propose an equal program of satisfaction. If he believed in that, he would not be a thief but rather would be seeking to join the flock.

We can think back to the passage in the Sermon on the Mount in which Jesus warns against false prophets, whom he analogizes as ravenous wolves in sheep's clothing (Mt. 7:15). He then shifts metaphors, telling his listeners that they will be able to tell the falsity from the fruit. In this parable, he articulates another defense adherents of his teaching will have: Once they have embraced the Jesusian teaching and have organized their affairs in accordance with it, they are unlikely to be drawn toward anyone who promises something different.

7.

ELABORATIONS

Many of the parables Jesus tells have the purpose and effect of restating or elaborating on some of the core elements of his political and social teaching. In the previous chapter, we saw the special attention Jesus gives to the propagation of his teaching. In fact, however, the propagation of the teaching and its substance are inseparably linked. The spread of *his* teaching is not transferable to the spread of *some other* teaching. In his view, the reason for the astounding promise of what he has to say in terms of its ability to reach people all over the world and over many generations—in principle, everyone, and in some cases whether or not they attribute what they believe to his influence—is that its substance (the specific terms of his guidance) strikes a deeply resonant chord in people. We know what that chord is because he explains it: It's the desire for righteousness or proper treatment at the hands of the political and social institutions with and through which one lives.

Jesus's parables about the substance of his teaching emphasize two main themes. First, he seeks to illustrate the value of his teaching, both in itself and as against other things one might choose to value, such as riches or worldly power. Second, he shows that the benefits of the teaching are achievable only by action in accordance with the responsibilities entailed in the teaching. In particular, Jesus is at pains in the parables to insist that no one is excluded, although he does not hesitate to point out that upon one's inclusion, one incurs exactly the same general obligations others have incurred before.

THE ABSOLUTE VALUE OF THE JESUSIAN TEACHING

The social and political order created in accordance with the Jesusian teaching—the community of goodwill—is mankind's most precious earthly possession. Two short parables in Matthew speak to Jesus's view of the inestimable value of his teaching, that of the hidden treasure (Mt. 13:24) and of the pearl (Mt. 13:45–46). In the first, a man discovers treasure in a field; he buries it and then sells everything he has in order to buy the field. In the second, a merchant looking to buy a pearl finds one of exceptional value; he, too, sells all he has in order to buy it. Jesus likens the kingdom of heaven to what happens in each story.

Note, first, that he does not liken the kingdom of heaven *just* to the pearl or to the treasure; rather, the simile for the kingdom is the whole action of the story. In both cases, a person discerns something of great value, the existence of which is unknown to others. The person who came upon it then gives up everything else of value to others—he sells all he has—for the sake of obtaining this one item, whose value he alone knows and appreciates. The kingdom of heaven, accordingly, is like the human acquisition of this thing of surpassing value, the Jesusian teaching. One might as well drop the figurative elements out: The kingdom of heaven, insofar as it manifests itself in this world, *is* the human acquisition of the Jesusian teaching.

How does the man in the field know the value of what he has come upon? How does the merchant? It is, somehow, self-evident to each. Neither needs a lecture on its value. To come upon the thing was, in each case, to get the point. Here we have a recapitulation of *hearing, knowing, becoming.* One has all the faculties one needs to understand the Jesusian teaching; it speaks to one's most primordial desire, the desire for righteousness, in a way no other ideas do.

Thanks to these parables, we can elaborate a bit on the element of *becoming*. The activity in these instances primarily consists of securing the acquisition of the Jesusian teaching. This is worth trading away everything else one has with a value in the marketplace. The point is not that the acquisition of the thing of highest value will necessarily take all that one has; instead, it is that one suffers no hesitation in deciding that *even if* it took everything, it would be worthwhile. All the things that are not part and parcel of the Jesusian teaching can be exchanged for possession of the Jesusian teaching with certain conviction that the deal is worthwhile.

The law also figures into these short parables. The man who found the treasure did not just steal it out of the field, nor did the merchant snatch the pearl and make a getaway. They each took steps to acquire what they wanted legally. An element of *becoming* is understanding and accepting that all the precepts of the Jesusian teaching are applicable; you can't simply pick and choose the ones that are to your advantage. The Jesusian teaching, illicitly acquired, is not really acquired at all.

At first, there seems to be an element of deception in these stories. Surely, the poor fellow who owned the land wouldn't have sold it if he had known it harbored such a treasure. Here, the figurative element of the story returns. The Jesusian teaching is not a material good. It is worth more than all material goods combined: As we have seen, the richest king who enjoys his riches at the expense of others, who selfishly satisfies the desire he feels for his mistaken idea of righteousness, is forever at risk. This is as true of the remaining dictators and warlords in our day as it was at the time of Jesus. Of course, those who have been through the Jesusian process of *hearing, knowing, becoming* attach a value to the teaching that others have yet to assign to it, simply because they have yet to find their way through the process. *Of course*, some will realize its true value before others do.

We should also ask ourselves what happens *next* in each of these two parables. Is the man who acquired the treasure to be presumed to horde it, to keep it to himself? Is the merchant, having found the perfect pearl, out of business? No, the answer is clearly that each has come upon a treasure that can enrich himself as well as others.[1] Jesus does not continue his similes past the point at which the analogy breaks down, but the point, amply described elsewhere (as in the case of "saltiness" and "shininess" we examined in our consideration of the Sermon on the Mount), is that upon possessing such a great treasure, one is able to share it with others in a way that does not diminish one's own possession of it. It is this willingness to share it that legitimizes the advantage one gets from it oneself. In our day, we are no less obliged to share the benefit of living in a community of goodwill, by extending it to others as far as we can.

THE COMPARATIVE VALUE OF THE TEACHING

If I happen to be rich beyond imagination or the most powerful person on earth, I may be quite content with matters as they stand and therefore unlikely to accept the claim that living life in a community of goodwill really does outstrip in benefits any other possible way of life. As far as aspirations go, some would no doubt prefer money and power in a world in which those things matter most rather than the least amount of money or power available to anyone in the community of goodwill.

Now, you could say that what's at issue here is really the luck of the draw and, accordingly, that political and social arrangements ought to be constructed so that no matter what kind of luck you have, you're still in the best position you could possibly be. That might be a good principle to adopt. Except, of course, that in the real world, we are already either rich or not rich, powerful or powerless, when confronted with the choice of whether to accept freely or reject freely the Jesusian teaching. The choice we face, in other words, is neither hypothetical

---

[1] The story of the hidden treasure in the noncanonical Gospel of Thomas continues with the statement attributed to Jesus that upon obtaining the treasure, the man is able to lend it out at interest—to enable it to (1) grow greater for him and (2) be of use to others.

nor speculative but comes to us as we are. Jesus understands that he needs to offer an account of why it makes sense for even the richest or most powerful person to accept the Jesusian teaching and the obligations that it entails toward others.

In the parable of the rich fool, Jesus tells the story of a man who has done well for himself in the world (Lk. 12:16–20). His land has produced a bumper crop, and he finds himself with a novel problem: what to do with all the produce. He resolves to tear down his old barns and build larger ones, so to store all the abundance. Jesus quotes him musing, "'And I will say to my soul, "Soul, you have many goods laid up for many years to come; take your ease, eat, drink and be merry"'" (Lk. 12:19). At which point God intervenes, telling the man that his soul is being called to account that very night and demanding to know from him, "Now who will own what you have prepared?" (Lk. 12:20).

The parable is, in outline, quite straightforward. The man's worldly success has preoccupied him at the expense of attention to his soul. In fact, the damage is worse than that. He has come to mistake the abundant satisfaction of his material needs for the sustenance of his soul. He vests his own sense of self-worth entirely in material prosperity. It validates him in his own eyes. Nothing else is required of him but adequate storage of his plenty, an action that is directed entirely toward his own satisfaction. He believes he has achieved it in the form of satiety and sees his task as its extension in time. This story echoes the passage in the Sermon on the Mount in which Jesus warns against storing up treasure on earth, where even at its most abundant it is subject to the ravages of destruction (Mt. 6:19–21).

The problem is that the true requirements of the soul are different. The intervention Jesus attributes to God at its end seems to mock the man by asking, "Now who will own what you have prepared?" The main point being: not you, you misguided fool. So, worldly pursuits and success are no proof against death; you can't take it with you. We should look more closely, however, at the question Jesus attributes to God. Obviously, the rich man's hope to feed his soul on his abundance hasn't worked out, since he's dead, but his bumper crop, all that he has managed to store in his bigger and bigger barns, presumably is not all going to be burnt up with him on his funeral pyre or buried in his tomb. His heirs are going to inherit it, as they will his land, the land that made him rich in the first place. The point of the question at the end of the parable is not that there is no answer to it. *Someone* will end up owning what the rich man has prepared. The point is that the rich man himself can give no answer to the question; he is speechless. Having thought only of himself and the attempt to satisfy his soul by providing it plenty of the things of this world, he has no frame of reference for relating that plenty to others.

He is not a malicious man; there is no indication here that he has obtained his abundance by unlawful means. Surely, he would bristle at the suggestion that he has done anyone wrong by acquiring what he has, that his success has come only with the corollary of the misery of others. Still, his only concern is himself; it is his gain and his alone that he thinks about. The rich man in this tale accordingly embodies an intermediate stage in the seeking of satisfaction for the primordial desire he feels for righteousness: He does not do so by oppressing others, at least in the context of what the law allows and requires. Neither does he do so, however, with regard for the satisfaction of others' desire for righteousness. Their desire is no concern of his; it doesn't register.

Or so he thinks. The pointed question he confronts at the end, the one that leaves him speechless and uncomprehending, opens a door for us. We can put ourselves in his place and see what he has failed to see. He is *in fact* not alone; surely, he would acknowledge a need to make provisions for his heirs. He needs to take others into consideration. And, of course, the moment he starts thinking about someone else is the moment at which he will cease to regard the satisfaction of his soul's desire as a matter that's only internal.

Jesus's story begins as a cautionary tale against placing too much store in material things, and it retains that element to the end. The most important message, however, comes from the way in which Jesus uses the rich fool's folly to direct us to think about satisfaction—not just in terms of providing for oneself but *necessarily* in terms of the impact of one's life on others.

We meet another rich man with a problem in the parable of the rich man and Lazarus (Lk. 16:19–31). Here, the man who had enjoyed the finest things in life ends up tormented in hell, but Lazarus, a beggar covered in sores who hoped only for crumbs from the rich man's table, is welcomed to the bosom of Abraham. When the rich man cries out for relief, Abraham tells him, "during your life you received your good things, and likewise Lazarus bad things; but now he is being comforted here, and you are in agony" (Lk. 16:25). The notion of such a reversal of fortune in the afterlife is hardly unique to the stories Jesus told, and indeed, if the depiction of such a reversal was all Jesus had in mind, then there would be little to discuss. The story would amount to a banal tale of the revenge of the have-nots against the haves, combined with an implicit admonition to the haves to behave themselves.

But that's hardly the end of this story. The rich man, in hell, implores Abraham to send Lazarus to warn his five living brothers about the peril they face, so they can avoid the rich man's eternal misery. Abraham responds that the brothers have Moses and the prophets to guide them in their conduct. The rich man says that if someone goes back to them from beyond the grave, then they will surely repent! Abraham says no, " 'If they do not listen to Moses and the Prophets, they will not be persuaded even if someone rises from the dead' " (Lk.16:31).

The rich man in this tale isn't merely a selfish fellow, forced to confront his selfishness. In his torment, he thinks of his brothers, whom he surely loves and would like to keep from harm. He wants to send them a warning: They must do right, lest they find themselves in his position. There is an impulse of generosity and of brotherly love in the heart of the rich man—all the more noteworthy because it will do nothing to alleviate his own torments in hell. The problem is that by the time he seeks to take action on the basis of this impulse, it is too late; and moreover, the obligation he feels toward others is too limited.

No doubt, the warm feelings he has toward his brothers from even the depths of hell were feelings he acted upon when he was alive: He treated his brothers as brothers, but he did not treat Lazarus this way. There was apparently no place for the beggar in the rich man's heart, let alone at the rich man's table. His generosity was too confined, too particular. What he needed to do was learn from the generous feelings he felt toward his brothers something about how he should act toward a neighbor, Lazarus, who was not his brother. Rather than simply consign Lazarus to a place on the other side of the gate, the rich man could have extended his brotherly relations to all his neighbors.

In the first part of the story, Lazarus hoped for no more than the crumbs from the rich man's table, which by implication weren't forthcoming. Jesus expects something from those with riches when they find someone like Lazarus at the gate.

And Lazarus is always at the gate. We see this problem acutely all around the world today. It would not be unreasonable to see the gate as simply that which separates, or rather seems to separate, those with an abundance from those who lack even a crumb. In this respect, the obligation of those inside the gate is to invite people in and to push the gate outward, with a view toward getting rid of it altogether: a world in which no one is in the condition of Lazarus.

This in turn points us away from the false impression of Jesus's story as a simple tale of comeuppance in the hereafter. Surely, Jesus is not suggesting that if Lazarus had been treated well, comforted, and cared for in the world by those who were better off than he—had he been elevated, in other words, from his position of abject poverty into better conditions—he could look forward to the torments of hell for eternity. It seems unlikely unless, having been uplifted, Lazarus himself developed the habits of the rich man in this parable, blithe indifference to the want of others. There might be special sanctions in such a case, given that Lazarus's indifference would be directed at those in a plight in which he recently found himself. (We will shortly hear a little more on that subject, in the parable of the unmerciful servant [Mt. 18:23–34].)

Furthermore, Jesus is not saying that if the rich man wants to reap a heavenly reward, then his obligation here is to transform himself and his brothers into beggars. He and his brothers need to care for Lazarus, but they need not and should not seek to turn themselves into Lazarus, thereby requiring the care of others. They should take care of themselves *as well as* Lazarus. The parable here echoes the intention of the Beatitudes, which, as we have seen, is to point to the *uplift* of the poor in spirit, such as Lazarus. This activity begins with mercy and extends to the reconfiguration, against resistance, of social and political affairs in such a fashion as to satisfy the primordial desire for righteousness that belongs to all those who, unlike Lazarus, have the capacity to reach beyond themselves.

By putting words into the mouth of Abraham, invoking Moses and the prophets, Jesus further suggests that the obligations upon the rich man in this tale ought to have been perfectly clear to him based on the provisions of the ancient law: He is surely thinking of the injunction to love your neighbor. The rich man loves his brothers, so he knows what it means to love, but he has failed to extend this love in accordance with the law. He has failed to see Lazarus as a neighbor or failed to take to heart the obligation to treat Lazarus as he would a brother, or both. It is, of course, entirely consistent with the Jesusian teaching on the ancient law—namely, that Jesus came not to annul it but to fulfill it—to regard those obligations as already incumbent on the rich man. In telling this parable itself, as an act of fulfillment of the law, Jesus makes the point explicit and, in addition, points to the outward extension of the obligation: When "all is accomplished," there will be no gate behind which the rich may repair to avoid the poor.

I have suggested that the desire of the rich man to warn his brothers as depicted here is an unselfish desire, in that it will bring the rich man no relief from the torments he feels in hell. But there is more at issue. The paradox of this story is that the dead man acts as if he were still among the living: By seeking to warn his brothers, he demonstrates that his frame of reference is still quite this-worldly, and his this-worldly act, though it does nothing to lessen his physical pain, nevertheless offers the prospect of assuaging his mind with the comfort that while he may have to suffer eternally, they need not—thanks to him!

In this story, however, it's too late. The rich man will not have the comfort that might come from the knowledge that his concern for others was efficacious. The only comfort he can take is that he tried. And insofar as this story stands as an affirmation of the Jesusian obligation to reach out, to seek to extend brotherly relations to neighbors and beyond, even to enemies, the parable of the rich man and Lazarus also reminds us that we will not necessarily have the pleasure of *succeeding* in doing so; only of *trying* by thinking of others.

Meanwhile, the living have to figure matters out for themselves. They have all that they need, Jesus says, and if the guidance of the fulfilled law as he presents it is not enough, emissaries from beyond the grave will not be persuasive either. Jesus makes a similar point in the Gospel according to John: "If I told you earthly things and you do not believe, how will you believe if I tell you heavenly things?" (Jn. 3:12).

There are several other Gospel passages in which Jesus warns that the possession of great material wealth can be an obstacle to taking possession of the greatest wealth, the Jesusian teaching. In one story (Mt. 19:6–26; Mk. 10:17–27; Lk. 18:18–27), a man approaches Jesus asking how to win eternal life. Jesus says the man should know: that he has to keep the commandments. This, the man says, he does. Then, Jesus says, the man should sell everything he has and follow Jesus. Unwilling to part with his possessions, the man leaves in dejection. As Jesus sees it, the man's problem is that material wealth is his top priority; it is more important for the man to keep his wealth than to fully embrace the Jesusian teaching. Oddly enough, rather than being the owner of his wealth, in the sense that he might feel himself free to do as he pleases with it—for example, putting it to work in the spread of the Jesusian teaching—it is his wealth that has a claim on him. Somehow, the man has his priorities so confused that he no longer understands that he is its master, not the other way around. Jesus sees this and radicalizes the question: He points to what will "complete" the man (Mt. 19:21) or provide what he "lack[s]" (Mk. 10:21; Lk. 18:22), and that is for him to give everything away. What he lacks and what completes him by this means is freedom, and specifically, freedom to embrace the Jesusian teaching.

The situation is, in its way, sadder than that of the rich fool and the rich man juxtaposed against Lazarus. The man in this story is not living in blissful ignorance of any other path, as are the other two (until it's too late); this man wants to do what's right, but he doesn't want it enough.

The story concludes with Jesus's observation that it is easier for a camel to pass through the eye of a needle than for a rich man to enter the kingdom. Who, then, can be saved, his astonished listeners ask him. Does that mean it's impossible? No, Jesus says—with people, a camel cannot pass through the eye of a needle, but "with God," all things are possible. A rich man *can* enter the kingdom if he accepts as his top priority the imperative of entry. His entry, not his wealth, must be what he prizes most, and the obligations upon him because of his wealth will be correspondingly great.

How great? Well, as Jesus notes on seeing rich people make their gifts to the temple treasury and then a poor widow putting in two small coins (Mk. 12:41–44; Lk. 21:1–4), she is the one who has given the most, since for her the gift did not come out of surplus but out of what she had to live on. The implication is that the rich need to contribute more than merely surplus, that which they have no real need of.

Given the dimension of poverty at the time of Jesus, it is perhaps unsurprising that he devotes so many lessons to the superior value of his teaching in relation to material wealth. But there are other aspects to earthly life that he also singles out for this comparative attention. One of these is raw political power, in the sense of the ability to muster force in support of one's wishes. In all four Gospel accounts (Mt. 26:51–54; Mk. 14:47, Lk. 22:49–51; Jn. 18:10–11), as he is being arrested, one of his followers (identified as Simon Peter in the Gospel of John) draws his sword and strikes a servant of the high priest. In the Matthew version, Jesus takes occasion to specifically renounce the use of force in the spread of his teaching. The teaching of Jesus, as we have seen throughout, is clearly meant to reshape the political and social world, but it is not meant to do so, and in fact cannot do so, in the manner of a conqueror with legions at his disposal (which Jesus said he could readily possess if he wished).

That's because the Jesusian teaching is inextricably linked to free acceptance by free people. Of their own volition, through the process of *hearing, knowing, becoming*, they must decide to set aside past slights or worse and to reach out in brotherly fashion to an expanding circle of their neighbors and on to their enemies. To the extent that they are successful, old enemies will cease to be enemies, and this world will accordingly be governed more in keeping with the new imperative to treat others as you wish to be treated yourself. Life in such a world, once again, is incomparably more valuable and worthwhile than life even as the strongest in a world in which the Jesusian teaching is unknown. Moreover, as we have seen, the world of the strong is actually weaker, over time, than the world of the Jesusian teaching; the properties of the latter fatally undermine the weak supports on which the former rests.

Perhaps falling just short of political power in the non-Jesusian world is something like fame or reputation: what others think of you. We have seen the lengths to which Jesus goes to caution against relying on the opinion of others as dispositive guidance on what to do. One must look, instead, within. This point comes through in the story of the instance in which Jesus catches two of his followers discussing the question of which of the two is the greatest (Mk. 9:33–37; Lk. 9:46–48).[2] In response, he tells them that whoever is the least will be the greatest. Their competition for honors threatens to undermine what should be their top priority, namely, living according to the principles Jesus sets forth. Note that Jesus does not seek to obliterate their ambition; rather, he seeks to channel it in a direction in which it can do good.

On numerous occasions in the Gospels, Jesus makes a statement to the effect that the last shall be first and the first shall be last. To the extent that people remain motivated by a desire to come out on top in one way or another—a sentiment Jesus does not endorse but does not disavow as long as what they want is a place of honor for the furtherance of his mission to fulfill the law—Jesus is willing to work with the human material on hand. To take an active role in being "the last" is socially beneficial even if the reason one performs in that role is to end up "the first." This prudential or pragmatic element of the Jesusian teaching is a subject we will explore more fully in the next chapter.

The Jesusian teaching outranks wealth, political power, and prestige in value, but there's another area of comparative judgment Jesus's statements compel us to face up to: The Jesusian teaching also outranks the claims of family—ties of blood and clan. In several passages that are troubling as a matter of first impression (Mt. 10:34–37; Lk. 12:51–53; Lk. 14:26), Jesus seems to scorn the reverence the ancient law requires of children toward parents as well as the seemingly natural attachment of parents toward children and siblings toward one another. For example, "He who loves his father or mother more than me is not worthy of me; and he who loves son or daughter more than me is not worthy of me" (Mt. 10:37).

The passage is readily explicable in terms of Jesus as son of God and savior, but again, we should not overlook the this-worldly meaning

---

[2] The Gospel according to Matthew has a version of the story that doesn't turn on a discussion among Jesus's disciples of who among them deserves top billing, but more generically on the question of who stands as greatest in the kingdom of heaven (Mt. 18:1–6). Stripped of the element of personal ambition, the story is less pointed.

of the statement. Here, the figure of Jesus also stands for the sub-stance of his teaching about how to live in the world. And the point emerges straightforwardly from that: Nothing trumps the Jesusian teaching in terms of the obligations it imposes on people (just as nothing exceeds in value the social and political benefits that accrue from living with others in accordance with the Jesusian teaching). The brotherly relations one has with one's blood brother must not entail a concert between brothers to work for their own advantage at the expense of other people. Otherwise, the obligation to extend brotherly relations outward would not and could not be fulfilled. The idea is not that you should repudiate your family; it's that your re-lations with your family should be aligned with your obligations toward others.

If they fail to align properly—and this, after your exhaustive ef-forts to be reconciled with your blood brother and all other kin, as Jesus has proposed—your higher obligation is toward action in accordance with the Jesusian teaching. If the price of doing "honor" to your father (Ex. 20:12; Deut. 5:16) is obeying his command to do wrong toward others, it is too high. That is not the honor a father properly demands, and once one has oneself gone through the process of *hearing, knowing, becoming*, one must reject any such demand from a parent. Obligations to family never amount to justification for joining a crime family, from the James–Younger Gang to the mafia to Saddam Hussein and his vi-cious sons Uday and Qusay.

It is obvious why Jesus does not acknowledge any exception here: He understands that any ambiguity is precisely of a character that un-scrupulous or simply misguided fathers (and other family members) will use to persuade sons and others to accept a world organized on the basis of deference to the will of a patriarch or to the supreme value of clan or tribe. The social and political implications of the corollary to his teaching Jesus spells out in these provocative passages are vast: He simultaneously rejects all *illegitimate* claims based on the obligation to honor one's father and on the imperative for brotherly relations among brothers while retaining the obligation for such honor and such relations *within* the framework of his teaching.

A passage from Luke repeats this point but with an additional twist relevant to our discussion of the comparative value of the Jesusian teaching against competing values: "If anyone comes to me, and does not hate his own father and mother and wife and children and brothers and sisters, yes, and even his own life, he cannot be my disciple" (Lk. 14:26). So, to the inferiority to the Jesusian teaching of wealth, power, prestige, and kinship, we add as well one's very life. But Jesus is not telling people to commit suicide or to risk their lives knowingly and gratuitously any more than he is enjoining people to hate their parents and their spouses and their children. What he is saying is that his teaching is more valuable to its adherents than "mere" life. Again, if the situation at hand should ever come down to a question of deciding in favor of action in accordance with the Jesusian teaching or of action to save one's own life at the expense of others, one will want to act in accordance with the Jesusian teaching.

I say "want to" because this is a decision people will reach freely. To take the preservation of one's life as the highest value is to substitute a kind of unfreedom for the freedom Jesus has found people to possess and which he seeks to secure. One becomes, in effect, a *slave* to the impulse for self-preservation: There is no higher value. The primordial desire for righteousness remains stuck in its most primitive form, similar to animal hunger or thirst. *My* satisfaction alone is at issue. All relations with others become matters of secondary importance. They are no more than a means to an end. Lost is what is distinctive about people—their ability to recognize that the desire for righteousness one feels can be compatible with the desire for righteousness another feels—and then others still, culminating in all others.

Modern societies based on individual rights sometimes have a hard time understanding why anyone would voluntarily risk dying for her country. An inalienable right to life is the first right one hears about in the Declaration of Independence, and the existence of the state, in

Hobbes's *Leviathan*, is first of all justified as a way to protect the lives of its citizens from a state of nature characterized by the struggle of all against all. Now, perhaps the state has "rights" of it own, such as to send you off to war. But it's unclear how this social contract is in your interest, if the result is your death.

But perhaps this framework for thinking about the question is wrong, at least in some cases. One might, after all, be willing to risk one's life for the sake of advancing or protecting a higher principle. Such, in many cases, is the willingness of those who put themselves in harm's way today, from the police and firefighters of 9/11 to the volunteers in today's military. Now, perhaps they put themselves at risk in the expectation (certainly the hope) that they won't, after all, die. Perhaps in thinking about the possibility of dying, they take consolation in their faith in an afterlife. Nevertheless, they risk an exit from the world at hand. Perhaps, however, the creation and protection of the Jesusian world, the expanding community of goodwill, is worth dying for in its own right. Jesus thought so.

THE UNITY AND UNIVERSALITY OF THE JESUSIAN TEACHING

Three of the Gospels include versions of one of Jesus's most famous observations, whose political overtones were indelibly etched on the American consciousness by Abraham Lincoln. Jesus says that a kingdom divided against itself cannot stand, and neither can a house divided against itself (Mt. 12:25; Mk. 3:24–25; Lk. 11:17). Lincoln's appropriation of the metaphor for the division of North and South in the Civil War seems entirely apposite. As a matter of practical politics, Jesus's observation is quite reliably true, regardless of the character of the "kingdom" in question: In the absence of unified political leadership in one form or another, the result will be division and chaos. This is true of the states of the Union in nineteenth-century America and of the mythical kingdom of united, peaceful England that King Lear sought to parcel out among his daughters.

But there is a deeper meaning to Jesus's observation, which relates to the specific content of the Jesusian teaching. The point is that the Jesusian teaching is indivisible from itself. It is a complete whole, one and the same wherever it is. Although people may adopt some of its elements more quickly than others, when "all is accomplished," the result is universal.

Consider a negative example. Let's suppose that Country A is, in general, Jesusian in its political and social structure and outlook, governed based on principles of equality in freedom, home to the Golden Rule as the principle people have in the main adopted as their *modus vivendi* (imperfectly, to be sure). Let's suppose Country B is quite the same. Now, is there anything we should be able to tell about the relations of Country A and Country B from what we know about the Jesusian character of their internal political arrangements? The answer is yes. For starters, Country A and Country B ought to be at peace with each other. They are both governed by the injunction to reach out in brotherly fashion not only to their neighbors but also to their enemies in case their relations were once characterized by hostility. (This is not to say that because they are governed in accordance with the Jesusian teaching they are *Christian* nations.)

Now if, as it happens, Country A and Country B do go to war, as in fact avowedly Christian nations have done historically with a frequency not obviously less than that of non-Christian countries, then we really are entitled to ask whether doing so can ever be Jesusian conduct. The answer is no. And the point is that the bloody division between the two means that the Jesusian "house" cannot stand. The "kingdom" of common adherence to the Jesusian teaching doesn't really obtain between the two, and rather than, for example, seeking to justify their own bellicosity by reference to the speck in their neighbor's eye, they each ought to attend to the log in their own.

We should not, however, lose sight of the way the Jesusian teaching spreads, which we looked at at some length in the previous chapter. The transmission is from person to person over time, and the "kingdom" exists in the relations between those who adhere to the Jesusian teaching even though there are others who still remain outside of those relations. Moreover, the fact that (by our assumptions) each of the citizens of Country A accepts the Jesusian teaching as far as what goes on within the borders of Country A is concerned, and the same in our example with respect to Country B, makes it *more* rather than less likely that the people within the borders of each will seek to reach across to one another.

It is incumbent on those who take Jesus's political teaching seriously to recognize divisions in the house or kingdom for what they are: matters to be overcome between people. Jesus tells a number of stories that illustrate the responsibilities people have toward others.

In the parable of the wise and foolish servants (Lk. 12:42–46; Mt. 24:45–51), Jesus tells a story about a slave whose master has left him in charge of the household while the owner goes away. His responsibilities as steward include seeing to it that the other slaves are properly fed. "Blessed," he says echoing the language of the Beatitudes, is the slave whose master, upon returning, finds the slave attending to his appointed responsibilities: "Truly I say to you that [the master] will put him in charge of all his possessions" (Lk. 12:44; Mt. 24:47). By contrast, the slave who takes his master's departure as an excuse for sloth and drunkenness is apt to find himself surprised by the return of his wrathful master, with grievous consequences.

To be put in charge in the manner of the slave here is to receive a grant of power and authority. We would be on target in thinking of the mayor of a big city or the president of a university or the CEO of a corporation. Those who find themselves so advantaged also find themselves with a choice: Will they exploit their advantage to satisfy their selfish aims, or will they understand that with power and authority comes responsibility? If they choose the former, they are likely to find themselves deposed by a higher power—that of the master, in the case of this story, or of the relevant higher authority in our modern examples: the voters, the board of directors, or trustees.

However, acting in fulfillment of one's responsibilities toward others leads, in Jesus's telling, to still more responsibilities: The good steward will get charge of all the master's possessions, but that makes more work for the steward. One might ask why more work is a good thing.

The answer is that this is not merely a tale about how a slave divides his master's food and wine. This is about maintaining proper relations among the householders. The goal is a well-run, orderly household, in which all present understand not only what they have coming to them but also their own responsibilities, including what they do *not* have coming to them. The good steward is the upholder and exemplar of this principle; he has found himself in the position of the guarantor that the satisfaction of one does not come at the expense of the satisfaction of another. Charged to take care of all the house's possessions upon first having faithfully executed his responsibility to see that those in the household are fed, in this story he is the embodiment of the Jesusian teaching. The work he must perform is the work each and every adherent of the teaching must perform. The addition of more responsibilities is an illustration of the principle of reaching out toward others.

We can think of the household as simply where we live, reminiscent of the conclusion to the Sermon on the Mount, where Jesus contrasts the prospects of a house built on a secure foundation with those of a house built on sand. The advantage of living in a house that functions as it should makes the work of ensuring that it is governed according to the Jesusian teaching worthwhile to all those called on to undertake it—which, as a practical matter, applies to most everyone. We are all charged with the responsibilities of the steward. These are preeminently our duties toward others, which go hand in hand with the advantages we enjoy.

If, in general, we can see the reach toward universality of the Jesusian teaching in the parable of the wise and foolish servants, two other parables emphasize that universality is something that applies not only "in general": It applies to each and every particular case. The parables of the lost sheep (Mt. 18:12–13; Lk. 15:4–7) and the lost coin (Lk. 15:8–9) tell of the diligent efforts of a shepherd to retrieve a sheep that has strayed from the flock and of a woman to find in her home a silver coin she has misplaced. When they manage to find the objects they are seeking, Jesus says, they rejoice.

The lost sheep and the lost coin have value to their custodians. It doesn't matter that the shepherd has ninety-nine sheep that are safe; still, he sets out to find the lost one. Similarly, the nine coins the woman has *not* lost do not lessen the diligence with which she applies herself to the task of finding the missing one. Jesus is, of course, propounding an analogy between the followers of his teaching and the flock in one story and a coin purse in the other. Again, as in the case of the wise steward, we see the shepherd and the woman as the embodiment of the Jesusian teaching: They are responsible for the proper order of the flock or for ensuring that the coins remain where they belong, in their purse. The advantage of these analogies is that we can see that the shepherd is not some sort of boss sheep or *übersheep*, any more than the woman is a coin herself. Yet insofar as the relations of people in this world are concerned, there is no radical, species-like disjunction between shepherd and sheep, purse owner and coin. No one has authority of that kind—or rather, everyone, in a collective sense, has the authority. The authority is the descriptive truth and utility of the Jesusian teaching to the community that adopts it. The shepherd and the woman, as in the case of the steward, correspond to the Jesusian teaching itself, as embodied in human form.

It is not good enough for the Jesusian teaching to settle for ninety-nine adherents when there are a hundred potential adherents, nor for nine coins in the purse when there could be ten. One could put it this way: It's good for the flock to be organized and safe, and *in general* the flock is organized and safe, but the mission of ensuring the order of the flock is incomplete so long as even a single sheep has strayed. The obligation to reach out is comprehensive.

We might profitably spend an additional moment on an element of both these stories that reinforces an important aspect of the Jesusian teaching. The premise of the story of the shepherd is that ninety-nine sheep are safe; the premise of the story of the woman is that nine of her ten coins are where they belong. The shepherd does not set out in search of the hundredth sheep to the peril of the ninety-nine, nor does the woman risk her nine coins in searching for the tenth. The point is that the proper arrangements among ninety-nine need to be *extended* to the hundredth.

As Jesus makes clear in several other parables, this lesson holds true regardless of who that hundredth is. Specifically, his injunction to reach out is comprehensively inclusive. In practical terms, this means that the obligation extends to those whom some might consider (and in Jesus's time certainly did consider) the lowest of the low. The parable of the great supper (Lk. 14:16–24; Mt. 22:2–10) drives this point home.

In Luke, a man is throwing a big dinner party (it's a king throwing a wedding banquet in Matthew, but we will follow the Luke version). When everything is ready, he sends out his slave to tell the guests who have been invited that it's time to come, but they answer the slave with excuses about how busy they are. So the master tells the slave, " 'Go out at once into the streets and lanes of the city and bring in here the poor and crippled and blind and lame' " (Lk. 14:21). After the slave does so, there is still room at the dinner, so the master sends the slave out again, this time to the highway, to fill up the house.

The parable has two elements. The first is the nonattendance of the finer folks in town, whom the host has invited: the well-heeled sort who have just bought new land or new oxen or have taken what may well be a second (or third or, in any case, yet another) wife. These were the people whom the host naturally thought to invite: his peers. In this-worldly terms, Jesus clearly intends us to see that attendance at the banquet is the embrace of his teaching and that the first natural movement of out-reach is to those who are in some way like oneself. Though the invited guests did indeed accept the invitation when it was issued, it's only now, as the slave goes forth to tell them the time for dinner has come, that they, one after another, back out. This would seem to be an indication of the distance one must travel in the process of *hearing, knowing, becoming*. The guests who said they would come but ended up with better things to do are reminiscent of the seed sown among the thorns in the parable of the sower and the seeds. They get the message but are tempted away from following through on it by the other influences life places before them.

An essential point of this parable is to flesh out what form those other influences may take. Here, the problem is caused by plenty. It is not as if any of the excuses Jesus has the guests offer describe something bad that has happened to them; in fact, it's just the opposite: a new piece of land, a new herd of oxen, a new wife—all good things. While each of these new acquisitions does indeed impose obligations on the person taking possession, the invited guests allow the new obligations con-nected to their material advantages to trump their other obligations. The temptations of this world are great for those who enjoy its fruits most bounteously. It's easy to forget about what one owes to others.

This acceptance and then rejection angers the host. (In the Mat-thew version, the invited guests not only spurn the slaves the king has sent out, they kill them, and so the king sends out his armies to wreak vengeance, destroying the malefactors and burning their cities.) So he directs the slave to "bring in here the poor and crippled and blind and lame" (Lk. 14:24). Since his wealthy peers have spurned him, he turns to the least fortunate of his neighbors, and when even this group does not fill his hall, he invites in strangers and foreigners off the road. In the end, he has swept the entire region with his invitations.

We should note that the man does not begin by inviting the lowest. It does not come spontaneously to him to fill up his house with the "the poor and crippled and blind and lame." This apparently occurs to him only after the well-heeled have spurned him, but this is not Jesus's way of saying you should begin your outreach with those who are most advantaged. Rather, it is a portrait of what comes most readily to the man's mind and of the ensuing awareness of the inadequacy of that initial impulse to the message Jesus conveys. What may begin with one's friends and peers does not end if they are unavailable.

Thanks in part to the more sanguinary details of the parable in the Matthew version and in part to the vow attributed to the host at the end of the Luke version—"none of those men who were invited shall taste of my dinner" (Lk. 14:24)—this parable is often read as a tale of comeuppance: The purpose of the host's act is not to *include* the disadvantaged but to undertake some sort of resentment-driven vicarious punishment of the well-heeled: Teach them a lesson. If we insist upon this reading—as opposed to taking a more benign view of the host, namely, as someone whose eyes have been opened to others, including the least advantaged, in a way they were not beforehand—then we have an element of the parable that addresses how good things sometimes happen for bad reasons, a theme we will to take up in the next chapter.

Without doubt, the problem of plenty is a real one. As this parable illustrates through the incomplete nature of the host's initial outreach and his peers' reaction, affluence offers people the temptation to ignore their obligations to others in pursuit of their own plenty. However, the notion that the invited guests, having made a mistake once, are accordingly forever excluded from admission to the social and political world of the "kingdom"—where the Jesusian teaching holds sway—runs counter to the well-established doctrine to try and try again. (How many times, Peter asks Jesus, am I supposed to forgive my brother? As many as seven times? "I do not say to you, up to seven times, but up to seventy times seven" [Mt. 18:21–22]). Rather than an administrator of some notional perfect justice, the host in this story seems better understood as someone whom circumstances have led through that process of *hearing, knowing, becoming,* by which people truly change the way they think and act toward others.

A number of stories in the Gospels concerning the actions of Jesus speak to the universality of his message. Early in his career, Luke reports, Jesus found himself thronged by people who had heard him or heard of him and wanted him to stay with them (Lk. 4:42–43). He tells them he has to preach "to the other cities also" (Lk. 4:43). His message is not just for local consumption. In three Gospels, religious leaders are scandalized that Jesus is dining with tax collectors and sinners (Mt. 9:10–13; Mk. 2:16–17; Lk. 5:30–32). Jesus tells them, "It is not those who are healthy who need a physician, but those who are sick; I did not come to call the righteous, but sinners" (Mk. 2:17). Here, we see that the imperative to take the Jesusian message to everyone may and will run afoul of the prejudices some harbor toward those whom they regard as lesser.

This point comes up again when Jesus dines in the house of a Pharisee and a woman described as a sinner anoints his feet with perfume (Lk. 7:36–50; similar stories appear at Mt. 26:6–13, Mk. 14:3–9, and Jn. 12:1–8). The Pharisee is appalled, but Jesus praises the woman for her faith. Needless to say, the prejudice others feel against those to whom one reaches out must not deter one from the effort. At another point, a number of children are swarming around Jesus, to the reported consternation of his disciples (Mt. 19:13–15; Mk. 10:13–16; Lk. 18:15–17). When the disciples try to shoo the children away, Jesus tells his followers that "the kingdom of heaven belongs to such as these" (Mt. 19:14)— meaning not only children but also others innocent of the ways of the world. Sophistication is not a prerequisite.

Another story about Jesus evokes a turning point in the universality of the message (Mt. 15:21–28; Mk. 7:24–30). A woman described as a Canaanite in Matthew and a Syrophoenician in Mark—a Gentile, that is, not a Jew—asks Jesus to help her daughter, whom the woman believes to be possessed by an unclean spirit. In the Matthew version, Jesus at first refuses, saying, "I was sent only to the lost sheep of the house of Israel" (Mt. 15:24). The woman persists, and Jesus replies metaphorically but with unmistakable clarity: "It is not good to take the children's bread and throw it to the dogs" (Mt. 15:26; Mk. 7:27). But the woman speaks up for herself, noting that dogs feed on the crumbs that fall under the table. Jesus, impressed by her reply, grants her her wish. This is the decisive moment at which Jesus makes it clear that his teaching is exclusive to no group; it is entirely a matter of its acceptance by those who hear it, and anyone who accepts it has a place.

THE GOOD SAMARITAN

The obligation *to* all is an obligation *of* all, as one of Jesus's most famous parables, that of the good Samaritan (Lk. 10:30–37), makes clear. The parable comes in response to a question a lawyer puts to Jesus. The lawyer has just cited the ancient law, from Deuteronomy 6:5 and Leviticus 19:18, enjoining the Israelites to love God with all their heart, soul, strength, and mind, and to love their neighbors as themselves, as the way to eternal life. Then, in a fashion that seems distinctly lawyerly in a thoroughly modern sense, the lawyer asks, "And who is my neighbor?" (Lk. 10:29).

In response to this, Jesus tells the story of a man who is beset by robbery on the road from Jerusalem to Jericho. They strip him, beat him, and leave him half-dead on the roadside. A priest—a man whose elite daily responsibility was to attend to the holy of holies in the temple—was traveling down the same road. Upon seeing the beaten man, the priest crossed to the other side of the road and passed him by. Next came a Levite, the name by which the class of priests' assistants in the temple were generally called. He, too, saw the beaten man and crossed the road to pass him by. Last, Jesus says, came a Samaritan; Jesus selects a member of a group with which the Jews of the day had no common dealings, each an enemy to the other. Yet the Samaritan, in Jesus's story, was the one who "felt compassion" (Lk. 10:33) for the beaten man, stopped, treated his wounds, and carried him to an inn, where the Samaritan paid the innkeeper to take care of the beaten man, promising more money for the innkeeper on the Samaritan's return journey. Jesus asks which of the three, the priest, the Levite, or the Samaritan, was the "neighbor" to the victim of the robbers. The lawyer gets the point—the Samaritan was the true neighbor—and Jesus tells him to act likewise.

In some respects, thanks in part to the spread of the Jesusian teaching down to our day, the shock value of Jesus's tale doesn't quite come through. The notion that Jesus casts a Samaritan in the role of hero, here the only true "neighbor," rather than the priest or Levite, high officials of the temple to which his listeners mainly belonged, cannot seem quite as scandalous to us as it must have to his listeners then. For surely it was surprising, a deliberate effort to break up a sense of complacency of a sort perhaps reflected in the smug, loophole-seeking question posed by the lawyer at the outset: Who's my neighbor? Meaning: In fact, I love my neighbor just fine. Jesus, of course, has in mind far more than an easygoing feeling of accommodation and comfort among those who have long habits of living together under the law, and he is certainly not going to let matters rest with a lawyer's narrow, lawyerly reading of the obligation to love one's neighbor. Jesus, after all, came to fulfill the law: in this case, to ask what "neighbor" *can* mean in order to derive what it *should* mean.

The truth is that while Jesus's story is scandalous, it is not implausible. There is nothing impossible to the notion that someone might be moved by the plight of another person left for dead on the side of the road and stop. Of course, there is nothing impossible or implausible in the notion of seeing someone suffering on the side of the road and crossing to avoid him, either. Recall the notorious 1964 murder of Kitty Genovese in New York City; numerous neighbors witnessed the attack or heard her screams but did nothing to help her or alert the police. Jesus is not necessarily posing a wild improbability (compassion) against a commonplace (indifference). But he does want to get at the issue of where the obligation to stop comes from and where it ends.

After all, if you saw your father on the roadside, you'd stop, and the same with your brother. Similarly, your neighbor, in the narrow sense of someone you know who lives near you. And from there, you may even be inclined or obliged to extend the obligation outward—to a sense of the term "neighbor" that includes all the members of your group or tribe, your fellow citizens, and the like. This is, after all, the holding of the ancient law.

Jesus is with you on reaching out. It is this injunction, after all, that the priest and the Levite of the parable fail to uphold. (The assumption here is that the victim was one of their own tribe, which Jesus seems to suggest both from the context of his dialogue with the lawyer and in noting that the victim was going from Jerusalem to Jericho.) Yet by introducing the element of tribe or identity group and juxtaposing members of one (Jewish priests and Levites) against members of another (Samaritans), Jesus seeks to shake up the too-easygoing sense of the law's obligation represented in the question of the lawyer. Although the priest and Levite have failed in their obligation to help a neighbor in a way that the Samaritan has not, the point of the story is to draw attention to the kindness a member of one group shows to the member of another—in this case, between groups known for the enmity between them.

All right, so you would stop for a member of your family or a friend. Even if, in accordance with the ancient law as Jesus sees it, you extend this obligation toward your neighbor and encompass all the members of your tribe or people, how does that make you any different from members of another tribe who feel a similar obligation toward their family and friends, neighbors, tribe, or people? As you would do with yours, so the others would do with theirs. The special privilege you accord to your own kith and kin is no mark of special virtue belonging to you and yours. Others feel the same pull toward their own.

In the Jesusian view, two things follow from this sense of connection to others. The first is that you *already know* what to do when you see someone, anyone, lying half-dead on the side of the road—namely, you should help—because you know what you would do if the person were a member of your family or a friend. You also know how you would like to be treated if you were in the place of the unfortunate person you have come across. There is no mystery here, no need for a special test to determine whether the person in question merits decent treatment at your hands because of some preexisting connection that would establish eligibility of special "neighbor's rights." The second is that in Jesus's view the point of the injunction to love your neighbor is not to set an *outward limit* on those eligible for decent treatment from you; it is to begin the extension of the circle of people due such treatment from you outward from the narrowest confines of family and friends. The Jesusian fulfillment of the ancient law is to point out that that outward extension need have no limit.

It is also worth noting that in the parable of the good Samaritan, the setting, the road between Jerusalem and Jericho, is a lawless environment. It takes place outside the reach of the political and social order that prevails in the towns—beyond the bounds of both the law of the occupying Roman authorities and the ancient law of the Hebrew scriptures, as well as the pattern of compliance with those laws among the people. The road is a place of danger; bandits and other predators lurk in wait for a traveler they deem weak enough to pick off. This is a kind of Hobbesian zone, where you are on your own in a struggle of all against all.

Such a condition of lawlessness stands in contrast to the backdrop against which Jesus elaborates most of his teaching—a world in which the ancient law is in force (albeit in some cases honored only incompletely or hypocritically). This different setting has a number of implications worth considering. Though the passersby are *outside* the world of law during the action of the parable, they *come from* a world of law. That's why they know, in principle, what they should do, whether they act on it or not: They do not leave the law entirely behind them. It travels along with them, so to speak. True, out on the road, there is no one to enforce the law: If in town, say, there is a legal obligation to come to the assistance of a stricken neighbor, on that roadside there would be no enforcement mechanism that could be brought to bear. Passersby are completely free to help or not.

Nevertheless, they may still feel the pull of the law, again whether they ultimately act on it or not.

Jesus's description of the priest and the Levite passing by "on the other side" of the road (Lk. 10:31, 32) keenly captures the psychology of the moment—the pull of the law the passersby feel. Why do they cross the road? They see the victim, and they understand full well the distress of the victim, but they cannot quite bring themselves to walk by the victim in close proximity. Were they truly indifferent, they could walk by without breaking stride or altering course so much as a step. Yet they feel they have to pass at a distance. They seek as much separation as they can. But no amount of distance will liberate them from the sense of obligation they feel, even as they choose not to act on it. It's not just some "other" they see along the road; it's a person who arouses in them a sense of interpersonal duty.

In this sense, the passersby have internalized the law; it is a part of them. They feel its pull apart from all external sanction or punishment. Their conduct, in this case, is without merit. But the very form their inaction takes—they cross the road to avoid a closer encounter with what they know they ought to do—reinforces Jesus's view of the possibility and promise the law holds.

A second point worth noting about the setting of lawlessness is that in such a lawless world, one lingers at one's peril. Perhaps one reason the priest and the Levite didn't stop is that they feared for their own lives and well-being at the hands of the very same robbers. Perhaps they thought that if they tarried, they would be putting themselves at greater risk. In this light, the conduct of the Samaritan stands out all the more. In stopping to help a stranger, he was accepting a risk to his own life. If that's true, then there would be a heroic element to the Samaritan's conduct that day. For the sake of what's right, he is willing to risk harm to himself. This brings to mind Jesus's declaration in the Beatitudes: "Blessed are those who have been persecuted for the sake of righteousness" (Mt. 5:10). In that instance, the issue was the way in which acting in behalf of what's right could bring the violence of the authorities upon you because of the threat you pose to their position of power and privilege. In this parable, the road is a place where, practically speaking at least, there are no authorities, and because of this, doing what's right entails additional risk.

Jesus doesn't say whether the man who fell victim to the thieves was rich or poor, and while this may be because the Samaritan (no less the priest and the Levite) couldn't tell, to Jesus, his personal finances do not matter. The obligation to help is present regardless of wealth or status. Even if the man was rich or powerful, he was brought low by the moment: This serves as a reminder of the precariousness of one's situation in the world, the way in which one can be transformed from high to low in an instant. The story also reminds us that riches and power are things of lesser value to the man lying beaten on the side of the road than the Jesusian willingness of the Samaritan to stop to help.

Jesus continues to emphasize this human connection between the high and the low in the story of judgment he tells about the division of the world between sheep and goats (Mt. 25:31–46). The sheep, who deserve favor and will inherit the kingdom, are those who have given the king food when he was hungry and drink when he was thirsty, who extended a welcome to the king when he was a stranger, who clothed him when he was naked, who visited him when he was sick and in prison. The righteous folks don't recall doing any such things for the king. The king explains: " 'Truly I say to you, to the extent that you did it to one of these brothers of mine, even the least, you did it to me' " (Mt. 25:40).

This story has two elements of particular concern to the this-worldly teaching of Jesus. The first, as we have anticipated, is Jesus's insistence that the obligation of each to each runs all the way down to "even the least." Now, some do not need food, drink, shelter, clothing, or comfort, but some do. The fact that some or even many *do not need them* does not overrule the obligation to those who *do*. Toward those who already have what they need, those who likewise have what they need still have certain obligations, as we saw above in the story of the great banquet. You do not discharge all of your obligations by associating exclusively with those who are similarly privileged. Even if such a thing were possible—and the chance you will one day run across someone in dire straits on the road from Jerusalem to Jericho suggests it is not, no matter that you cross the road to avoid too close an encounter—it would not be sufficient by the reckoning Jesus proposes here.

In these examples, it's important to consider the literal meaning of Jesus's language as well as the figurative. For many people, food, clothing, shelter, and the like are very much at issue. That's still true today, though fortunately to a significantly lesser extent as the Jesusian teaching has spread. Nevertheless, we should also understand that the kingdom the "sheep" will inherit—the same kingdom the "gentle" or meek will inherit, per the Beatitudes (Mt. 5:5), the one Jesus describes here as "prepared for you from the foundation of the world" (Mt. 25:34)—is one where "even the least" need to be welcomed. They may not be able to get there on their own. Accordingly, it is up to those who are capable of getting there on their own, those who have felt the desire for righteousness and are willing to act on it—perhaps at risk to themselves—to speak up for "the least."

The second element of concern to Jesus's this-worldly teaching is the figure of the king. Just as the "kingdom of heaven" has earthly relevance as the community of goodwill, so the king here needs to be understood not solely as a divine judge but also as the embodiment of the Jesusian teaching. In Jesus's story, the king, the highest of the high, identifies himself with the lowest of the low and knows the right way to treat them. To the extent others understand and act in accordance with the teaching and therefore help its "reign" to spread, they partake collectively of the king's kingliness. Jesus certainly does not endow such a collective body with anything like a right of final judgment over other people—in fact, he warns against precisely such illegitimate arrogation of the authority to condemn, as we have seen, in favor of the imperative to reach out again and again. He does contend, however, that those who embody the Jesusian teaching *know what is required of them.* They know this through the application of the Golden Rule, and therefore, they recognize that all obligations are not fulfilled until they are fulfilled to "even the least." And as a corporate body, they understand their obligation to remove the faults they themselves have. They are capable of judging their own conduct and knowing when it comes up short.

8.

BAD ACTORS

Jesus provides descriptions in his parables of some of the difficult characters certain to be encountered as his teaching spreads. The characters we meet in his stories are of a sort familiar to us today. He gives guidance for how to cope with them—in some cases, how to turn the actions of bad actors to the advantage of the spread of the teaching, with (preferably) or without (if necessary) reforming the character of the bad actors.

Such characters play crucial roles in two of Jesus's most brilliant parables, the prodigal son (Lk. 15:11–32) and the vineyard workers (Mt. 20:1–5), in which he warns of the greatest and most persistent source of resistance to the spread of his teaching. In a way, it is the final human failing, the last barrier in people's hearts to full acceptance of the responsibilities of the Jesusian teaching. As such, it is of especially keen importance to a modern world based on Jesusian principles.

The term for this last wall of resistance is "resentment." Although that sounds like rather a mild problem or condition from which to find oneself suffering, its importance is profound for the social and political order of the Jesusian teaching.

THE "BAD PERSON"

In the Beatitudes, as we have seen, Jesus offers a typology of the "good person" based on progress from passivity to activity. We have seen that it is possible to turn around the categories of the Beatitudes and thereby perceive more clearly a typology of the "bad person" as well. Some of Jesus's parables seem tailor-made to illustrate the types of "bad person" one encounters.

We begin with an especially egregious example, the parable of the evil tenants (Mk. 12:1–11; Mt. 21:33–46; Lk. 20:9–16). The three Gospel versions differ only slightly. In Mark, a man has planted a vineyard and outfitted it for the production of wine, then rented it to vinegrowers as he departs on a journey. Come the harvest, the owner sends his slave to claim the owner's share, but the vine-growers beat the slave and send him away. The owner sends another slave, and the growers beat him even worse. The owner sends a third, and this time the growers kill the slave. Finally, the owner dispatches his "beloved son" in the belief that "They will respect my son"; the growers this time are jubilant. They say: "This is the heir; come, let us kill him and the inheritance will be ours!" (Mk. 12:6–7). They do so. Jesus asks, "What will the owner of the vineyard do? He will come and destroy the vine-growers, and will give the vineyard to others" (Mk. 12:9).

The sheer outrageousness of the conduct of the tenant-farmers is breathtaking. If we take the vineyard itself to represent the Jesusian teaching in the world, then we see that the tenants are would-be usurpers. They want to take advantage of the fruit of the Jesusian teaching, in this case a well-designed vineyard, without adhering to the principles that made it what it was. The owner has struck a bargain with them, but they will not uphold their end.

The tenants act as if they own the vineyard. Adherents of the Jesusian teaching do not *own* the Jesusian teaching: It is theirs in the sense that they possess it, and in the sense that they have the responsibility to propagate it—to carry it forward in time and space through the process of *hearing, knowing, becoming.* But it is not theirs in the sense of something they are free to modify as they wish. The point about the Jesusian teaching is that it offers precise instructions about how people must arrange their social and political affairs in order to achieve the satisfaction of the desire for righteousness of each and all. This guidance is not oppressive, except toward those who would like to obtain advantages for themselves at the expense of others, but its elements are not optional. The vineyard owner in this story has something rightfully coming to him, and the tenants want to keep it for themselves. In fact, they want the whole vineyard for themselves, quite as if they were the ones who planted it and equipped it for winemaking.

The parable is a study in incorrigibility. The owner sends a representative on four occasions, the last time his own son. Nevertheless, the tenants' treatment of the emissaries grows worse with the arrival of each. They kill the last two, and in the case of the son, they throw his body out of the vineyard, denying him even a proper burial. Perhaps they think that the arrival of the son means that the owner is dead, and in killing the son, they hope to obtain title to the vineyard by virtue of their possession of it in the absence of a legal heir to the owner. It is a brazen and wicked plan.

In the case of the parable of the sheep and shepherd from chapter one, the problem was faithful sheep—adherents of the Jesusian teaching—pursued by a false shepherd. The sincerity of their adherence to the Jesusian teaching affords them a measure of protection against the blandishments of those seeking to subvert it. Here, the problem lies with the flock, the tenants. They moved into the property under false pretenses. Whatever their promises, they never really became adherents of the Jesusian teaching: They never were willing to abide by the terms of their agreement for use of the property. The emissaries from the owner seek, quite rightly, to enter by the door, but they are rebuffed, abused, and worse. Jesus makes it clear that the tenants forfeit all claim to continue to cultivate the vineyard, to profit from the initial investment of another whom they now spurn.

At the end of the story, Jesus shifts the narrative voice. He is no longer telling the story as if describing something that actually happened; instead, he poses a question to his listeners, then answers it: "What will the owner of the vineyard do?" The owner will return and destroy the tenants, that's what, and then offer the vineyard to others willing to abide by the terms of their agreement. (In the Matthew version, it is Jesus's listeners who provide the answer that the owner will "bring the wretches to a wretched end" [Mt. 21:41] and rent the vineyard to others.) Those who have spurned the Jesusian teaching will be dealt with harshly indeed. They have been warned.

The shift in voice (or speaker) is an answer to an interesting problem the parable poses by implication. Surely, we are right to be distressed about what happens to the owner's representatives. Surely, Jesus's story is meant to provoke anger toward the tenants among his listeners—as, indeed, it does, and not just in the explicit Matthew version. The anger is in accordance with ordinary human feeling and with the ancient law, but it is a bit of a problem with regard to the Jesusian teaching itself.

This problem is one we have encountered before: What should we do with the bad fish in the parable of the net and fish or the barren fig tree in the parable known by that name: When do you give up? We know that some behavior is entirely incompatible with the Jesusian teaching. In fact, it would be hard to come up with a better illustration of such behavior than we find in this parable. Yet Jesus puts some distance between himself and the vineyard owner at the end when he asks, "What will he do?" as if the owner were not a character Jesus had created but a person with a will and volition of his own. Jesus does not dispatch the owner on a mission of vengeance in Jesus's own voice, with his approval. The Jesusian teaching is a little more difficult than that. Although Jesus amply recognizes that much of what human beings are capable of doing is entirely incompatible with his teaching, he withholds his final assent to the conclusion that one must give up. Clearly, he does expect people to give up—and with reason, as this parable shows. But how much more quickly, even prematurely, would people give up on one another if encouraged to do so? The risk of undermining the teaching in this way is great, the more so as the teaching spreads and acquires power in its own right.

In addition, we must recall that as far as the spread of the Jesusian teaching in this world is concerned, there is no all-powerful vineyard owner waiting in the wings to wreak vengeance on those who spurn the obligations that come with the enjoyment of life in a world laid out in accordance with Jesusian principles. Or rather, *we* are the vineyard owner, the adherents of the teaching, and our claim to righteousness is best vindicated by our adherence to the teaching. At the same time, we are not wrong to be angry, and Jesus lets the story come to an end without condemning the conclusion that the evil tenants have to be destroyed, even if he does not explicitly endorse it.

While not all of the conduct Jesus describes is as bad as that of the tenants, some does arouse our ire as readers of and listeners to Jesus's stories. One such is the parable of the unmerciful servant (Mt. 18:23–34), which serves as a perfect illustration of the inversion of the Golden Rule. Here, a king decides to settle accounts with his slaves, and upon determining that one of them owes him a great deal of money, the king decides to sell the slave and his family to make good on the debts. The slave falls prostrate before the king and begs for forbearance, promising to make good on his debt. The king, Jesus says, "felt compassion and released him and forgave him the debt" (Mt. 18:27). Lo and behold, the slave then goes out and finds another slave who owes the first slave money—a tiny fraction of the sum at issue between the first slave and the king. The second slave throws himself on the ground before the first, pleading for patience and promising repayment. The first slave is unmoved and has the second thrown into debtor's prison. The king's other slaves, having seen what happened and feeling sorry for the second slave, go to the king and tell the tale. The angry king summons the first slave, demanding of him, " 'Should you not also have had mercy on your fellow slave, in the same way that

I had mercy on you?' " (Mt. 18:33). The king then hands him over for imprisonment and torture until the original debt is fully repaid.

Here, we see a portrait of someone in a position to grant mercy and who has himself benefited from a grant of mercy. It's the benefit that the servant has already received that produces the outrage. The Golden Rule tells us to treat others the way we wish to be treated ourselves; here is a case in which the servant *has been treated as he wished* and refuses to extend the same treatment to another. No wonder the king is angry.

As we have seen, the key to the earthly progress of the Jesusian teaching is to make the first move—to treat people as *you would wish* to be treated before they have treated you in such fashion. In the parables of the evil tenants and the unmerciful servant, we have cases of the harsh condemnation due to those who, having been the beneficiary of someone else's going first, decline to follow through with others. Note that what's at issue here is not a reciprocal gesture—an instance in which the slave might be moved to show mercy toward the king, in a kind of quid pro quo. Rather, it is the thwarting of the outward extension of the lesson of mercy—its general application, as the Jesusian teaching requires.

HYPOCRISY

Two of Jesus's parables, that of the Pharisee and the tax collector (Lk. 18:10–14) and that of the two sons (Mt. 21:28–31), amplify the lessons he taught about hypocrisy in the Sermon on the Mount. They also portray the inversion of a quality of character Jesus pronounces "blessed" in the Beatitudes, the "pure in heart."

Jesus tells of a Pharisee and a tax collector who go to the temple to pray. The contrast between a senior religious official of the day and the holder of a despised office of the Roman occupation could not be greater, especially in the setting of the temple. In prayer, the Pharisee says, " 'God, I thank you that I am not like the other people: swindlers, unjust, adulterers, or even like this tax collector' " (Lk. 18:11). He then notes that he fasts twice a week and pays all the tithes he owes. The tax collector, meanwhile, in praying merely berates himself as a sinner, asking God's mercy, as he beats his breast. Jesus says that the tax collector, not the Pharisee, went home justified that day.

The Pharisee takes his frame of reference from those around him, comparing himself to others and finding the others wanting. He is far more interested in the specks in the eyes of others, and so he misses the log in his own, generating a point of view that avoids a candid assessment of his faults and ascribes purity to his own heart based on a comparison with the bad conduct of others. That's exactly the passageway to an impure heart, one incapable of examining itself honestly. Self-justification follows from the inability to perceive in others anything except what flatters oneself.

The harm you do to yourself thereby is bad enough: You have placed a massive obstacle in the way of your ability to identify and fix your own faults. You also do a grave injury to others, since you take the whole of a person before you and transform him or her into an abstraction: the embodiment of a negative quality. There is no human fellow-feeling in the process, no empathy, no hint of looking within yourself in order to ask how you would wish to be thought of and treated if the situation were reversed. In addition, the characteristics you abstract you select exactly because they are negative, which you take as a positive for you. It's the zero-sum approach to human interaction; my gain is your loss, and vice versa. As we have seen, this is exactly the human trait that Jesus has set himself the task of transforming in the social and political world.

The Pharisee in this story looks at a man he recognizes as a tax collector and sees nothing else. He misses the evident piety of the man, a product (in Jesus's telling) not of the tax collector's desire to be seen as pious, like the Pharisee, but of genuine remorse, a man aware of the things he has done wrong and regretful about them. This piety, the Pharisee cannot see. In identifying the man as a tax collector, the Pharisee thinks he knows as much as he needs to in order to judge him harshly.

Though Jesus says that it's the tax collector, not the Pharisee, who "went to his house justified" (Lk. 18:14) that day, we must be careful not to allow the negative reaction we feel toward the Pharisee to discolor our impression of the tax collector. Yes, Jesus is drawing a contrast between the lifetime of other-directed false piety of the Pharisee and the moment of genuine remorse for bad conduct in the case of the tax collector. But it is, precisely, a moment. Having depicted a man, the Pharisee, who judges people on the basis of abstractions, Jesus is not going to do the same, only selecting the positive qualities. Jesus doesn't say the tax collector is *thereafter* justified. He says *went home that day*. The tax collector has made a start by expressing contrition for his wrongdoing, looking within himself honestly, and finding himself wanting. He has taken a leap and seems ready to embrace the Jesusian teaching, but in order to do that, the tax collector is going to have to change his ways.

In the parable of the two sons, Jesus tells of a father who owns a vineyard, where he tells his sons to go to work one day. The first son refuses, but then regrets what he said and goes to work. The second says he will go to work, but then doesn't. Jesus then asks, which of the two did his father's will? He concludes with the observation that tax collectors and prostitutes will enter the kingdom of God before those to whom he is speaking that day, the high priests and elders of the temple.

In this story, Jesus invites us to draw the distinction between declaration and reality: We ought to live up to what we profess. The second son is clearly at fault for his failure to do so, and Jesus likens him to those in his temple audience whom he believes say one thing but do another. There is an additional element to the story, however, and that's the way the heart works on the first son. He at first rejects his father's request. Perhaps he felt it was beneath him to go work in the vineyard, or perhaps it was just easier not to. On further reflection, he regrets his initial avowal and does go to work. He, like the tax collector in the previous parable, is able to look at himself honestly and see his own errors.

The problem of hypocrisy is front and center in the eight woes that Jesus pronounces upon the temple religious establishment as well (Mt. 23:13–33). Most of the pronouncements begin, "Woe to you, scribes and Pharisees, hypocrites!" Again, the sense of "hypocrite" is the term's classical meaning: someone playing a role, acting in a fashion that has no correspondence to what's really going on within. Jesus has just admonished his listeners to do what the scribes and Pharisees say, not what they actually do. He offers a withering bill of particulars whose general pattern is meticulous attention to appearances coupled with inner debasement. On the outside, the cup is clean and the temple is white, but inside is nothing but self-indulgence and impurity.

There are certain parallels here between the characteristics underlying the woes Jesus pronounces and those of the "bad person" we were able to discern by looking at the qualities opposite the ones Jesus sets forth in the Beatitudes. To "shut off the kingdom of heaven from people" (Mt. 23:13) is to eschew the pursuit of universal satisfaction of the desire for righteousness in favor of the maintenance of one's position of privilege. Jesus also points out there that in so doing, the scribes and Pharisees shut themselves out of the kingdom as well, so their misdeeds are ultimately as harmful to themselves as anyone else.

Of particular interest is the last woe Jesus pronounces: He rebukes the scribes and Pharisees for their arrogant claim that, in words he puts in their mouths: "'If we had been living in the days of our fathers, we would not have been partners with them in shedding the blood of the prophets'" (Mt. 6:30). It is, in a way, an ultimate form of hypocrisy to revisit the past in the spirit of the present in order to compare oneself favorably to those who have come before. Jesus's evocation of the failure to recognize the prophets for who they were at the time echoes a point he has made elsewhere with the witty observation that a prophet is not without honor except among those who have known him close at hand (Mt. 13:57; Mk. 6:4). He points to the very human failing underlying the nostrum that familiarity breeds contempt (or worse), but he will not countenance people looking back and smugly deciding that they would never have fallen prey to such feelings. This is no virtue but merely acting a part: the role of the most virtuous.

THE FINAL HUMAN FAILING

The last two parables we will consider are those of the vineyard workers and of the prodigal son. Although they are rich in meaning on their own, they share an important theme: the danger of resentment. It is, again, a product of taking one's bearings by means of others, only this time in a highly refined form, one in which even if the approval of others were forthcoming, it would not be enough to neutralize the poison. Having assigned oneself, for one reason or another, a status of superiority with regard to someone else, one *simply cannot stand* the elevation of the other to a position equal to one's own.

In the parable of the vineyard workers, Jesus says that the kingdom of heaven can be analogized to a man who goes out to the marketplace early in the morning to hire workers for his vineyard. He makes a deal with them to pay each a denarius to work in the vineyard that day. A couple of hours later, he goes out again and finds some men standing idle. He offers them work as well, promising to pay them what is fair, and off they go to the vineyard. The same again three hours later and three hours after that. Finally, he goes out at the eleventh hour and hires still more men. In the evening, he tells his foreman to pay the laborers, starting with the last to arrive and ending with the first. When those who had worked only since the eleventh hour each receive a denarius, those who were working longer think they are about to be paid more. But each of them as well gets a single denarius. "When they received it, they grumbled at the landowner, saying, 'These last men have worked only one hour, and you have made them equal to us who have borne the burden and the scorching heat of the day'" (Mt. 20:11–12). The landowner rebukes them, pointing out that they had agreed to work for the day for a single denarius. "'Take what is yours and go, but I wish to give to this last man the same as to you. Is it not lawful for me to do what I wish with what is my own? Or is your eye envious because I am generous?'" (Mt. 20:14–15).

In the parable of the prodigal son, Jesus tells of a man with two sons, the younger of whom asks his father if he may collect right now his share of his inheritance. His father agrees, dividing his wealth between the two sons. The younger son then leaves on a journey to a far country, "and there he squandered his estate with loose living" (Lk. 15:13). He hires himself out at labor, but the earnings are slim, and he muses that the men who work for his father have more to eat than he. He decides to go home and apologize for his misdeeds, asking his father to take him back not as a son but merely as a worker. His father sees him coming and runs out to embrace him. The younger son apologizes as he had planned. Rather than being angry, his father orders the slaves to fetch his son fine clothes and to prepare a feast of celebration.

The elder son, meanwhile, has been out in the fields, and as he approaches the family house on the way in for the evening, he hears the music of the celebration. The elder son dispatches a servant to find out what's going on, and the servant comes back with news of the return of the younger brother and of the feast of celebration the father has prepared. The elder son "became angry and was not willing to go in; and his father came out and began pleading with him. But he answered and said to his father, 'Look! For so many years I have been serving you and I have never neglected a command of yours; and yet you have never given me a young goat, so that I might celebrate with my friends; but when this son of yours came, who has devoured your wealth with prostitutes, you killed the fattened calf for him.' And he said to him, 'Son, you have always been with me, and all that is mine is yours. But we had to celebrate and rejoice, for this brother of yours was dead and has begun to live, and was lost and has been found'" (Lk. 15:28–32).

The figures of the vineyard owner and the father in these parables evoke the actualization of the Jesusian teaching in this world. To toil in the vineyard in exchange for the wage the owner offers is to participate in the world of the Jesusian teaching, the "kingdom" as it is realized by those who act on Jesus's guidance for political and social arrangements. To go to the feast the father throws to welcome the return of his prodigal son, the same: entry into the kingdom.

The emphasis in the parable of the vineyard workers is on the toils; the emphasis in the parable of the prodigal son is on the rewards. The former speaks, first of all, to the responsibilities that fall upon one in the Jesusian world; the latter to the rewards one enjoys by entering and living in such a world. But the parable of the vineyard workers is not missing the element of reward: it comes in the form of a denarius for each, the pay for the day. Nor is the element of responsibility absent from the parable of the prodigal son: The returning son must, indeed, come back; he begs his father's forgiveness and seeks to rejoin his household not in his previous capacity as second son but as a mere laborer in hope of enough to eat; he claims no entitlement, but professes a willingness to toil.

The prodigal son has lived a life of dissipation and ended up in a bad way: hard up for his daily bread. The vineyard workers have put in their time under the hot sun and are looking forward to their compensation. The son, having rewarded himself with his inheritance and wasted it, finds himself in a condition of dire want and is ready to work; the vineyard workers, having spent their day doing what is required of them, are ready to reap their reward.

With these examples, Jesus shows the connection of what you have coming to you and what the obligations on you are, looked at from two different but complementary perspectives. For those who fulfill their obligations, there is a reward; for those who reap a reward, there are obligations. As we have seen, the desire to reap a reward without fulfilling the obligations—to enjoy the benefits of living in a world organized according to the Jesusian teaching without accepting the responsibilities—is ultimately a losing proposition. There is no world of the Jesusian teaching apart from people's adherence to their responsibilities, and here we see the willingness of the prodigal son to accept his responsibilities in the end, thereby returning to the good graces of his father, as well as the willingness of the vineyard workers to toil in exchange for the reward promised to them.

But we might ask: What other option do they have? Won't the men in the marketplace go hungry if they don't accept work? Won't the prodigal son eke out only the barest of subsistence if he doesn't return home? But, of course, they have other options: They might, for example, turn to a life of crime. This is a real choice, though, of course, undesirable consequences may follow from it, such as getting caught and being punished. They choose, however, not the *lawless* life—in the extreme case, the struggle of all against all, at the end of which the strongest rules absolutely for as long as he remains strongest—but life in the world of law. There are certain benefits that come from living in a world of law, but along with them come certain obligations: To begin with, you are likely going to have to go to work for your daily bread.

There is nothing here to suggest that the world of law cannot be improved upon: that the world of law will always and everywhere require daylong, back-breaking labor from anyone who wishes daily bread, and that nothing more than daily bread will ever be forthcoming in exchange for such labor. One could say that the figures of the father and the vineyard owner, who enjoy great prosperity and yet represent admirable characters in Jesus's telling, point to the possibility of something more than mere subsistence. The well-off, too, in the Jesusian teaching, have obligations—in many respects, greater in accordance with their wealth. Furthermore, one could say that the mutual benefit two people enjoy when they act in accordance with the Golden Rule has the potential for beneficial economic consequences as well as social and political consequences. In the meantime, in these stories, we find a place in the world of law for hard work to yield daily bread, if no more, and the choice of the vineyard workers and the prodigal son to accept that bargain.

More trouble arises, however. In the case of the prodigal son, it comes from the attitude of the elder brother. In the case of the vineyard workers, it comes from those who have been toiling in the vineyard since daybreak. The elder son sees the feast his father has thrown for his no-account brother. Those who have been toiling in the vineyard since morning see those who arrived only at the eleventh hour walk away with the same wage the early starters were promised.

Both the elder son and the all-day workers see this as truly, profoundly, and deeply unfair. How come they, who have been good or worked longer and harder, get something comparatively lesser than those who have been bad or have barely broken a sweat? The elder son is angry, and he vents it toward his father; the vineyard workers "grumble" to the vineyard owner. They are offended by what they take to be the application of a mistaken principle of justice or fairness by the person with the power to have done things differently.

These responses do not exhaust the emotional content of the stories, however. Both parties are feeling something else beside anger at the father or the vineyard owner, even though this other feeling goes unexpressed—in fact, one could say that the unexpressed feeling is deeper and is the real internal source for the expression of anger. That's the feeling of *resentment* the elder son and the early-arriving workers feel toward the prodigal brother and the eleventh-hour arrivals in the vineyard.

The father tries to reassure his elder son by pointing out that everything that is the father's is the elder son's as well. Jesus intends us to regard this as reasonable. He likewise intends us to conclude that the vineyard owner's rejoinder is reasonable: Those who started at the first hour were promised a denarius and will receive what they were promised. Why should it matter to them if the owner chooses to be generous with those who went to work later? It's also worth noting that no one was getting rich on a denarius a day. The sum would be about enough for one's daily bread; one-tenth of that, or a proportionate share for those who came last, would not be. The vineyard owner is making sure everyone gets enough to live on. But the reasonableness, even justice, of these replies does not really respond to the emotional tug of resentment pulling at the elder son and the earlier arrivals at the vineyard.

After all, while the prodigal son was out squandering his inheritance on loose living and having a good time, the elder son was being a good boy. While the early vineyard workers were toiling, the ones who showed up later were idle and perhaps even enjoying their hours of leisure. There is an element of envy to the feelings of the elder brother and the early workers. Perhaps they would have preferred to be carousing or lolling themselves. Perhaps they would prefer, at that very moment, to be free and at leisure for a good time.

Alternatively, maybe they would not have preferred these things. Maybe they realize that they have enjoyed benefits from being good and doing what is required of them. Here, we begin to see the stakes for the future of the Jesusian teaching. Jesus intends us to understand the world of the father and the vineyard owner as the world in which his teaching holds sway, with a due balance of benefits received and responsibilities incurred and fulfilled. The elder son has enjoyed those benefits. Likewise, the vineyard workers who came early to earn their daily bread and reap the benefits have had to fulfill their responsibilities. In the case of the workers, they toil in the vineyard. The elder son has his responsibilities, too: He was out in the field when his brother turned up. His is not, nor could it be, a purely hedonistic life of leisure in his father's house. The Jesusian teaching describes a world in which no one is exempt from the obligations of the Golden Rule, of reaching out to others.

So it's not simple envy, in the sense of *I want what you have.* The elder son and the early workers *already have earned* what the prodigal son and the eleventh-hour arrivals now wish for and aspire to: a chance to rejoin the father's house, a chance to earn one's daily bread. If anything, the elder son and the early arrivals became objects of emulation for the younger son and the workers arriving later. They sought for themselves what the elder son and early arrivals had. They were perhaps even envious of the elder son and the vineyard workers in precisely the sense of *I want what you have.*

The "envy" the prodigal son feels toward his older brother and that which the idle would-be workers in the marketplace feel toward those who have a job leads in a very different direction from the "envy" of the elder brother and the early arrivals in the vineyard. In the case of the former, it leads to an enthusiastic acceptance, on merely the hope or possibility of a benefit, of the responsibilities already demanded of the latter. The prodigal son doesn't demand recognition as his father's son; he seeks only the place of a servant. The eleventh-hour arrivals go to work not on the promise of a specified amount of compensation, but out of gratitude for *anything* they might get at the end of the day. Their "envy" produces a desire to be deemed worthy of the benefits others, fortunate in their eyes, are able to obtain. The "envy" of the elder brother and the early arrivals is entirely negative; it yields no aspiration. The elder brother and the early arrivals perhaps *wish to have been* the younger brother or the late arrivals without now wishing to be them. They wish they'd been out having a good time, or so they tell themselves, and yet still be able to claim a place at the father's table or the wage for a day's labor in the vineyard. They see how others arrive late to a set of responsibilities they have long embraced, with equal benefit thereafter, and the image wreaks havoc on their sense of themselves, releasing a poison within them.

In the end, the elder brother and the prodigal son are *entirely in agreement* about how to live and what kind of life is the right kind of life. The same is true of the vineyard workers who came early and those who came at the eleventh hour. They all accept that the Jesusian teaching is on the mark. For the elder son and the early arrivals, however, the full measure of benefit that living in accordance with the Jesusian teaching produces, which they once deemed adequate, now seems insufficient. They seek a special status because they arrived at the Jesusian teaching sooner than others, who now stand to benefit no less than they.

With these slighted feelings, they miss the point of the Jesusian teaching. They only *seem* to have embraced it; they have heard it, and they know what it says well enough to declare for it; but they have not yet become one with it. *Hearing, knowing, becoming*: For them, the process has been truncated, as the thorns choke the wheat. Their desire for righteousness has not come fully into alignment with the desire for righteousness of others. They cannot make the leap that will let them put aside the past for the sake of the present and the future. Rather than *welcome* the new arrivals, as they should, they complain about the fairness of a process that lets newcomers arrive at all.

Through all this, it's striking how little it takes to prick this sense of grievance, this resentment. With the vineyard workers, we see that it is not only those who arrived at dawn who resent the equal benefit of those who arrived at the eleventh hour; those who arrived in the third, the sixth, and even the ninth hour resent the later of the latecomers. No doubt the earliest arrivals were resentful of those who came next, yet received the same benefit.

And what do the resentful *do*? Well, perhaps they fly into a murderous rage, either against the principle of justice that governs the world in which they live (the law Jesus has "fulfill[ed]," that is) or against those who, in their view, have benefited from the principle somehow unfairly. But to do so would be to reject the Jesusian teaching root and branch—to repudiate it. Some may choose this course, and that would certainly be a challenge for the Jesusian teaching's prospects in this world. However, it's not really what Jesus is getting at here. He has in mind something subtler and more insidious.

Oddly enough, the answer to the question of what the resentful do about their resentment may well be: nothing. The elder son doesn't dare tell his father to send his younger brother packing, and it seems more plausible than not that after his father explains himself, the elder son goes to the party after all. He respects his father; this respect is the basis of his complaint against his disrespectful, prodigal brother. Similarly, the early arrivals in the vineyard don't see themselves in a position to demand of the owner more than he promised them. They complain and feel wronged, but they cannot turn their complaints into an agenda because they accept outwardly what they cannot accept inwardly: the truth and beneficiality of the Jesusian teaching.

Thus, the final obstacle the Jesusian teaching encounters: acceptance in principle and in fact but rejection from within, a lingering feeling of resentment and selfish righteousness that severs the connection between even the best of conduct—right conduct toward others in accordance with the principles Jesus has set forth—and the inner sense of oneness with the teaching that yields true satisfaction of the desire for righteousness.

9.

PRUDENCE AND PRAGMATISM

Much of what Jesus says in the Sermon on the Mount focuses on the origin of his teaching in the law and the necessity of grounding its spread in a world of law: These concerns reflect his counsel of pragmatism and prudence in ensuring that his teaching takes root. He reinforces this point in several parables. Insofar as the protection of the community of goodwill and its further spread are matters of concern for us today, we need to be especially attentive to this underappreciated element of the Jesusian teaching. The right place to begin is by dispelling a common misimpression of what the qualities of prudence and pragmatism imply.

Prudence is a quality people often associate with timidity—half-measures from those who lack the courage of their convictions. Indeed, those who are timid often seek to hide their fearfulness under the mantle of prudence. Similarly, people sometimes consider pragmatic action to be the opposite of principled action.

Jesus counsels prudence and pragmatism not out of timidity, but out of a calculation of how best to ensure that the principles of his thisworldly teaching spread as far and fast, and take root as firmly, as possible.

In this world, as we have seen, his teaching does not take mankind as a blank slate on which anything can be inscribed. Rather, he takes as his starting point the world in which people live, the world of law, but also a world in which people are hardly perfect in their adherence to the law—the existing law, let alone the fulfilled law.

Unwilling to sacrifice the achievement that such a world represents, Jesus isn't proposing to go back to the world out of which the law emerged, a struggle of all against all, and start over. That's because the principles he offers for the organization of political and social relations require law. Going back to the beginning would represent no gain and entail much human misery.

At the same time, Jesus understands his own radicalism perfectly well—the way in which his fulfillment of the law is calling forth a vast change in political and social relations. He knows that this is not an automatic process; it depends on people. In order to realize the benefits of his teaching in this world, they must freely accept the responsibilities that go along with the benefits. This process of *hearing, knowing, becoming* takes people from where they are, a world that knows law but only a law that has yet to reach the fullness of its potential, and brings them to the "kingdom," in which they can participate on earth to the extent that they are able to arrange their earthly affairs in accordance with what Jesus says. To eschew the idea of beginning where people are and leading them along from there, to call for the overthrow of the existing law or to take people as something other than the flawed beings they are, is to run the considerable risk that the result will not be Jesusian but anarchical, a regression to a lawless time.

THE OLD LAW IN THE "KINGDOM"

No Gospel story is more famous in evoking the relationship between the teaching of Jesus and the law as it stands than that of the challenge posed to Jesus by the Pharisees and the Herodians over whether it is lawful to pay the Roman poll tax (Mt. 22:15–22; Mk. 12:13–17; Lk.

20:20–26). Those who have come to test him include representatives of the temple priests as well as the royal court. Their objective, which Jesus perceives from the beginning as hostile, is to get him to say something that will amount to sedition against Rome—or in the alternative, something they can use against Jesus, perhaps some way of faulting his own piety on the same grounds of hypocrisy on which he has been skewering them. Jesus asks them to bring him a denarius, and when they do, asks whose face is on the coin. Caesar's, they say. "Then render to Caesar the things that are Caesar's; and to God the things that are God's" (Mt. 22:21; Mk. 12:17; Lk. 20:25).

From the context of the story, it is clear his contemporaries well understand that Jesus is no friend of the Roman occupation, just as he is no ally of the reigning temple and court elites. However, as with the Sermon on the Mount, when he was keen to assure his audience that he did not come to "abolish" the old law of the Torah, here he wittily presents assurance that a rebellion against Roman rule is not on his agenda, either. In both cases, he speaks truly, in the sense that the literal meaning of his words accurately reflects his guidance. The message in this case reinforces his sense of where one's "treasure" truly lies: It is not a matter of riches you store up, but of where your heart is, and as far as this world is concerned, whether you treat other people in accordance with his guidance.

Still, Jesus's words here do carry a strong sense of irony in that he knows the revolutionary implications that his teachings bring not only in spiritual matters but also in this-worldly affairs. Despite this awareness, he also knows that his revolution will not take place by means of a revolt against the Roman tax system. For Jesus, the way the revolution works is not necessarily or even optimally through open defiance of or confrontation with existing political and worldly powers. It works internally, awakening the conditions within people in accordance with which they seek to change their relations with one another. It is a process that occurs from person to person over space and time.

A rebellion against the Roman poll tax—and there can be no missing the whiff of resistance to it among those Jesus has been preaching to in Galilee and Judea—would not serve the spread of the Jesusian teaching. In the first place, such a rebellion would fail, with grave consequences for those participating in it (a subject that Jesus takes up, as we shall shortly see, in the brief parable of the two kings). Furthermore, it would be misconstrued. The revolution Jesus proposes is not about keeping your money; it's about something far more important, and money is only a good symbol for his revolution to the extent that it signifies that which is most highly valued—the Jesusian teaching itself, not the coins. Finally, the revolution Jesus propounds is not simply one of demanding one's due—a revolution of selfishness. It is also about accepting one's responsibilities. Only by means of the latter can one bring about the conditions in which the desire for righteousness can be broadly, indeed universally, satisfied. Those responsibilities entail at a minimum a wary or prudent respect for the ancient law and temporal law as it exists, even though one is well aware that the law will, in time, change—and one should work for that change, if one is up to the task, even at risk of persecution for the sake of righteousness.

Sometimes Jesus's depiction of the deference due to the old law comes across as truly harsh. Consider, for example, the conclusion of the Matthew version of the parable of the great supper (Mt. 22:11–14) (see chapter 7). In this version, it's the king who's throwing what turns out to be a wedding feast, and after the poor have been invited in to take the place of those who were invited but declined to show up, the king takes a look at the guests and discovers one who is not dressed suitably for the occasion. The king confronts him: " 'Friend, how did you come in here without wedding clothes?' And the man was speechless" (Mt. 22:12). The king then has his servants tie the guest up and throw him out.

This sharp rebuke helps emphasize several key points. The first is that upon entry to the banquet, which we understand here as participation in the world ordered according to the Jesusian teaching, there are indeed obligations on everyone—including, as in this case, those invited in off the streets. In the Matthew version of the story, those who end up at the banquet include "both evil and good" (Mt. 22:10). (The emphasis therefore differs from that of the Luke version, where the presumption is that the "poor and crippled and blind and lame" are all worthy; their problem is that they have been too long excluded.) The net cast by the king to fill his wedding hall has drawn in both the worthy and the unworthy. We come upon a truth that is not especially pleasant to contemplate, but for which we have been prepared: In the exercise of our obligation to reach out, we will find ourselves inviting in people who have no intention of abiding by the principles of the Jesusian teaching. They will seek its benefits without being willing to pay the costs; they want the privileges without the obligation.

In this case, the obligation seems to be an outgrowth of the old customs and ways: One must put on proper attire for a wedding. It is, no doubt, a way of honoring the bride and bridegroom, as well as the host, *as well as the law and custom that underlie marriage itself*. To appear without wedding clothes is, perhaps, to express contempt for one and all of the above. All are invited, but those who participate in the banquet owe an obligation to that old law and custom as well.

Even so, this does not end the matter. The king in Jesus's story, on spying the ill-dressed guest, doesn't simply throw him out on the street straightaway. Rather, the king asks the man how he happened to come in without proper wedding clothes. The guest is speechless in response. He has nothing to say.

This speechlessness speaks volumes. It is quite plausible that the reason he is shabbily attired is that he is too poor to afford wedding clothes, and if he explained that to the king, the king himself might have been willing to provide them. But the guest has *no good reason*, no way to justify himself, and he knows it. Invitation to the banquet is not carte blanche to do as one pleases—to eat, drink, and be merry without regard to the rules of the occasion, the law and customs of a wedding feast. These rules must be followed, and those who flout them or show contempt for them have no place at the table. An exception may even be possible, as the question of the king suggests—here, perhaps, we have an indication of how the Jesusian teaching acts to fulfill the law, by allowing a guest who has reason to be ill-dressed to be excused for his violation of the ancient law strictly construed.

We should not conclude from this story that final judgment of worthiness or unworthiness belongs to the people who embrace the Jesusian teaching; it doesn't. The fact that certain conduct is unacceptable does not relieve one from the obligation to try again with the person who misbehaves. Nevertheless, the problem of dealing with those who seek the benefits of living in a society and polity ordered according to Jesus's guidance, but without incurring the corresponding obligations, is one Jesus acknowledges people must cope with.

In the parable of the ten bridesmaids (Mt. 25:1–13), we see similar considerations at work. Jesus says that the bridegroom was delayed en route to the wedding, and the ten bridesmaids went out to meet him, taking their lamps with them against nightfall. The prudent ones also took along flasks of oil for the lamps; the foolish ones did not, presumably figuring there was enough inside the lamps already. Waiting for the groom, the bridesmaids fell asleep, and when a cry went up that the groom was coming at last, all ten hastened to trim their lamps. The foolish ones, seeing that their lamps were now going out for want of oil, asked the prudent ones to give them some. The prudent ones refused, saying that if they gave any away, they would not have enough for themselves. The prudent ones told the foolish ones to go out and buy more. While the foolish bridesmaids were gone buying oil, the groom arrived, and the five prudent bridesmaids went into the wedding feast with him. When the five other bridesmaids returned, the master of the house spurned them and denied them admission.

Once again, we have a wedding, and once again, we have an egregious violation of custom, this time on the part of the five foolish bridesmaids. Their task is to wait for the groom and enter the feast with him. Five of them are up to the task. They have made sufficient preparations to fulfill their responsibilities without any difficulty. Since they don't know when the bridegroom will arrive, they bring extra oil—enough, one supposes, to last them through the whole night if need be. The other five, the foolish ones, don't, apparently figuring the bridegroom will arrive before their lamps run out or not even thinking twice about it. What the relevance of the lit lamps is to the customs of the ceremony, Jesus doesn't say, but it really doesn't matter. The story invites us to assume that the lit lamps are in some way important and understood by everyone as such; they are part of the customary procedure, and this is, in the first instance, a story about the importance of custom.

We can take the wedding feast in this parable as metaphorically equivalent to the wedding feast in the Matthew version of the parable of the great supper: For purposes of this-worldly consideration, this is the place where the Jesusian teaching has been embraced. Again, the Jesusian feast takes place against a backdrop of law and custom. There is no admittance to the feast in defiance of the law and custom, yet this is what the foolish bridesmaids seek. They failed to meet their responsibilities and duties, and in so doing, forfeited their claim to the benefits and pleasures of the Jesusian feast.

The fault of the ill-attired guest in the previous parable was apparently that he did not care about his customary responsibilities: hence his speechlessness. Here, the fault of the foolish bridesmaids is not that they don't care. It's that they are too hasty. We can imagine that bringing along a flask of spare oil was a bit of a bother. You'd have to find a flask and then fill it from the barrel, or something like that, and it would clearly be a matter of greater short-term convenience to content oneself with the oil already in the lamp. The prudent ones made additional preparations to ensure that they could fulfill their responsibilities. The foolish ones didn't.

They are not, however, speechless as their lamps are flickering from lack of oil. They beg the other five for oil. They see their error. But the ones with extra oil refuse them. While this conduct on the part of the five bridesmaids Jesus describes as prudent at first seems selfish or harsh, it is necessary: In order for the customs to be maintained, the bridesmaids need their lit lamps to enter with the groom. The five with flasks don't believe they have enough extra to accommodate the others; if they did, they would be obliged to be generous. The letter of the law, according to which the foolish bridesmaids have no claim on the others' oil, gets trumped by the Jesusian obligation to reach out first. It's the Golden Rule.

There is no extra oil, however. The five who have enough could split what they have, but then rather than five bridesmaids ready to go in with the groom in accordance with the customs of the wedding feast, all ten would be equal in running out beforehand. But that is not Jesus's position here. If it were, it would point to a willingness to throw the law over altogether and substitute a radical new doctrine for the one that has long governed in this particular place and time. Jesus is unwilling to do that—notwithstanding what we can rightly take as his primary wish for the adoption of his teaching as far and wide, by as many people, as possible. The obligations due for admission to the Jesusian feast are the obligations imposed by the old law. The fact that Jesus has acted to "fulfill" the ancient law does not exempt one from following the provisions of the ancient law, not in this case. Again, in this-worldly terms, this is no final judgment on the foolish bridesmaids; likely, they will bring along extra oil the next time someone asks them to serve in that capacity. But this parable in conjunction with the story of the ill-dressed guest does make rather explicit the proposition that those who are unwilling to abide by their obligations have failed to earn a place at the Jesusian feast. This lesson is no less relevant to the spread of the Jesusian teaching today than it was in Jesus's time.

RESOURCES AND AMBITION

Ultimately, what distinguishes the five prudent (or "wise") bridesmaids from the five foolish ones is not that they are any better at predicting the unknown—in this case, when the bridegroom will return. It's that they are better prepared. They are forward-looking. They anticipate difficulties that may lie ahead as they pursue their desire and plan for how to cope with them.

In two parables offered in succession (Lk. 14:28–30, 31–32), Jesus offers further counsel along the same lines. During the story of the tower builder, Jesus asks his listeners, " 'Which one of you, when he wants to build a tower, does not first sit down and calculate the cost to see if he has enough to complete it?' " (Lk. 14:28). If not, he says, the would-be builder will earn the ridicule of those who see the half-built tower. Similarly, though with a twist, Jesus asks what king seeks to do battle with another before first assessing the strength of his army compared to the other king's? And when his forces don't measure up, "he sends a delegation and asks for terms of peace" (Lk. 14:32).

A tower is the product of an act of construction. A war is a contest between competing camps. Both are germane to Jesus's teaching. Those who are seeking to spread his teaching want to build something, a world in which Jesus's ideas about how social and political affairs should be organized hold sway. In spreading it, they come up against other contending ideas about how the world should be organized. In both of these metaphors, however, Jesus offers what seems as a matter of first impression to be rather pessimistic counsel: If you can't finish building the tower, don't start it; if your enemy has you outnumbered two-to-one, don't fight.

First impressions fail to do full justice to Jesus's meaning in both stories. The point about the tower is that you should scale your ambitions to your resources: There is nothing quite so boldly conspicuous as a great tower. Of course, if you are capable of acting on and extending the Jesusian teaching in the way in which a tower dominates a landscape, by all means, do so. But what if you are not? Well, the alternative is not to do nothing. It's to do what you *can*. One needs to take stock in advance.

The danger of failing to do so comes through in the story about the king contemplating a battle. It's not just that the king who goes up against an enemy twice as strong will not win: It's that he will lose and may lose everything. If you have some resources at your disposal, but not enough to build a great tower, then if you start building such a tower, you end up with nothing. If, however, you set your sights more modestly, in line with your capacity, then you may end up building a smaller but perfectly sturdy and durable structure that will reflect well on you.

All the more striking, in its way, is Jesus's endorsement of the weaker king's decision to seek peace. Jesus has already made clear what the stakes are: very likely, a defeat, not to say a rout. Under those circumstances, it is better to seek what one can get in exchange for sparing the stronger the trouble of a fight. Such a course at least has the potential to *preserve* what the weaker king has to a degree that would be impossible if matters came to blows. Jesus's story illustrates that an important part of his message is to protect the gains that his teaching has made in the world. The radicalism of the teaching itself demands prudent implementation. This was true in the case of the two wedding parables we have just examined, in which Jesus explored the ongoing importance of law and custom, and it is true here, where we come to a greater appreciation of the stakes.

Just as there is such a thing as excessive and imprudent zeal, so too is there such a thing as too much caution, an unwillingness to take risks of any sort for the sake of the spread of the political and social arrangements Jesus advocates. It remains a central imperative of the Jesusian teaching to seek its spread, as we have seen, and in fact there is no "static" version of the Jesusian teaching according to which one is relieved of any and all responsibility to reach out to others. One can always do *something*, and one must. But one must make the determination of *what to do* in the light of circumstances.

A GOOD USE FOR BAD THINGS

Circumstances for the spread and adoption of the Jesusian teaching may be adverse, but that does not mean one must wait for ideal conditions. In the parable of the talents (Mt. 25:14–30; Lk. 19:12–27), Jesus tells the story of a vaguely disreputable man who is leaving on a journey. Before going, he puts his money into the hands of his slaves. Several of the slaves invest the money successfully, and on the return of their master present him with the profits. One slave, however, afraid of the harshness of his master's judgment, has done nothing with the money entrusted to him but keep it safe, returning it to him when he gets back. The master is furious at the waste of opportunity and casts the slave out, giving the money to the most successful of the other slaves.

Although the master in the tale is an unsympathetic character—he is a man his slaves know to be a "hard man" (Mt. 25:24)—he is nevertheless an enabler of something good. The money given to the slaves represents an opportunity for them to do good by making more money in the marketplace. Jesus points here at two different ways of pursuing gain. One, on the basis of which the master has earned the reputation he acknowledges, is by reaping where you don't sow, which at best would be parasitical on the labor of others but more plausibly simply entails theft. Needless to say, this is not praiseworthy. The other way would be to *earn* money, which some of the slaves do by putting to use the talents the master provides. Jesus presents the gain made by this means as praiseworthy.

Now, the master in the tale simply wants gain. It is apparently of no concern to him how he gets it or how his slaves get it. In fact, he says that anybody who knows his reputation knows what it is he cares about. He then rewards the slaves who make a gain for him and punishes the one who doesn't. The fear of *losing* his master's money led the slave to bury it for safekeeping rather than invest it, but the master is not content merely with what he has; he wants more.

The twofold challenge for the slaves in the parable, then, is how to satisfy the greedy master without duplicating his character flaws. The slaves want the praise of the master and the advantage of rewards from the master, but not by any and all means the master himself would use. Some of them figure out how to deliver; one of them remains paralyzed with fear and fails. It's not that the action of the latter is wrong in the way that reaping where you did not sow is; it's that his action is ill-considered on prudential grounds. He failed to understand how he could make legitimate gains even in the context of his thrall to a master whose own legitimacy is very much in question.

The challenge for the Jesusian teaching often takes this form: how to make the most of imperfect circumstances and live in a world whose standards of judgment aren't necessarily compatible with those that you embrace and seek to spread. However, the solution is not to bury the asset with which you have been entrusted, any more than you would light a lamp and then hide it under a basket. You need to make prudent use of what you have.

Jesus offers another story about making the most of what you have to work with in the tale of the unjust steward (Lk. 16:1–13). A rich man hears a report that his manager has been squandering his possessions. He confronts the manager, demands an accounting, and dismisses him. The manager, desperately worried for his livelihood, hits upon a scheme that will get him a job in some other household. He contacts the people who are in debt to his master and discounts what they owe by large percentages. "And his master praised the unrighteous manager because he had acted shrewdly" (Lk. 16:8). Apparently, he got to keep his job after all.

If we look at this story as a profile of the manager, we have a case in which criminal cunning finds itself rewarded. The manager had no business writing down the debts owed to his master in order to pocket a personal gain, namely, future employment by someone with whom he conspired in fraud.

We must not neglect the rich man himself, however. He has heard an accusation against his manager and has confronted him with it. He then finds out about the fraud and conspiracy. Rather than feeling that this merely confirms the accusation against his manager, he takes this as evidence of the shrewdness of his manager, and therefore, presumably, of his suitability in his current job. Here, the discovery is the rich man's: At first, the rich man is worried that the manager is acting out of self-interest rather than in the rich man's interest. The manager is desperately worried for his livelihood, describing himself as "not strong enough to dig" and "ashamed to beg" (Lk. 16:3). The rich man then sees the manager solve the problem of future employment and decides the manager is so shrewd he deserves praise, not dismissal. The manager demonstrates through self-interested action a quality, shrewdness, by which the master can profit as well.

The manager was accused of acting out of self-interest by wasting his master's goods. The manager goes on to prove the charge against himself, but in doing so, he paradoxically demonstrates to the master that he is capable of taking very good care of the master's goods indeed. The manager shows himself to be shrewd, and the master shows himself to be shrewd in recognizing the shrewdness of the manager. The result is satisfactory to both.

While Jesus doesn't say whether the original accusation the rich man heard against the manager was just or unjust, clearly, relations between the two were poisoned. Yet rather than accept that outcome as the final result, the rich man discovers something in the manager's ability that is of great use. Beginning with the worst suspicions of each other, they end up in a situation from which they both benefit. The parable is one of reconciliation, and the process is anything but pretty. In spite of that, the outcome is better than any alternative ending. Such is the power of the Jesusian injunction to be reconciled.

In the concluding passages, Jesus says: "Make friends for yourselves by means of the wealth of unrighteousness" (Lk. 16:9). The shrewdness here is not an end in itself, but it does serve as a means to an end. The "wealth of unrighteousness" is not an insurmountable liability in the pursuit of right conduct; it can constitute the path to the highest earthly end, reconciliation. Hence, Jesus's observation that "ye cannot serve God and mammon" (Lk. 16:13, KJV). If one serves "mammon," then either the rich man gets defrauded and the dismissed manager gets a new job based on his dishonesty, or the manager gets caught in his fraud and goes to his ruin, something worse than the ditch-digging he says he isn't strong enough to do and the begging he says he is ashamed to engage in. But if one places the principles of the Jesusian teaching at the forefront and serves them, the result is beneficial not just to one or the other but to both.

In the parable of the unjust judge (Lk. 18:1–5), Jesus offers another example of how an imperfect situation can nevertheless result in a favorable outcome. Here, Jesus describes a judge who is repeatedly importuned by a widow seeking legal protection from an opponent. Jesus says that at first, the judge was unwilling to grant her request, "but afterward he said to himself, 'Even though I do not fear God nor respect man, yet because this widow bothers me, I will give her legal protection, otherwise by continually coming she will wear me out'" (Lk. 18:4–5).

The first element of Jesus's message is unmistakable: Persist. It is entirely possible that by persisting, you will get what you seek notwithstanding initial resistance. Indeed, you may get what you seek mainly because the person whom you are pestering tires of being pestered. Insofar as Jesus associates his message with what the woman seeks over and over again, the this-worldly implication is clear. While it would obviously be better if the judge saw the merit of the woman's claim and granted her the relief she sought on that basis, it is still a gain for her when he grants it just to be rid of her. One might refine the point further: It's the judge's loss, not the woman's, that he grants her request only to be rid of her. In so doing, he continues in his ways, impervious to justice, though for her, justice has been done. One can get something positive out of an unjust judge as one can get something positive out of the unjust master in the parable of the talents.

This does not, however, exhaust the meaning of the tale. The judge begins as a figure of authority in this world who neither "fear[s] God nor respect[s] man." The ancient law has no meaning for him as God's law; the idea of justice as something owed to people in accordance with the law is likewise a matter of indifference to him. He doesn't especially care. The story seems to indicate that he rules in the cases he hears on the basis of what is convenient for him. At the conclusion, he finds for the woman because he wants to be rid of a pest; she is a pain to him, and that's exactly how he thinks about judging. His task in court is to find the result that gives *him* the most pleasure or least pain. There is no higher standard the judge applies. A result that would be inconvenient to him is a result that he will not reach.

Of course, initially, he found against the woman. No great surprise there: Women possessed extraordinarily few rights enforceable in court—although, to be sure, widows did enjoy certain enforceable claims on the estates of their husbands. Despite the legitimacy of some such claims, this judge rejected hers. Now, perhaps he would not have done so had he known then how difficult she was going to be, but he could not be expected to foretell the future. Nevertheless, his willingness to change his mind under her pressure indicates that he was not especially attached to his initial ruling. And after all, the first ruling might well have been every bit as capricious as his final ruling: made in response to whatever pleasure/pain calculus applied the first day she came to court.

A problem remains, however. If in the end the judge is receptive to this woman's cause because she is persistent, then he might well be receptive to anyone else's cause on the same grounds. Jesus's telling of this story has led us to the justified assumption that the woman has right on her side. Her rightness, though, has no impact on the judge, and so we have to leave open the possibility that the next insistent petitioner will pursue a manifestly unjust judgment and nevertheless prevail with a judge who is merely interested in his own convenience.

That's a risk. This judge affords us no protection from such an outcome. But, interestingly, something else inherent in the situation does—not a guarantee, but at least a measure of protection. We must look again at the persistence of the woman. Obviously, what she seeks is to her advantage and contrary to the interest of her opponent. She seeks to benefit from the judge, but it is not merely the pursuit of an advantage that takes her to court time and again. It is her sense of justice; she believes she is right.

But where is her opponent? Why isn't he equally as persistent in opposing her and upholding the initial judgment in his favor? That might just have something to do with her opponent's realization that right is *not* on his side. The woman goes to *court*. She seeks to have her case decided by a judge. She may or may not know that the judge doesn't really care about justice, but she knows what a court is for, namely, to do justice, even if the judge in this court is not doing justice to her. She keeps coming back because she understands perfectly well that justice has not yet been done, and therefore, the court has not performed its proper function. One certainly cannot rule out someone going to court to try to obtain an unjust advantage over another person. Upon losing, however, such a person would not be especially likely to come back again and again, begging the judge to reconsider. It's not so much a question of whether the malefactor has the nerve to persist. Let's assume that he is a thoroughly horrible fellow, without the least scruple or sense of conscience. To put it bluntly, if you are looking to do someone an injustice or to take advantage of that person for your own selfish reasons, there are more productive places to pursue such a scheme than a court of law, where you risk having your nefarious plans exposed in a setting that will cause you the gravest consequences.

People know what courts are supposed to be for: the enforcement of law and the administration of justice. That's why they knock on the courthouse door when they have been done wrong even if they suspect that the court will not be receptive to them. They appear in court to seek justice, and if the court is unforthcoming, they appeal the judgment of the court in the name of justice.

Persistence is a quality that can be put into service for what's just and fair or what's unjust and unfair. What Jesus suggests here is that the Jesusian teaching will create people who are more persistent out of a sense of the justice of their cause than are those who are merely seeking advantage for themselves. This gives the Jesusian teaching an advantage even with judges whose judgment is based not on law or justice but the calculation of their own advantage.

One additional possibility is worth considering in relation to this short but thematically rich tale. Suppose the judge's initial ruling was not derived from whatever happened to be convenient for him, but was rather a correct ruling, one based on the law as he correctly interpreted it. In Jesus's view, the persistence of the woman would then run counter to the law, but not counter to what is just and fair. The law does not *define* what is just and fair. From Jesus's perspective, the law is subject to *question* as to whether it is just and fair. We have seen in the Sermon on the Mount that Jesus tells people to settle their quarrels before they get to court. That's because a settlement that they themselves agree to is one they will each perceive as fair. In court, you run three risks: a dishonest judge, perhaps like the one in this case, who rules against you for his own gain or convenience or pleasure; an honest but all-too-human judge, whose imperfect administration of the law results in your disadvantage; and even an honest judge who rules against you correctly in accordance with a law that somehow doesn't or shouldn't apply in your case. In the last instance, persistence in pursuit of *justice* will be different from persistence on behalf of a legally correct outcome because of a deficiency of the law—either its application to a particular case or in general. Jesus encourages this sort of persistence as well, as befits his intention to "fulfill" the law.

THE DEATH OF JESUS

We come to a curious paradox: If Jesus counsels, as he does, a measure of prudence and pragmatism in relation to worldly authority as well as respect for the old law and temporal law, and if he teaches (as he does) that even those who are not favorably disposed toward the Jesusian teaching can be induced in some cases to serve its ends by means of a certain worldly cunning, what are we to make of Jesus's death at the hands of the worldly authorities? Was he better at counseling prudence than applying it in his own case?

Jesus taught by his words and by the example of how he lived, including his death by crucifixion. The last words of Jesus, dying on the cross, are given in John as, "It is finished" (Jn. 19:30). *What* is finished? The answer may refer to Jesus's suffering, but the context suggests otherwise. The Gospels describe Jesus thirsting on the cross and being given vinegar to drink, an echo of Psalms 69:21: "They also gave me gall for my food / And for my thirst they gave me vinegar to drink." The vinegar given to Jesus on the cross is presented as a fulfillment of this scripture. What is "finished" at this point is accordingly not merely his suffering nor merely a life, but also his teaching about how people should live in the world. He came to say what he said, and prior to his death, he did so. It is abundantly clear, as we have seen, that he fully understood the radicalism of what he was saying in the context of its times, and indeed of all time. Had he been cut down early in his ministry in Capernaum, we would have a very different set of problems on our hands today; but, of course, in this case especially, such a speculative exercise in alternate history makes no sense whatsoever.

After the Resurrection scenes in the Gospels, most of the words attributed to Jesus in Matthew, Luke, and John[1] are directed at persuading his disciples that the man they see before them is indeed Jesus. The three Gospels describe Jesus as eating, showing his wounds from the cross, performing miracles to acquire food, and describing the ways his Resurrection fulfills scripture. Jesus also talks about what happens next and exhorts his followers to carry on. What we do not find in these scenes, not to put too fine a point on it, is anything that decisively alters, amends, or adds to the political teaching Jesus set out before his

---

[1] The earliest versions of the Gospel According to Mark provide no account of interaction with the risen Christ described in Mark 16:9–20. Later manuscripts add a passage in which Jesus instructs his disciples to go all over the world and preach the gospel, mentioning some signs by which believers will be known, including the ability to cast out demons, speak in tongues, and pick up poisonous snakes.

death—his instruction on how people should organize their affairs in this world. No more sermons; no more parables; no more debates with Pharisees and Sadducees; no more instructions delivered to the general public.

In Matthew, Jesus tells his followers to baptize people "in the name of the Father and of the Son and of the Holy Spirit, teaching them to observe all that I have commanded you" (Mt. 28:19–20). John describes the scene as follows: "[Jesus said,] 'Peace be with you; as the Father has sent me, I also send you.' And when he had said this, he breathed on them, and said to them, 'Receive the Holy Spirit' " (Jn. 20:20–22). In the context of the political teaching of Jesus, this Spirit is that part of the Jesusian teaching about how to live in this world that makes people want not just to live according to the teaching themselves but to spread it. That means both geographically—to "all nations" in Matthew—and over time: Jesus exhorts Peter to "Tend my lambs" and "Shepherd my sheep" (Jn. 21:15–16), then concludes, "Truly, truly, I say to you, when you were younger, you used to gird yourself and walk wherever you wished; but when you grow old, you will stretch out your hands and someone else will gird you, and bring you where you do not wish to go" (Jn. 21:18). That younger person will presumably have girded himself or herself before performing the service to the old person and will continue to do so until too old and in need of help going where he or she no longer can. It is a striking image emphasizing what Jesus made clear in his public ministry before his death: that his is a teaching for all people and all time and that it is borne freely by free people.

His freely accepted death completes the political teaching of Jesus.[2] The unarmed prophet who could have commanded legions instead allows himself to be arrested, tortured, and executed in order to make the point that the truth that makes you free must be freely chosen. Jesus dies a free man because he knows this truth and cannot be made to

---

[2] Christianity, of course, begins with the Resurrection.

deny it. In accepting death, he shows that the freedom you have because you know the truth cannot be undone by coercive authority, even in its most flagrant form—execution by crucifixion. Jesus lived an exemplary life of freedom and died free as well. The Resurrection provides an image of the ultimate triumph over death in a world to come, but it in no way diminishes Jesus's this-worldly triumph over death in freedom.

The question of whether to die in freedom or live in fear is one that will recur. The challenge of the cross is not unique to Jesus. Others have faced and will face equally horrible persecution and execution because of their advocacy of what's right. Jesus speaks of this in various Gospel passages generally taken to reflect his eschatological concerns—the imminent coming of the end times, final judgment, and the reign of God on earth. But the words attributed to him have resonance at all times in which what's right is in danger.

As he notes in Mark, "When you hear of wars and rumors of wars, do not be frightened; those things must take place; but that is not yet the end. For nation will rise up against nation, and kingdom against kingdom. . . . These things are merely the beginning of birth pangs" (Mk. 13:7–8). The struggle for the triumph of right, the Jesusian teaching in this world, is certain to be long and difficult, requiring sacrifice on the part of those who believe in it. As he notes, "Greater love has no one than this, that one lay down his life for his friends. You are my friends if you do what I command you" (Jn. 15:13–14). Of course, what he "commands"—or "enjoins" or "charges," if you prefer, because the choice of whether to accept such a "command" belongs solely to the person who hears it—is that people make friends with their neighbors, extending such brotherly relations outward in a widening circle that reaches out even to their old enemies. Finally, "A pupil is not above his teacher; but everyone, after he has been fully trained, will be like his teacher" (Lk. 6:40). Jesus's free acceptance of his death for the sake of the advance of his teaching is one that others have been and will yet be called on to emulate.

Completed by his death, the political teaching of Jesus for this world lives on in empowering freedom through truth, in the sense that his teaching continues to resonate in the lives of people after he is gone. "[Y]ou will know the truth, and the truth will make you free" (Jn. 8:32). The teaching, the truth, is alive in the world. In this earthly sense, Jesus remains in the world as a teacher—beyond the confines of his own life on earth.

PART III

THE JESUSIAN TEACHING AND THE PRESENT MOMENT

10

THE MODERN WORLD

The political teaching of Jesus is a fully realized account of universal freedom. This freedom is constituted by each person's acceptance of the equal freedom of everyone else. Acceptance takes on the practical, everyday form of treating others the way you would like to be treated. It is undeniable that the world of today has not yet achieved the full potential of his teachings, but it is also undeniable that we have made strides in his direction.

This is, in the first instance, a world of the "fulfill[ed]" law: Jesus has taken the existing law as his point of departure and developed it to its fullest potential, a proposed idea of justice that people will recognize universally as true and beneficial. In such a world, people freely accept this fulfilled law because they believe the law articulates correct principles that are good to comply with. They recognize that the benefits or rights they enjoy socially and politically come with a prior set of responsibilities they must meet in order to enjoy the benefits. If they fail to do so, the world they wish will simply *not be*—action in fulfillment of their responsibilities is what constitutes or creates the world of rights and benefits. Law therefore transcends its ancient association with coercive power—people conduct themselves in accordance with the law not because they will be punished if they don't, but because they want to.

How, if not by the fiat of the law or the weight of the customs of the society in which they live bearing down on them, do people know what to do in order to fulfill their responsibilities toward others? Not by looking for the applause or approval of others for their action, but by looking within themselves. The purpose of such inner examination is not selfish, but to draw closer to others. One first seeks and removes the impediments *within oneself* to the improvement of relations with others. Then one reaches out to them. The basic principle of outreach is the Golden Rule, according to which the answer to the question *How would I like to be treated?*, obtained through inner examination, yields the answer to the question *How should I treat others?* Note that this is not an activity that takes up merely a part of the day. It is the principle that is to guide all your interactions with everyone else.

As such, the Jesusian teaching takes us beyond the world of law. Jesus shows that the essential strength of the law is also its inherent drawback; it articulates rules for judgment that are meant to apply to numerous different cases. Jesus calls attention to a way in which people can transcend the law without contradicting its restrictions. They do this by making friends: settling the disputes between one another in a manner that is acceptable to all involved. The Golden Rule in action is a principle of interaction according to which any given two people can achieve friendly relations—or even better relations, without limit. If I want someone to treat me better than in a merely civil or cordial fashion, I begin by treating the other person better. If the other shares my view of the possibilities that inhere in the Golden Rule, that person will do likewise.

This is something the law can never do in regulating people's conduct. The law is a great *No*: "Thou shalt not. . . ." A court can tell you when you have failed to fulfill your obligations to others in accordance with the law, and it can sanction you for doing so as harshly as society wishes. But its action is negative. Jesus, by contrast, grounds the interaction between people on a positive principle.

While the Golden Rule includes the idea *Do not treat others in a way you would not wish to be treated*, it also says a great deal more. If

I merely refrain from striking you on the right cheek because I wouldn't like you to strike me on the right cheek or face the legal consequences for slapping you, then that is a victory for the distinctly pre-Jesusian rule of law. Jesus extols the potential benefit for both of us if I do *something good* for you, instead of simply refraining from doing something bad. He encourages you and me both to seek something better than that between us.

In its ultimate form, that seeking of "something better" expresses itself as love.

The ancient law, as we have seen, already holds that you should love your neighbor as you do yourself. Internal self-regard becomes a touchstone for the development of regard for others. This is especially important because it tamps down selfish self-regard, a love of self that can be satisfied only at the expense of others: If you can't apply your love of yourself to your neighbors, you love yourself too much. This moderating principle doesn't require you to abjure all love of self—only that portion of it which might interfere with love of others.

We can see, therefore, that the ancient law already embodies a certain principle of equality. Indeed, Jesus excoriates the people of his time for their failure to live up to their obligations under the ancient law. The "woes" he pronounces on the scribes and Pharisees, who have special responsibility with respect to the law, speak to this sort of failure. Yet inadequate compliance does not end the matter: The "fulfill[ment]" of the law Jesus came to offer doesn't consist merely in an exhortation to comply with the law as it is.

Jesus offers two main refinements. First, the principle of equality in the ancient law applies, precisely, to those on whom the ancient law is binding, the Israelites. The law of the Torah does not bind others. They are outside its ambit.[1] Recall the lawyer who asked the lawyerly

---

[1] Some read the Noahide covenant, God's promise and injunction to mankind after the flood, as the universalization of the principle of equality first implied in the creation of man in the image of God.

question of who counts as a neighbor. Jesus's answer there and elsewhere is that in principle, everyone does: People should seek to extend their neighborly relations ever outward.

Second, Jesus recognizes that what the law can do for relations between people is limited. To get the law right—to have good law—is no small thing. At the time Jesus presented his teaching to "fulfill" the law, there was clearly still a long way to go before "all is accomplished" in the sense that the full potential of law has been realized, and we are not there yet.

Even the completion and universal extension of the law as a voluntarily shared idea of right conduct do not do full justice to what Jesus is getting at. People need more than law; they need forgiveness for their inevitable shortcomings. They want to be treated not just according to the letter of the law but with a certain measure of generosity, so that their good qualities get taken into account even when the law is passing judgment on their failings. People cannot find this kind of satisfaction without love, and love is something the law cannot provide. Where there is love between people, law will be unnecessary; the mutual quest for a more intimate connection and reconciliation supersedes the law. Of course, this love, no less than love of self, must not be of a kind that can be satisfied only at the expense of others. But love is capable of opening new vistas between those who share it without compromising essential obligations toward others.

The political teachings of Jesus encompass not just law but love. He provides a mechanism, the Golden Rule, for the outward extension of brotherly relations and for the deepening of these relations into something that substitutes an affirmative striving for the well-being of others for the stony "thou shalt not" of law. The desire for righteousness that people feel as primordial and that Jesus says "shall be satisfied" *cannot* be satisfied without law. Once people understand that the only way anyone's desire for righteousness can truly be satisfied is through the satisfaction of everyone's desire for righteousness, then this desire can be satisfied with *but one* law, a law that tells us how to love:

"In everything, therefore, treat people the same way you want them to treat you."

KINGDOM WITHOUT A KING

We have discussed the question of whether the "kingdom of heaven" to which Jesus frequently refers (also the "kingdom of God") has a this-worldly element that must be considered. But there's another aspect of the problem that is relevant to the extension of the political teaching of Jesus down to the present: Does the "kingdom" require a king?

The political importance of this question couldn't be more obvious. Should we reason by analogy from an other-worldly kingdom in which God rules to conclude that Jesus is suggesting that people are best off ruled by a king? But to ask this question is to see the problem with the analogy: An earthly king would be like God exactly how?

Now, again, if the question is solely one of the Second Coming of Christ to earth or some other version of the arrival of God to sit as ruler of earth[2]—if, in short, the earthly king is the same as the heavenly king—then the analogy poses no problems because the earthly king is *like* God in all respects, being either God or an aspect of God's divine being. This would also end our this-worldly investigation of the question. However, insofar as we have also understood Jesus to be describing a "kingdom" that is already coming into being in this world with the spread of the Jesusian teaching, then we at once come upon the problem that no human king in this world could ever come close to the divine perfection contemplated in the king of heaven. Omniscience and omnipotence—sorry, these are not properties of earthly kings, no matter how wise or how powerful they are.

Of course, kings have long sought to justify their rule and their dynastic succession by some supposed "divine right," and attempts to overthrow kings have historically been treated as offenses against an

---

[2] For example, in accordance with Isaiah 2:2–4.

order extending from God in heaven down to people on earth—far more serious than routine lawbreaking. Furthermore, a king is not just the current victor in the struggle of all against all. A king is different from a tyrant in that the king propounds the law or acts in accordance with law, whereas a tyrant rules lawlessly. A proper king is not just ruler over his subjects for his own benefit but for theirs as well. He has great responsibilities as well as the privileges and benefits of his high place.

Ironically, these attempts to defend kings as somehow connected to the divine actually reinforce how different earthly kings are from God or any idea of God as a divine being, all-knowing and all-powerful. The answer to the question of whether Jesus is suggesting that people are best off ruled by a king on earth then becomes "not necessarily" because even the best possible earthly king bears no comparison to the king of heaven.

Would Jesus have a preference for rule by a king over other kinds of governance? Or would he prefer some other kind of government over a king, even the best possible earthly king? The question is important because, nowadays, most people who live under democratic governments wouldn't consider for a moment replacing them with a monarchy. Their sense of what freedom and equality mean would not allow for any such thing. In the Western world, royalty, where it still exists, is a residual institution, disconnected from current politics. Kings and queens speak for the past, the history and tradition of various countries, and only very little to current problems. Although other parts of the world still have rulers who style themselves "king," those among us who value freedom and equality tend to dismiss their claims to rule by any kind of right as post-facto rationalizations for the power they wield and its historical origins.

How consistent is this modern conclusion with the Jesusian teaching? One finds no direct support in the statements the Gospels attributed to Jesus for anything like democratic government. In fact, Jesus expresses a general level of wariness of popular opinion: He warns people against using the opinion of others as their lodestone. In the parable of the evil tenants, as we have seen, a mob takes over the vineyard and does violence to its rightful owner's representatives. We have also seen Jesus warning against the popular wide path through the large gate.

At the same time, there is no suggestion in the Jesusian teaching that a widely shared opinion is bad simply because it is widely shared. Jesus had in mind, after all, the spread of his teaching about how to live in the world to as many people as possible. Insofar as its essence is its voluntary acceptance, Jesus envisioned people weighing it for themselves in this world and deciding that what he offered was a true description of the possibilities here and one they would find it beneficial to be a part of.

So we begin to draw a little closer to the essence of the problem: It's not whether a majority decides one way or the other that makes something right or wrong; it's whether something is right or wrong that should determine whether a majority decides in its favor—or only a minority, or even a king on his earthly throne, or even a single person with the ability to participate in the process of *hearing, knowing, becoming*.

According to Jesus, the first question when thinking about how you should act toward someone else is "what's right?," which you can ordinarily figure out by asking yourself how you would like to be treated if the situations were reversed. Now, of course, we know that the historical world has been and remains full of conflict: I may know what the right thing to do is based on the Golden Rule, but some aspect of the political or social order in which I find myself situated may tell me to do something else. But here, in the gap between what I know is right and what the situation allows, I find an agenda for political action: I know what needs changing and why. Jesus has extraordinary confidence in the ability of ordinary people to reach such judgments. Of course, the road ahead can be fraught with danger, and Jesus is likewise aware that some people will not be up to the challenge of pursuing this-worldly justice against those who obtain satisfaction for themselves at the expense of others. In the Beatitudes, he identifies this activity as the responsibility of what I have called the "good person," and he affords the highest place in his typology of the "good person" to those who find themselves persecuted for their efforts to advance his teaching.

We have also seen that Jesus is prudent and pragmatic in his approach to the this-worldly spread of his teaching. He carefully delineates obstacles likely to be encountered and shows how they can be overcome. Unwilling to risk slipping into conditions of anarchy, he pays necessary deference to the past in the form of the old law, while simultaneously seeking to move from the world of the old law to the world of the radical Jesusian "fulfill[ment]" of the law. We should think about the figure of the king in this light as well. At the time when Jesus propounded his teaching, the choice was not between a king and a modern, Western-style democracy. Instead, the politics of the day involved all sorts of dodgy questions about the relationship of the Roman occupation to the throne of Herod, the interaction of the political elites and the temple elites, the question of ancient enmity between peoples, and so on. At the moment when he propounded his teaching, its most urgent task was its spread beyond the handful of his closest followers. At once, it had political and social implications; but these implications didn't turn into an imperative for an immediate "power to the people"–style political revolution and would have been ill-served by an attempt to link them to such a program (which is not to suggest that a revolution is *never* a good idea).

The Jesusian teaching did not seek its realization as an earthly kingdom in the sense of its enactment or adoption as law in the domain of an earthly king. The "kingdom of heaven" on earth is a matter, first of all, of affinity among people as a result of their right conduct toward each other. A real-world king might play a role in facilitating such relations or hindering them, and various kings have done one or the other—or both, if the issues involved are multifaceted. But there is no expectation in the Jesusian teaching that its adoption will come or can come as a result of its imposition by even the best of kings; it is the working of "people power" from one person to another over space and time that brings it about. Under some circumstances, the Jesusian teaching may be able to spread only slowly; in others, rapid propagation may be possible. The key constraint is that the "free and voluntary" requirement must remain.

As the political teaching spreads and the principle of free acceptance of equality in freedom takes greater root, it becomes possible to ask what kinds of political arrangements are most likely to ensure that people adhere to the fundamental principle. At such a point—at which Western societies arrived after considerable struggle in the twentieth century—the modern idea of democracy emerged as the answer to this question. The reason for this has two aspects, opposite sides of a coin. First, freedom in the Jesusian sense generates the logical conclusion that insofar as people need political mechanisms to settle the disputes among them, they each deserve an equal share in the decision. Second, there is no basis for the conclusion that one person has a justifiable claim to exclude others from a say in the decision.

We must be careful here, however. Democracy is a means to an end, the preservation and extension of the Jesusian principle of freedom and equality. In modern societies, democracy may in fact be the *only possible* means to that end. That being said, democracy in itself is not the end, especially if majorities vote to satisfy themselves at the expense of minorities. The only proper route to the satisfaction of the primordial desire for righteousness is the satisfaction of *everyone*'s desire for righteousness. There is always a test to be applied to political arrangements—the extent to which they conform to the "fulfill[ed]" law in this regard. Democracy, too, is always subject to this scrutiny.

The principle that no democracy can rightly overturn is the Jesusian principle of equality in freedom as encapsulated in the Golden Rule. We can therefore say that this principle takes precedence over all others pertaining to the political and social arrangements of this world.

Indeed, it was this principle that led to the conclusion that for modern societies, democracy is the only way to go. This principle is not necessarily *chronologically* prior to democracy, in the sense that one must always wait until people share the principle before attempting to put a democratic government in place. In some cases, democratic self-government has helped people find their way to the principle of equality in freedom. But the principle does not come from or grow out of democracy.

A key characteristic of democracy is that majorities accept that they may one day be minorities, and so they govern with a measure of restraint. Minorities accept democracy because they expect the restraint of the majority and realize that in the future they are free to contest the majority. In other words, those who find political satisfaction in a properly functioning democracy do so not as members of the majority or the minority but more or less unanimously. Which is to say, once again, that there is a principle underlying democracy, and not just any principle, but the principle of freedom in equality: It is a law, in fact the fulfillment of the possibility of law. What makes it a law is not coercive power associated with its promulgation or extension in space and time, but rather its free acceptance by people as both true and beneficial. The lawgiver in question was Jesus. The this-worldly sense in which Jesus might be construed as "king," or even "king of kings," is as the giver of the law accepted down to our day.

A World without Enemies

Jesus counsels forgiveness, reconciliation, self-correction, turning the other cheek, mercy, peacemaking—what seems at times an infinite mandate to reach out to others, owing to the possibility that one more effort will produce the reciprocation that is at the heart of the benefit to be won from the Jesusian teaching. But there is a very serious practical problem: What if reaching out exposes you to destruction? Indeed, what if the very act of reaching out in accordance with Jesus's teaching is the means by which those who do not share the principle of freedom in equality, preferring instead the pursuit of their own satisfaction at the expense of others, obtain the access they need to harm you or impose their will on you precisely through this outreach? We have seen how small a problem this is when the injury to you is on a par with a slap to the cheek, but what about something far worse—something, at the limit, that seeks the extinguishing of the Jesusian teaching of universal equality in freedom and the substitution for it of some other principle of political and social organization? And what if there is a realistic prospect of the success of that competing principle?

This is, in my view, the most difficult question posed by the political teachings of Jesus. Over and over again, in scene after scene and saying after saying, he reaffirms the necessity of continuing to reach out. To be sure, Jesus speaks of a divine reward that will come to those who follow his teaching, as well as eternal punishment for those who do not. Perhaps that is the last word on the matter and the only possible solution to the problem. If so, there is no more to say with respect to the this-worldly teachings we have been investigating. Yet there is more to say beyond simply that the punishment Jesus describes as God's to administer in the next world has no analogue in this world.

The analogue would, of course, be death. Imprisonment, even under conditions of torture or humiliation, would not quite be the same: Jesus tells those who are persecuted for his sake to rejoice; the point is that the freedom that is essentially one's own, intrinsic to each person, cannot be taken away. But a life can be put to an untimely end, and with it, whatever freedom means to that person in this world. This might happen in wartime or as a legally sanctioned punishment for a crime. It might also be an act of self-defense. Murder, of course, is forbidden. But is there, in the Jesusian teaching, ever any basis on which to distinguish from simple murder and killing in wartime or the death penalty or homicide in self-defense?

One may search the words of Jesus in the Gospels high and low without ever finding a plain basis for making such a distinction. There is a certain amount of violent language attributed to Jesus in the Gospels, especially his remark, "Do not think that I came to bring peace on the earth; I did not come to bring peace, but a sword" (Mt. 10:34). But notwithstanding the historically not-infrequent interpretation of this passage as a mandate to take up arms to advance the Christian faith, doing so requires the suppression of the plain meaning of far more numerous passages reaffirming the need to keep reaching out. A reading of this passage that is more consistent with the rest of Jesus's statements would note that it is the task of people to make peace on earth among themselves. The peace Jesus *did not* come to bring would seem to be the peace of submission, acquiescence in a world organized according to the principle of the advantage of the strong over the weak, and the sword is in this sense something more powerful than brute strength, namely, the Jesusian teaching.

There is another sword that is not quite so metaphorical, and this sword is the one Peter uses to strike the servant of the high priest at the time of Jesus's arrest. While Jesus objects in no uncertain terms to the use of the sword at that time, surely Peter did not produce his weapon out of nowhere. It would seem likely that he carried it routinely, at least in situations that brought some risk to the person of Jesus—and, if so, it would be hard to avoid the implication that Jesus didn't mind. Is this a hint of a possible acceptance of self-defense? After all, one need not use the sword to defend with a sword: Its mere presence would likely have a certain deterrent effect on some potential harmdoers. While it is impossible to make a persuasive case for aggressive war in supposed furtherance of the teaching of Jesus, it is not quite so hard to make a case for self-defense where the teaching of Jesus is gravely threatened. (That's a separate question from whether the person of Jesus was to be defended with the sword in the garden that night.)

When Jesus tells Peter (Peter again) that he should forgive his brother seventy times seven times, we have what sounds at first like an injunction for infinite outreach, but actually says 490 times. That's a finite number used in a fashion to invite the figurative reading of *as many times as necessary.* Yet it is a finite number, which again hints at the possibility of a limit without saying so directly.

And in another puzzling passage (Mk. 11:12–14, 20–21; Mt. 21:18–20), Jesus, on his way into Jerusalem and hungry, sees a fig tree, which turns out to have no fruit on it, only leaves. Jesus curses the tree, pronouncing that it never again bear fruit. In the Matthew version, the tree at once withers. The Mark version has an additional and troubling element, namely, figs are out of season. Rather than withering instantly, what happens in Mark is that as Jesus is leaving Jerusalem later that night, Peter (Peter yet again) spots the tree Jesus earlier cursed and point outs that it has withered. Why does Jesus curse the fig tree? Especially if it's not the season for the fig tree to bear fruit? What fault has the fig tree displayed? Inevitably, the story recalls the parable of the barren fig tree (Lk. 13:6–9) we have examined, where the point is to try again to get the tree in the vineyard to bear fruit. Do we have a hint, once again, about a time at which, having exhausted all effort, one must give up?

Surely, it did not escape the attention of Jesus that people are indeed inclined to defend themselves when threatened. No less so, nations. It seems implausible in the extreme that he expected his teaching would suddenly eradicate that propensity. Certainly, it had no such effect. There is a radical pacifism to the Jesusian teaching, but it is an endpoint—the condition in which those who live according to the teaching find themselves with respect to one another once they have embraced the teaching, and complete only at the point at which all nations, one way or another, embrace the teaching. In the meantime, Jesus's profound expression of patience and his understanding of the importance of prudence and pragmatic considerations suggest he understood perfectly well that a condition of universal and perpetual peace was not imminent.

Why, then, didn't he say so? The answer, it seems to me, is that had he done so, he would have been thought to sanction striking out at one's enemies or striking back at them, and he didn't wish to grant such approval. In the first place, to offer such permission at some point, even after the requirement of a certain specified amount of outreach and quantity of forgiveness has been met, would be to invite its abuse. If Jesus had said outright that the four hundred ninety-first offense was one too many, deserving not forgiveness but furious revenge, then clever people would ask what, really, the difference was between the four hundred ninety-first and the four hundred ninetieth or the two hundredth or the tenth—or, on the strength of one's supposed ability to read the intention of the other, the first.

The number is transparently arbitrary, after all. The eventually forthcoming permission settles the matter in principle—after a point, forgiveness is not required. So then the question becomes not whether but when. Instead of seeking opportunities for setting the past aside and going forward together, one is busy checking off the boxes one needs to before one can do what one has really wanted to do all along, namely, strike back.

Second, Jesus's blanket refusal of permission to strike back, notwithstanding the reasons to think he knew perfectly well that people would continue to strike back when threatened, forces those who accept the premise of his political teaching, equality in freedom, and would like to think they are in compliance with it, to confront the challenges they face as generously as they possibly can. It may be that necessity is a defense, but it is a defense of an action that *needs defending*, not one that is self-justifying or self-evidently justified. It is not a defense one should be able to make effortlessly. To strike and kill someone as an enemy really is to obliterate all earthly possibility of the relations of equality in freedom one takes as the touchstone of one's political and social arrangements. One may have to do so, but it should never be done lightly. The way to spread the Jesusian teaching is not to give people a choice between accepting it or death. One can all too well imagine what kind of misbegotten holocaust could ensue from such reasoning and accordingly why Jesus would want to leave that door closed. Those who accept the essential organizing principle for this world of universal equality in freedom may find themselves in exceptional circumstances, but he insists that in accordance with his teaching, they view such cases as exceptional and not routine.

But haven't we, then, accepted a modification of the basic principle, according to which reaching out to extend relations of equality in freedom gives way in certain circumstances to a higher need of self-defense? Is this something Jesus really anticipated and acquiesced in on pragmatic and prudential grounds, and, if so, doesn't it force a radical revision of our assessment of his priorities, to the point at which the whole edifice of his political teaching about how to live in the world comes into question? Alternatively, perhaps the exceptional case we have been discussing is something we have read into the Jesusian teaching that isn't really there, in which case Jesus was ultimately indifferent to the capacity of people to defend his teaching in this world against its obliteration by its enemies, who by his own descriptions will be brutal, wily, and persistent. We would have to recur to the position that the only matter of consequence to Jesus was the next world, and therefore, all the things he said that sound like a discussion of how people should and can live in this world in relations of brotherhood, as we have been discussing, are no more than an elaborate tent for salvation. In other words, what Jesus said might be true but beneficial not in this world, only in the next.

We can reach this conclusion, however, only by *underestimating* the ambition of the political teachings of Jesus. In its broadest possible terms, what Jesus is proposing is *a world without enemies*. This category of relations, the enemy, dates to the origin of the human: Cain slays Abel. Or, as we have discussed, relations of enmity are different from the animal predator/prey relationship in that they are not merely natural; they involve *recognizing* or *identifying* another person as an enemy. Even though this hostility may take the form of a struggle to the death, it is nevertheless a condition of mutual relationship. In it, Jesus sees possibility: the possibility of taking that relationship and turning it into something positive, namely, a relationship of equality in freedom freely accepted by the parties.

The ancient world could imagine no future without the category of enemy. This is the meaning of Deuteronomy 23:6, in which the Lord admonishes the Israelites *never* to seek the peace or prosperity of the Ammonites or Moabites because of what they did to the Israelites. Here is a principle of permanent apartness, irreconcilable difference, necessary Otherness at the heart of politics in the broadest sense. This is what Jesus seeks to do away with, and it is the ultimate reason he withholds consent from the abandonment of the effort to reach out to others. It was a simple matter of fact that conflict and enmity would persist past the time of Jesus, as he was well aware. But he also anticipated an effect his teaching to deepen and extend brotherly relations and to reach out to enemies would have over time: It would improve the quality of relations among people in a way they would understand and appreciate, and in doing so, it would constrict over time the sphere in which relations of enmity operate, ultimately squeezing the category of "enemy" out of politics altogether. When "all is accomplished" in accordance with Jesus's "fulfill[ment]" of the law, when the principle of equality in freedom attains its universal potential, there are no more enemies.

More to the point, *wherever* people adopt the principle of equality in freedom, the category of enemy disappears among them. The Jesusian teaching then calls on them to seek the spread of this principle by reaching out to others.

In our day, the principle of equality in freedom governs most of the modern world. It is for this reason that we can say with some degree of confidence that so long as this principle holds among people, the United States will never go to war with Germany or France, nor will France ever go to war with Germany again—more broadly, the United States and Europe and other countries as well have achieved a permanent peace. As it happens, there is no point in history prior to the end of World War II at which one could make the same observation about any such group of countries. What we are talking about is the history of violent political conflict and organized warfare since the beginning of time. And in this area, among these people, it is over.

We must face up to the times in which we live and make radical claims when it is reasonable to do so—when radical changes in the international environment have taken place. They have. It is not a given that the principle of equality in freedom, the Jesusian teaching, will forever remain what it is today, namely, the freely accepted choice of so many people, but so long as it is, this peace will persist. And it is the legacy of the teaching about how to live in this world that Jesus espoused some two thousand years ago. The test of our legacy will be our ability to preserve it and extend it further.

11

MIRACLES AND THE MIRACULOUS

Throughout this book, we have paid close attention to the words of Jesus, but the Gospels also describe a number of extraordinary *deeds* of Jesus, namely, the miracles.

Since our approach has been to focus on the political teaching of Jesus rather than the Christian religious teaching as such, the subject of miracles, which presumably are the product of divine intervention in earthly affairs, would seem to be out of bounds, at least as a matter of first impression. Miracles are things that only God does, or the Son of God, or angels, or those in and through whom the Holy Spirit is acting. Scripture is also fairly clear in suggesting that some people called on demons to perform, shall we say, "anti-miracles."

For our purposes, we can confine ourselves to a single question: Is the political teaching of Jesus we have been exploring in any way dependent on miraculous deeds for its truth or validity? Of course, the Gospels report that miracles perceived firsthand and tales of the miraculous lent authority to the teaching of Jesus in his day, and these tales continue to inspire many down to our own, validating divine claims. The central organizing principle of the Christian religion is the story of the miracle of Jesus's Resurrection. However, miracles are perceived firsthand not universally but locally, after which they become stories, tales of the miraculous. Acceptance of the political teaching of Jesus or of the religious teaching of Jesus does not depend on personally bearing witness to a miracle nor, arguably, on the spread of tales of the miraculous. By now, it is at least as arguable that belief in the divinity of Jesus bolsters faith in the truth of the miracles as that the tales of the miraculous prove the divinity of Jesus.

But controversy over miracles is hardly new. If Jesus did deeds possible only with divine intervention, beyond the capacity of mere mortal man, then it could hardly be said that people universally accepted this divine quality of his at the time. As people wondered who he really was and in some cases rejected his divinity, so the miracles attributed to him were also controversial. We would err if we read into this anything like a modern, rationalist perspective. Nevertheless, surely it's true that some people simply didn't believe the stories. Others, as noted, attributed the ability to perform them to demonic forces. In both cases, the doubts go hand in hand with skepticism that Jesus was the Messiah, the Son of God, the Christ. Though the Gospels suggest that Jesus's miraculous deeds won many over, the Gospels are quite clear that these deeds did not win everyone over—though this fact is in no way telling with regard to either the divinity of Jesus or, more important for our purposes here, the validity of his teaching.

We might go on to ask whether anything about our subject, the political teachings of Jesus, requires *further* miracles, or whether instead the words as they have come down to us are adequate to form a coherent whole, regardless of the possibility that the words of Jesus commanded authority in their day because of the demonstration effect of miraculous deeds. In my view, the words are enough with respect to the political teaching (though not, of course, with respect to the religious teaching). Nothing further in the way of additional miracles is required. Of course, one need not rule out the possibility, anticipated in 's commission to his disciples to go forth, preach, and heal the sick, that the spread of the teaching of Jesus might produce miracles, or at least results that people describe as miraculous, even down to our day. However, to acknowledge such a possibility is not to say that the spread of the teaching of Jesus is the only possible source for or explanation of such miracles, if they are indeed miracles.

A contrary view would necessarily seem to embody a paradox: If we cannot accept the teaching on the terms in which Jesus presents it—namely, its plausibility as universal truth for all time and all people—of what recourse is the divinity of Jesus? Here, we would be relying on the *authority* of the Christ as divine being to make up for, in essence, the deficient or unconvincing character of the teaching. But if Jesus is divine, then the teaching cannot be deficient. It may be that we should listen to Jesus because he is the Son of God and performed miracles, but it may be that we should listen to him also because he has something to teach us, solely on the merits of the teaching itself.

If the political teaching constitutes a coherent whole in the absence of miracles, then we could stick with the coherent whole it forms and not bother ourselves about miracles and the miraculous. From the onset, we've acknowledged that we are dealing with a *part* of the teaching of Jesus, the part about how people should live on earth—the political teaching. The question of the miracles is really no different from the question of the immortal soul and divine judgment. These are essential elements of Jesus's religious teaching, and there can be no expectation of Christian salvation in the absence of not only good conduct but also faith. But again, this is the religious question.

And yet I do not think, finally, that we have exhausted the this-worldly aspects of the question of miracles and the miraculous. Most of the miracles of Jesus and his disciples described in the Gospels concern healing the sick (including bringing the dead back to life) and feeding the hungry. If these were occasions of divine intervention, they were mostly directed at very worldly, practical concerns. If they were displays designed to show people an aspect of Jesus's exceptional being, they did so by focusing on a very specific problem at hand: This one was a paralytic (e.g., Mt: 9:2); this one had leprosy (e.g., Mk. 1:40–42); this one was blind (e.g., Lk. 18:35–43); this one died much too young (e.g., Mk. 5:22–24, 35–43); the wedding feast ran out of wine (Jn. 2:1–10); the nets were empty after a full day of fishing (e.g., Lk. 5:4–7). The miracle is not a display or show in the manner of a magician. The miracle *is* the practical result.

In some cases, Jesus seems at pains to explicitly distance himself from the miracle achieved. Such is the case in the story of the centurion who beseeches Jesus on behalf of an ailing servant; the servant isn't even present for his healing (Mt. 8:5–13; Lk. 7:1–10). In the Luke version of the story, only when emissaries later reach the centurion's home do they find the servant cured (Lk. 7:10). Jesus tells some of those he has cured not to tell anyone what happened (e.g., Mt. 8:4; Mk. 1:44), though clearly, some do, unable to contain themselves (e.g., Mk. 1:45). When Jesus feeds five thousand (e.g., Lk. 9:12–17), he has his disciples distribute the multiplying quantities of loaves and fish to people in small groups, without ceremony. In the John version of the story, the people understand this as a "sign" (Jn. 6:14), but in the other three versions, it is unclear that the people being fed are aware of the miracle that has produced the food. Nor does anyone actually observe Jesus's Resurrection (e.g., Mt. 28:1–7). It's the open tomb they find.

There are only two apparent exceptions to this pattern. One is the curse Jesus places on a fig tree, which we considered in the previous chapter. The other is the account of Jesus's walking on water (e.g., Mt. 14:24–34): This miracle appears to the disciples, who witness it first as a display of uncanny power. Here, too, however, the practical aspect emerges: The disciples are in a small boat trying to cross the sea of Galilee, "a long distance from the land, battered by waves; for the wind was contrary" (Mt. 14:24). Jesus calms the wind, enabling them to reach Gennesaret safely. Results matter most. As Jesus notes, "Truly, truly I say to you, you seek me, not because you saw signs, but because you ate of the loaves and were filled" (Jn. 6:26).

And, of course, Jesus declines to produce signs on demand, for example, in his encounter with Herod (Lk. 23:8–11) or at the time of his temptation by Satan in the desert (e.g., Mt. 4:5–7). In certain respects, the miracles depicted in the Gospels are noteworthy for their modesty and localization, not for high impact and visibility. Let's just note that in the Gospels, the sea does not part, nor does writing mysteriously appear on a wall, nor does a voice speak from the sky such that an entire nation hears it. Sometimes, it seems as if Jesus deliberately diverts attention away from any special ability he has to produce signs and wonders. He calls on his disciples to go out and perform cures (Mt. 10:8; Lk. 9:2) as if doing so is a perfectly straightforward activity.

At some risk of overstatement, we may venture the conclusion that Jesus wishes to be listened to and believed and to have his guidance on how to live in this world accepted, not on the strength of *what he can do because he is who he is* but on the strength of *what he says*. Again, the voluntary element of adherence to his teaching comes to the forefront. Moreover, as we have seen in our discussion of the parable of the rich man and Lazarus, Jesus observes that those who are not persuaded by the law and the prophets are not likely to be persuaded even by visitors from beyond the grave. And the character of his teaching is such that in accordance with it, people other than he will be able to perform miracles as well.

Jesus's miracles remind us—or at least they should—of a time when one's daily bread was in no sense a sure thing, when such horrible diseases as leprosy ravaged mankind, when parents could have no routine expectation that mothers would survive childbirth or that children would live to adulthood.

What I would like to suggest by way of a conclusion is that in the prosperous, developed world—the world in which the political teaching of Jesus is most firmly entrenched—we have now solved many of the problems that gave rise to a felt need for miracles. The miraculous is now ordinary, enjoyed to a point at which it is hardly worth remarking. Our ability to do certain remarkable things—curing forms of cancer, making people's daily bread available at reasonable cost at the

corner supermarket, saving babies born seventeen weeks prematurely—
is, it seems to me, in no small measure a product of the beneficial effects of the Jesusian teaching. Rather than finding ourselves in a world
in which my gain is your loss, my freedom is your oppression, we have
cultivated a habit of cooperation based on trust. True, we have contracts and legal means for their enforcement, but we have more than
that: an ethic that calls for the consideration of the wishes and needs of
others in pursuing our own wishes and needs. In short, we pursue the
satisfaction of our desire for righteousness cooperatively, in a way that
allows, at least in principle, for the satisfaction of the properly construed desire for righteousness of everyone. There is no point in curing
the sick if the sick don't matter, nor is there much point to the elaborate web of social arrangements necessary for transactions to take place
at the supermarket if you can't get past the conclusion that the way to
get your daily bread is to take it from those who are weaker than you.

Of course, the prosperous, developed world is not the whole world.
For huge numbers of people, daily bread is not forthcoming, disease is
rampant, mothers die in childbirth, and children succumb to disease
and malnourishment. Warlords and tyrants oppress the weak. Politics is
a life-or-death affair, close to a struggle of all against all. People are
driven from their homes, separated from their families, slaughtered on
the basis of tribe or faith. There are wars and rumors of war: want and
terror.

In short, for much of the world of today, human misery is not dis-
tinguishable from that of two millennia ago, if indeed it is not worse.

It seems to me that people in this condition are no less in need of
miracles than were the people of Jesus's time. It also seems to me that
it is within our capacity to provide some. In Jesusian terms, those who
have much justify their abundance only to the extent they are willing to
exert themselves on behalf of those who have little or nothing. *In everything, therefore, treat people the same way you want them to treat you. . . .*
If this statement stands as the summary principle underlying the success
and prosperity of much of the world today, as I think it does, then those

who live in that part of the world and benefit accordingly would be well advised to accept an obligation to continue to reach out to others.

And if such outreach as the provision of medicine for the sick, food and clean water for the hungry and thirsty, shelter for the homeless, armistice for the war-ravaged, safe haven for the targets of genocide, support for the oppressed and persecuted—and satisfaction for those who desire righteousness—sometimes seems to those on the receiving end to be a *miraculous* intervention, as we know it does, well, who can object? Not I. Nor would I be troubled by the suggestion that the best and ultimate explanation for the working of such miracles down to our day and into the future is the spread of the political teachings of Jesus.

ACKNOWLEDGMENTS

One approaches the main source material for this book in full knowledge that the canonical Christian Gospels are not exactly neglected works. To the extent that I have had something new to say about the teaching of Jesus, or at least a new way of saying something, it emerges against the backdrop of a literature of interpretation, exegesis, influence, and even opposition that is simply staggering in breadth, volume, and in many cases profundity. Readers who are familiar with that literature, especially the major philosophical works that have taken up themes Jesus addressed, will no doubt have detected the resonance of some of those works in this book. I have a vague intention of someday doing up an annotated copy of the manuscript, spelling out and exploring some of the connections and the secondary questions they raise. But I decided early on that the clarity of this presentation would have been impeded rather than enhanced by its attachment to such an apparatus.

I have mainly relied on the New American Standard Bible, and I am grateful to the copyright holder, the Lockman Foundation, for its generous rules regarding quotation. There are two online resources that I have used extensively and deserve special mention. One is BibleGateway.com, a ministry of Gospel Communications International. Its text search function through major translations and its cross-referencing are superb.

The other is the Interlinear Study Bible available at StudyLight.org, a nondenominational Christian Internet ministry, which offers the capability of direct word-by-word comparison of English translations with the Greek and Hebrew originals in a form that far surpasses anything achievable in print.

I am in debt to Kenneth Anderson, Peter Berkowitz, Mary Eberstadt, Lee Harris, Joe Loconte, John Podhoretz, and Gary Schmitt, who read all or parts of the draft manuscript at various stages and provided comments that immensely improved what appears here. Thanks also go to Tony Corn, E. J. Dionne, Andrew Ferguson, Christopher Hitchens, Steven Menashi, Cheryl Miller, Kori Schake, and Richard Starr for offering useful suggestions in the formative stages of the project. Thanks to Charles Kitchen for research assistance in the early going and especially to Samantha Sault for carefully reviewing the manuscript and references. Thanks as well to the Rev. Msgr. V. James Lockman for his invitation to present some of my research in a talk at the Church of the Annunciation in Washington, D.C., the first public airing of the material.

Thanks to Joni Evans, Jonathan Pecarsky, and Mel Berger of the William Morris Agency, who saw me through, respectively, the beginning, middle, and end of the project.

I am grateful to Judith Regan for seeing potential in this project. At HarperCollins, much gratitude to Cal Morgan, who understood at once what I was hoping to do in this book and is a superb editor. Matt Harper's incisive and unbashful editorial guidance helped me clear up a number of passages that needed more work.

My professional home is the Hoover Institution, Stanford University. There is simply nowhere better. This book falls under the rubric of Hoover's initiative on individualism and American values. My thanks to John Raisian, Hoover's director, for his support. At Hoover's small Washington, D.C., office, where I spend most of the year, thanks as well to Rachel Abrams and Sharon Ragland and to my former colleague there, Kelly Dillon.

I hope the writing of this book hasn't been too burdensome on the family: my wife, Tina, and our daughters, Abby and Molly. If it was, they didn't complain, for which I thank them much. Long ago, Tina brought home for me the truth of the remark that being alone is a deficient mode of being with. This book is for her.

INDEX